# BIBLE AND LITERATURE
## SERIES

### Editor
### David M. Gunn

FOR JANICE

# Irony In The Old Testament

EDWIN M. GOOD

*Wenigstens Selbstironie sollte der Sünder haben —
also jedermann.*

WILHELM BUSCH

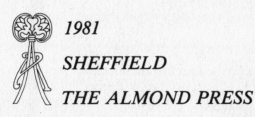

1981

SHEFFIELD

THE ALMOND PRESS

The quotation from Tablet XI of "The Gilgamesh Epic" is reprinted by permission of Princeton University Press from J. B. Pritchard, ed., *Ancient Near Eastern Texts Relating to the Old Testament*. Copyright, 1950, by Princeton University Press.

First published in 1965 by The Westminster Press, Philadelphia, Pennsylvania. This edition published by arrangement with The Westminster Press.

SECOND EDITION

Published by
The Almond Press
P.O. Box 208
Sheffield S10 5DW
England

**British Library Cataloguing in Publication Data**

Good, Edwin M.
 Irony in the Old Testament. – 2nd ed. – (Bible and
 literature series ISSN 0260-4493; 3)
 1. Irony
 I. Title  II. Series
 221.6'6   BS1171
 ISBN 0-907459-05-6

Printed in Great Britain
by Redwood Burn Limited
Trowbridge & Esher
1981

# CONTENTS

# PREFACE TO THE SECOND EDITION

WHEN REPUBLICATION of this book was first proposed, I began to think of what I would like to change. It was soon clear that some of my changes of mind since 1965 would involve not merely touching up and referring to works that have appeared in the interim but completely rethinking and rewriting some parts. The upshot is that, save for the correction of a few errors, the text remains intact.

I may nevertheless set down some brief notes on what I might have changed had I the chance. I would attempt to avoid the unthinking use of the masculine generics, "he" and "man." When I wrote the book, the issue had never occurred to me. Second, I would make a much sterner effort to maintain the Hebrew text without emendation. Reading over the book again in 1981, I am dismayed by the many alterations I made in the text.

I suspect that the flaws in the first chapter could be removed only by rewriting it. The issues in irony set out there still seem to me the right ones, though they could have been stated more cogently and illustrated more aptly. Omission of reference to "Romantic irony" was criticized; one reviewer remarked that I mentioned Donald Duck but not Kierkegaard. I am convinced that in its usual forms, including Kierkegaard's *(The Concept of*

*Irony* first appeared in English several years after this book was published), Romantic irony was not what I called irony but was rather a lofty, often sarcastic invective. I wish I had done better by the Greeks. My reading in the classics has widened considerably since 1965, and on p. 30 I would refer to Thucydides rather than to Reinhold Niebuhr.

The chapters on Jonah and Saul I would leave nearly as they are, though I would make reference in the latter to Herbert A. Lindenberger's remarkable novel, *Saul's Fall.* Several literary studies of parts of Genesis that have appeared since 1965 would have influenced revision, especially Robert Alter's studies of narrative and J. P. Fokkelman's superb *Narrative Art in Genesis.* And I think I now see more clearly the interweaving lines of the Abraham story.

The most extensive revisions would come in the chapter on Isaiah. It rests on a distinction between the words of Isaiah and later additions that I now find not useful, requiring knowledge accessible only by circular reasoning, hence not accessible as knowledge. Giving up that distinction would probably force a total recasting of the chapter.

The chapter on Qoheleth has always in some ways been my favorite, and the affection has persisted through long enough acquaintance with its blemishes that I doubt that anyone has any objection that I have not myself had at one time or another. For revision I would have searched Qoheleth more closely for a coherent structure. As for Job, no one is ever finished with it. I have stated in print that I would not now use the word "faith" for Job's final state of mind, a word too loaded with Christian and Protestant connotations. Some other subsequent findings make me think the essay a bit superficial. I hope in the future to make up the lack with a book on Job, which will not exhaust Job but will probably exhaust me.

Finally, if I could, I would omit the Epilogue. Very soon after publication I thought it a premature leap from literary criticism to theology, and I do not now wish to make that transition, while not objecting if others do. I request the reader, then, to read the Epilogue, if at all, as reflecting a mind-set 16 years old.

In the first preface, I disclaimed raising the banner for a new school of interpretation, although little literary criticism of the Hebrew Bible was then going on. I still reject that intent, partly because I distrust schools, having seen so many of them degenerate into clubs that talk only to their own members, partly because, to my delight, literary-critical work on the Hebrew Bible has expanded greatly. No banner being needed, far be it from me to wave one. And, although revision would reflect a sharper critical method, I would remain stubbornly eclectic. One may find useful questions and, now and again, helpful answers from New Criticism, myth criticism, semiotics, structuralism, phenomenology, and rhetorical criticism, but none seems to me to hold the sole means of getting out of a text everything that is in it.

One of the fruits of this narrow entry into literary criticism for me has been a continuing interest in the play of the aesthetic imagination in the religious traditions of both West and East. Some expeditions into those bracing climates have persuaded me that scholars of religion have examined the aesthetic side of the human spirit much less that they ought. I do not mean that art, literature, and music are simply encoded verbal thoughts, religious "ideas" to be deciphered in the aesthetic artifact. Products of the aesthetic imagination are not reducible to ideas or thought, even when, as in literature, they are verbally formed. Rather, a sense of the central importance of beauty is to be found, I think, in every culture, rendering the aesthetic imagination crucial to the religious expressions of human meaning. Wonder and delight in the presence of the beautiful are indispensable to a profound humanity.

Stanford, California, March 1981                         Edwin M. Good

# PREFACE TO THE FIRST EDITION

BIBLICAL CRITICS are not, generally speaking, literary critics. We have taken literary criticism to mean the distinction of sources, the analysis of forms, the separation of secondary from primary materials, and theological exegesis. These are all worthwhile and necessary tasks, but they do not comprise literary criticism. We have failed, however, to raise the genuinely literary question about the Bible. I mean that we have been so concerned (and properly concerned) with its truth, both factual and religious, that we have not investigated the literary means the Biblical writers use to convey their truth. Form criticism is a step in the right direction, but on the one hand it has been bedeviled by an unfortunate formalism, while on the other hand it has used literary observations for nonliterary purposes. We have, in other words, been so eager to *interpret* the Bible that we have sometimes forgotten to *read* it, to read it in the same way that we read *The Divine Comedy,* for example, or *Othello,* or *The Waste Land.*

I am not raising the standard for a new "school" of Old Testament studies. Nor am I attempting what is ordinarily done in college courses entitled "The English Bible as Literature." Yet the Bible *is* literature, whatever else it may be. Those of us who pretend to scholarly expertise in the field have often snickered discreetly up our sleeves at Mary Ellen Chase and those like her who have tried to read the Bible, taking seriously the fact that we have it on printed pages. But we have failed to give them the help that we, with our specialized knowledge, could have rendered. They have at least posed the genuinely literary question, and our judgments of their failures must stand equally as judgments of our own failures to deal with important matters.

The present book is only a start on an aspect of this entire field. To say that Old Testament writers use irony is to make an affirmation about the Old Testament's literary quality. It is to ask, *How* do Old Testament writers say what they say? No study of literature can afford to ignore that question. And to investigate irony is, I think, to enter upon the question at a peculiarly sensitive point. Irony is a hallmark of sophisticated subtlety. If, in fact, Old Testament writers sometimes express their ideas by irony, the possibility opens that they have said something different from, or more complex than, what we had supposed. I claim no revolutionary disclosures in the pages that follow. But here and there points of interpretation over which exegetes have wrangled seem to me to be cleared up by the recognition of irony. As the epilogue will show, I am inclined to think that the presence of irony in the Old Testament casts a new light on the theological task of interpretation.

But I have by no means finished the job. The essays that follow are substantially independent, unified only by the considerations of the opening attempt at definition and by the fact that I have investigated each body of material for the irony present in it. I have not sought to draw interconnections otherwise among the books treated. Nor have I expounded all the irony that the Old Testament holds. Perhaps the major gap is the omission of any treatment of The Book of Jeremiah, but further illumination on the Old Testament's irony would come also from Deutero-Isaiah (Isa., chs. 40 to 55), from Micah and other of the shorter prophetic books, from Judges, from Exodus, from The Proverbs, and even from The Psalms. It would take another volume. I do not promise another volume, though my interest in the question is not exhausted by this one.

It is a necessary pleasure to nod graciously in a preface to those who have afforded indispensable help with the book. Dr. Elmer M. Grieder, of the Stanford University Libraries, went out of his way to find me a place to work without interruption. Prof. Samuel Terrien gave me encouragement and help at a distance, in addition to teaching me most of what I know about The Book of Job. Prof. James Muilenburg gave me salutary warnings of dangers along with the example of his own interest in this kind of question. Prof. Sheldon H. Blank kindly sent me a copy of an unpublished paper together with his own encouragement. Friends and acquaintances too numerous to name have supported me by their solicitude and their eagerness to see the finished product. The Stanford Philological Association and the Stanford Research Club opened their platforms to me so that I might test my thoughts on their competent minds. By no means least, I must be grateful to several classes of Stanford undergraduates who suffered without complaint my constant reference to the project.

In particular, my thanks are due to Rev. Ralph R. Sundquist, Jr., who graciously relieved me of the proofreading and of the preparation of the Index at a time when travel in Europe would have made these tasks very difficult to accomplish.

Authors' wives always make life serene and keep children out from underfoot during the gestations of books. My wife did that, but she has also ridden close herd on my prose — close enough to be sometimes painful — so that its literary infelicities remain in spite of her efforts to reform me. The dedication to her, far from being a dutiful gesture, represents literally inexpressible gratitude.

E. M. G.

# ABBREVIATIONS

ANET    *Ancient Near Eastern Texts Relating to the Old Testament,* ed. by James B. Pritchard (2d ed., Princeton University Press, 1955)

AQHT    " The Tale of Aqhat," a Ugaritic legend

ATD    Das Alte Testament Deutsch

BJ    La Sainte Bible (Bible de Jerusalem)

CB    The Cambridge Bible

CBQ    *Catholic Biblical Quarterly*

HAT    *Handbuch zum Alten Testament*

HKAT    *Handkommentar zum Alten Testament*

IB    *The Interpreter's Bible*

ICC    The International Critical Commentary

IDB    *The Interpreter's Dictionary of the Bible*

JBL    *Journal of Biblical Literature*

JNES    *Journal of Near Eastern Studies*

K–B    Ludwig Koehler and Walter Baumgartner, *Lexicon in Veteris Testamenti Libros* (2d ed., E. J. Brill, Leiden, 1958)

LD    Lectio Divina

LXX    The Septuagint

MT    Masoretic Text

RPh    *Revue Philosophique*

RSV    Revised Standard Version of the Holy Bible

TR    *Theologische Rundschau*

VT    *Vetus Testamentum*

ZAW    *Zeitschrift für die alttestamentliche Wissenschaft*

# I

## THE IDENTIFICATION
## OF IRONY

Iᴿᴼɴʏ, like love, is more readily recognized than defined. In
that, it is like any controlling attitude toward life, be it religion,
be it philosophy, be it the comic or the tragic. Who can *define*
religion? Who can comprise philosophy in a sentence or comedy
in a paragraph? I do not mean that these attitudes toward life
are disparate and mutually exclusive. There is, after all, such a
thing as religious philosophy, though some philosophers and
theologians may plead its bastardy. There are dramas labeled by
their authors " tragicomedy." But our subject is primarily irony
and only secondarily tragedy, comedy, or philosophy, although
in the present book the irony has principally to do with religion.

### Sᴏᴍᴇ Pᴏɪɴᴛᴇʀs ᴛᴏ Iʀᴏɴʏ

A mere etymology will not tell us what irony is, but the word's
origin may cast some light on its meaning. *Eirōneia* is a Greek
word, though irony is by no means, as one writer has suggested,
a Greek thing.[1] The word is an abstraction from the term used
to designate one of the characters in the earliest Greek comedy.

[1] J. A. K. Thomson, *Irony: An Historical Introduction* (Harvard University
Press, 1927), p. 2. I regret beginning with a disagreement with Mr. Thomson,
whose book is vastly illuminating on irony in classical literature. I am greatly in
his debt throughout the entire first part of this chapter.

The comedy presented the conflict (*agōn*) between two characters, the one called the *alazōn*, the other, the *eirōn*. The *alazōn*, we are told, may be called the "impostor," the *eirōn*, the "ironical man." The *alazōn* is the pompous fool, the pretender who affects to be more than he actually is. The *eirōn*, his antagonist, is the sly, shrewd dissimulator, who poses as less than he is. The conflict ends, of course, in the pricking of the *alazōn's* bubble, the triumph of the *eirōn*. Therein lies its comedy, for the spectator knows without doubt which character is the impostor, which the ironical man, and he knows what the end will be. The comedy lies in watching the impostor exposed and deflated by the machinations of the ironical man.

Irony, then, begins in conflict, a conflict marked by the perception of the distance between pretense and reality. It is not confined to Greek comedy, of course. Charlie Chaplin was the very image of the *eirōn*, the little man, the flat-footed nobody, apparently at the mercy of any power that sought control over him but, in the end, the unaccountable victor over everyone. Donald Duck is surely the *alazōn*, thoroughly impressed with himself, usually defeated, humiliated, but ready to puff himself up again and again. Low humor of all kinds demonstrates the conflict between the impostor and the ironical man. The *alazōn* invariably slips on a banana peel, the *eirōn* may miss it. To be sure, when slapstick gets to the pie-throwing stage, the carnage is general, and even the *eirōn* may sputter with meringue. But the laughter comes from seeing it on the face of the exposed *alazōn*.

Irony, however, is too sensitive a tool to be blunted forever on the Keystone Cops. Ironic comedy can be subtle indeed, and few writers have been as sharply ironic as Aristophanes. *Lysistrata* is surely the most devastatingly ironic satire on war the world has ever seen. Yet when Aristophanes turns the light of irony on Socrates in *The Clouds*, we sense a kind of double irony; for

Socrates himself was a master of irony.[2] Only an accomplished ironist could have spoken as Socrates did to the Athenian court that was trying him for high treason.[3]

What effect my accusers had upon you, Men of Athens, I know not. As for me, they well-nigh made me forget who I was, so telling were their speeches! And yet, so to say, not one atom of truth did they utter. But that which astonished me most among all their fabrications was this, that they said you must be on your guard, and not be deceived by me, as I was a masterly speaker. That they should not be ashamed when they were promptly going to be caught by me in a lie, through the fact, since I shall show myself to be no orator at all, therein methought they reached the very height of their effrontery; unless perchance what they call masterly speaker means the one who tells the truth. If that is what they are saying, then I will admit I am an orator, though not of the sort they describe.

That is the first paragraph of the *Apology*. Read also the last, after the sentence of death has been voted.

When my sons grow up, then, Gentlemen, I ask you to punish them, you hurting them the same as I hurt you, if they seem to care for money, or aught else, more than they care for virtue. And if they pretend to be somewhat when they are nothing, do you upbraid them as I upbraided you, for not regarding as important what they ought to think so, and for thinking they have worth when they do not. If you do that, I shall have received just treatment from you, and my sons as well.

And now the time has come for our departure, I to die, and

---

[2] It would be pleasant to believe the story that when *The Clouds* was performed in Athens, Socrates stood up in the audience so that people could see the original of the caricature they saw on the stage. In the play, Socrates is the *alazōn*, the butt, therefore, of Aristophanes' *eirōneia*.

[3] Quotations are from the translation by Lane Cooper, *Plato on the Trial and Death of Socrates: Euthyphro, Apology, Crito, Phaedo* (Cornell University Press, 1941).

you to live. Which of us goes to meet the better lot is hidden from all unless it be known to God.

Socrates sees the contradiction between pretense and reality, and, even faced with death, smiles at the incongruity. Whether these are his actual words or whether Plato has constructed the speech, partly from memory (he was present) and partly from the sense of what would be fitting, need not concern us. Socrates has been accused of putting on ironical airs, of deceiving his hearers by pretending to be less than he is, as the proper *eirōn* always does. And by doing precisely that in his whole speech of defense, he turns the irony upon his accusers.

Some of you, perhaps, will take me to be joking, but be assured that I shall tell you the simple truth. The fact is, fellow citizens, that I have got this name through my possession of a certain wisdom. What sort of wisdom is it? A wisdom, doubtless, that appertains to man. With respect to this, perhaps, I actually am wise; whereas those others whom I just now mentioned may possibly be wise with a wisdom more than human, or else I do not know what to say of it; as for me, I certainly do not possess it, and whoever says I do is lying, and seeks to injure me.

We might almost hear the voice of Erasmus' Folly here. *The Praise of Folly* takes the form and title of " encomium," a speech of fulsome praise.[4] The speech to which the jester in cap and bells calls all the dullards to listen is self-praise, the demonstration of her claim that she, Folly, is the guiding spirit behind all that the world takes to be great and dignified. Put in the mouth of Folly, the boast is ostensibly to be dismissed as mere fun and

[4] The Latin title of *The Praise of Folly* is *Encomium Moriae*, which is a Latinization of the Greek *Egkōmion mōria*. In *Moriae*, as is well known, we have a pun on the name of Sir Thomas More, to whom the book is dedicated. The best translation of *The Praise of Folly* is by Hoyt Hopewell Hudson (Princeton University Press, 1941).

foolishness. Yet the perceptive reader is invited to glimpse behind the mask of Folly the face of truth, and Folly's dissimulation, her pretense to speak nothing but what her name implies, is the vehicle for Erasmus' hilariously biting satire on the times. Folly is the *eirōn,* the shrewd critic masquerading as the wide-eyed innocent.

The irony of which we have so far spoken is a criticism. It exposes falsehood and stupidity, recognizes foolishness and pretense. It mocks those who think they are something when they are actually nothing.

Another kind of irony is noticeable among the Greeks, though it is by no means confined to them and probably did not come into existence with them. It is usually called "tragic irony."[5] Where the irony in comedy lies in seeing the pretensions of the impostor exposed as folly, the irony in tragedy lies in seeing the truly great fall beneath destiny because they sought to be too great. The word for it is *hybris:* overstepping the proper bounds. We might almost call it "impropriety," had the word not become so trivialized in English. *Hybris* in tragedy is the counterpart of *alazoneia* in comedy.[6] Its tragic character arises not from the imposture whose exposure is sheer pleasure but from genuine greatness, whose downfall inspires, in Aristotle's words, "pity and terror." The irony is in the way the audience sees the downfall coming, hears it adumbrated in speech, follows it to its awful conclusion, knowing all the while what the dramatist's characters do not know, perceiving therefore the tragic overtones and under-

[5] The term "tragic irony" was first used in an essay on Sophoclean tragedy by Bishop Thirlwall in 1833. Cf. the appreciation of Thirlwall's essay in G. G. Sedgewick, *Of Irony, Especially in Drama* (University of Toronto Press, 1948), pp. 19–23. See also Norman Knox, *The Word Irony and Its Context, 1500–1755* (Duke University Press, 1961).

[6] Cf. F. M. Cornford, *The Origin of Attic Comedy* (Doubleday & Company, Inc., Anchor Book, 1961; originally published by Cambridge University Press, Cambridge, 1914), pp. 181–184. J. A. K. Thomson, *op. cit.,* p. 34, makes the same point in dependence on Cornford.

tones that take the dramatis personae by surprise.

The irony in Greek tragedy is so striking because, unlike modern drama, the spectators know the plot in advance. They know before the watchman appears on the wall that Agamemnon will be killed by Clytemnestra. They know that Oedipus is married to his mother, that Medea will destroy all that Jason holds dear. The audience wonders not how it will all turn out, but how the dramatist will manipulate the characters, when he will accomplish the action. Only so can we understand the *Agamemnon* of Aeschylus, for example, which consists from beginning to end of interminably long speeches. All know that something crucial, Clytemnestra's murder of Agamemnon, must happen. But nothing happens. The watchman tells his story, the chorus speaks its 217-line narrative ode, Clytemnestra and the chorus converse about the victory at Troy, and the chorus muses again on the war. The herald appears and is interrogated by the chorus, repeating the facts of victory. He is entrusted by Clytemnestra with a message to Agamemnon; then, urged by the chorus, he recounts the storm at sea that decimated the returning host. The chorus muses again on Helen and on *hybris* and on justice, and at last, at line 782, Agamemnon enters. He prepares to resume his rule, threatening retribution on malcontents of whom he is but vaguely aware; he is greeted effusively by his wife, who orders her maidens to lay down the scarlet carpet for Agamemnon's triumphal entrance into the house. Agamemnon is worried by this stroke: " Such state becomes the gods and none beside." She insists; he demurs. But at last, giving in, he bares his feet, and then, at line 974 (the play has 1,673 lines), the only onstage *action* of the whole drama takes place: Agamemnon treads on the scarlet carpet. Everything has led up to this final act of overstepping the bounds, and from it swiftly comes the great man's fall. The irony, then, lies in the characters' preparation for the fall, Clytemnestra deliberately manipulating it, the chorus dimly sensing its inevitability, Agamemnon unwittingly blundering ahead. Everything depends on the means Aeschylus uses to adumbrate and then to present the foregone conclusion.[7]

The impact of this irony comes through the disparity between what the tragic hero on the stage knows and what we know. We watch him act in genuine greatness, but see his action go too far. We know he will surpass his bounds; he does not. We can only watch in pity and terror as the inexorable happens. Everything in Greek tragedy is laid out for us by the dramatist. Nothing is hidden.[8] We are told all, and because we are told all, the irony of the drama is fully disclosed to us. The test of the dramatist's art, then, is neither plot nor characters, whether plausible or implausible, whether interesting or uninteresting. The test becomes the way in which the dramatist presses the story upon us, the manner by which he conveys to us what we already know.

The irony in modern drama proceeds on a different course. The dramatist assumes that we do not know the story beforehand, and the irony is felt as we respond to the play as a whole.[9] Looking back over it, we perceive the incongruities of action and speech. This kind of drama is founded on the philosophic premise that the work of art is to effect a reaction from its totality. We are to reflect upon it all, turn it over in our minds, understand it, as it were, ex post facto. When we leave the theater or lay the book down, the experience has only begun.

The philosophic base of Greek tragedy was that the artistic experience was to be complete on leaving the theater. The catharsis

[7] This analysis of the *Agamemnon* is dependent on J. A. K. Thomson, *op. cit.*, pp. 39–53.

[8] Erich Auerbach, *Mimesis: The Representation of Reality in Western Literature* (Doubleday & Company, Inc., Anchor Book, 1953), ch. 1, posits this as the controlling character of Greek literature. He illustrates the principle with an episode from the Odyssey, but it certainly applies equally to tragedy.

[9] This is also true of dramas we know perfectly well, e.g., *Hamlet*. Shakespeare does not require knowledge of anything outside the play itself, whereas the Greek tragedies do.

was finished; understanding had been achieved. The drama
was constructed to have its effect as it went along. The tragedian
assumed that his audiences possessed a framework of knowledge and understanding, knowledge of the story and understanding of the way the world spins. All had that in common —
the author, the characters, and the audience. The audience was
required to listen, to fit each piece of insight into the existent
structure as the play went along. The play finished, the structure was complete, and the audience understood.

This is the way with folk art. We do not wait in suspense
while John Henry has his contest with the drill in the folk song.
John Henry is a great man, the greatest of all the " steel-driving "
men. We know beforehand that he will undertake the contest
with the steam drill, that he will push his greatness just too far
and, winning the race, will be struck down by the nemesis of
death. The stark verses pile up the tragic irony, with the hero's
ironic boast, the portraits of the wife and the son, and finally
the tragic victory of man over machine. But the irony lies further
in the fact that the victorious man has been too victorious, has
tempted fate, and has been crushed by it.

A similar motif is present in what is surely the most neglected
masterpiece of the world's literature, the Babylonian Epic of
Gilgamesh.[10] Centered on the search by Gilgamesh, King of
Uruk, for a way to transcend mortal limitations, the epic recounts battles, journeys, a great friendship, and mystic wisdom.
Gilgamesh finally comes to the dwelling of Utnapishtim, the sole
survivor of the worldwide flood, who has been granted divinity

---

[10] The best translation is that in *ANET*, pp. 72–99, which is reprinted in
Isaac Mendelsohn, ed., *Religions of the Ancient Near East* (Liberal Arts Press,
1953), pp. 47–115. See also the translations by N. K. Sandars, *The Epic of Gilgamesh* (Penguin Books, Inc., 1960), and Alexander Heidel, *The Gilgamesh Epic
and Old Testament Parallels* (The University of Chicago Press, 1946). It is not
too much to say that the Gilgamesh Epic must rank with Homer, the Scandinavian
sagas, the Mahabharata, and the Chanson de Roland among the greatest epics of
literature.

because he had evaded destruction. With Utnapishtim's gift of
a plant guaranteeing immortality, Gilgamesh seems to have succeeded in his quest. But at almost the last instant, the plant is
stolen by a snake, and Gilgamesh returns to Uruk aware fully of
his unbreachable limits. They are symbolized in the last lines of
the poem with hauntingly ironic resignation by the description
of the limits of Uruk:

Go up, Urshanabi, walk on the ramparts of Uruk.
Inspect the base terrace, examine its brickwork,
　If its brickwork is not of burnt brick,
And if the Seven Wise Ones laid not its foundation!
One " sar " is city, one sar orchards,
　One sar margin land; (further) the *precinct* of the Temple of
　　Ishtar.
Three sar and the *precinct* comprise Uruk.[11]

Irony, then, is present both in the tragic and in the comic. Indeed, it forms one of the bridges between the two.[12] It is therefore clear that we cannot simply classify irony as a category of
laughter. Its appearance in tragedy forbids that, but at the same
time its place in comedy and its sometimes humorous character
restrain us from confining irony to " tragic irony."

The effect of irony in Plato's *Apology* indicates that there is
an ironic mode of speech, an ironic manner of making a point.
Socrates illustrates it; Folly illustrates it. Dictionaries can be very
pedestrian about it: that figure of speech " in which the intended
meaning is the opposite of that expressed in the word used " (*New*

---

[11] Translation from *ANET*, p. 97. The " sar " may be a land measure. The
italicization of " precinct " means that the word's meaning is uncertain.

[12] So Northrop Frye, *Anatomy of Criticism* (Princeton University Press, 1957),
p. 162. Frye identifies four categories of narrative literature: the tragic; the
comic; the romantic; and the ironic, or satiric. To use the analogy of a circle,
tragedy lies between romance on the one side and irony on the other, opposite to
comedy. Hence, in Frye's scheme, romance and irony are the opposite bridges between comedy and tragedy.

*English Dictionary*). To say one thing and mean another, generally the opposite — that is sufficient definition of irony for most people. Its recognition often depends on sensitivity to a tone of voice. Gilbert Highet refers to a sermon by the medieval Dominican, John Bromyard, which calls money a more powerful god than God, for " it can make the lame walk, set captives free, cause the deaf judge to hear and the dumb advocate to speak." [13] It would be difficult to miss the irony of that. Or of Housman:

> Malt does more than Milton can
> To justify God's ways to man. [14]

But it is not hard to miss this, from Montaigne: " God is kind 'to those from whom he takes life by degrees; that is the only blessing of old age. The final death will be less complete and hurtful; it will dispatch only the half or quarter of a man." [15] Is that meant ironically at all?

I think it is, though we cannot be utterly certain. Is not a source of irony's attraction and repellence alike that it may plausibly be taken literally, invites us to take it literally, makes a certain sense when taken literally? Yet a nagging doubt hints at a meaning hidden behind the mask. Sometimes, as with Erasmus' Folly, we are invited to look behind the mask, but the invitation may be entirely in the tone of voice. Only if we could hear Montaigne speak those words, inflecting them in order to convey his meaning, could we be sure whether or not he intended them ironically.

Another form of irony uses the suspicion that a thing means more than it says. Irony as understatement is technically called

[13] Gilbert Highet, *The Anatomy of Satire* (Princeton University Press, 1962), p. 46, relying upon G. R. Owst, *Literature and Pulpit in Medieval England* (Cambridge University Press, Cambridge, 1933).

[14] *A Shropshire Lad*, LXII.

[15] *Essays*, Book III, 13: " Of Experience," tr. by E. J. Trechmann (Modern Library, Inc., 1946), p. 974.

litotes. Aristotle defines *eirōneia* in the *Nichomachean Ethics* as a "pretence tending toward the underside" of truth.[16] Montaigne provides us with another instance: "It is not enough for a sober understanding to judge us simply by our external actions: we must sound the innermost recesses, and observe the springs which give the swing. But since it is a high and hazardous undertaking, I would rather that fewer people meddled with it."[17] Chaucer's description of the Clerk of Oxenford is an example:

> As len*e* was his hors as is a rake,
> And he was not right fat, I undertake.[18]

Jonathan Swift provided a clear, though macabre, instance of understatement, with his essay *A Modest Proposal for Preventing the Children of Poor People in Ireland from Being a Burden to Their Parents or Country, and for Making Them Beneficial to the Public* (1729). The very title is ironic, for the "modest proposal" was that, since Ireland was starving, the children should be slaughtered and eaten. The tone of utter rationality, the list of benefits to be gained from the scheme, the careful disclaimer of all views of the matter that might border on cruelty ("which, I confess, has always been with me the strongest objection against any project, how well soever intended"), mark the understatement of the whole satire.

There, perhaps, is the real irony of the *Modest Proposal:* Swift knows that no one will take the "substantive" part of it seriously, that it is by no means a viable option for the solution of the Irish question. And by reducing all alternative solutions to absurdity with this one, he sharpens the issue unbearably. Yet one might almost feel, as Gilbert Highet says, that the Nazis fiendishly misunderstood Swift, for their "final solution to the

---

[16] *Nich. Eth.* II. vii. 12, quoted by G. G. Sedgewick, *op. cit.,* p. 7.
[17] *Essays,* Book II, 1: "Of the Inconsistency of Our Action," *ed. cit.,* p. 283.
[18] *Canterbury Tales,* "Prologue" (J. M. Dent & Co., London, 1908).

Jewish problem" followed lines not dissimilar to the *Proposal,*
without, however, confining attention to the children.[19]

We may wonder how anyone could find the heart to laugh
even on the periphery of such a thing. But that is precisely the
point of irony. It clarifies with extreme sharpness the incongruity
involved in a matter of great moment. Hence, as A. R. Thompson says, there is in irony a laughter that hurts, as opposed to
the laughter of comedy, which satisfies.[20] "To perceive it," he
continues, "one must be detached and cool; to feel it one must
be pained for a person or ideal gone amiss." [21] There was a few
years ago an irrepressible irony in the spectacle of moral theologians solemnly debating whether a man would be ethically
justified in shooting persons who tried to enter his bomb shelter.
It is not amusing that some divines actually argued the affirmative, nor that some, without humor, defended the negative. It
might be urged that merely to raise the question shows a serious
moral insensitivity, if not degeneration. The moral degeneration,
however, probably lies in the possibility that bomb shelters might
turn out to be useful rather than in the niceties of admission to
them. It is painful to see an international situation in which anyone would dream of arguing the point. And the hurt arises from
commitment to the ideal of international peace, to a vision of
truth.

In exactly the same way, we must perceive irony in the bomb-
ing of Negro churches in the Bible Belt. It exhibits the incongruity between allegation and practice, between vociferous allegiance to a God of love and justice and mob action against a

[19] Highet, *op. cit.,* p. 61. That is not precisely what Professor Highet says. I
refer to him because he points out the connection.

[20] A. R. Thompson, *The Dry Mock: A Study of Irony in Drama* (University
of California Press, 1948), ch. 2, pp. 15–48, *passim.* I would not oppose irony to
comedy in general.

[21] *Ibid.,* p. 15. Cf. also Georges Palante, "L'Ironie: étude psychologique,"
*RPh,* Vol. 61 (1906), p. 152: "Irony is the passionate daughter of sorrow; but
it is also the proud daughter of cold intellect."

minority. Bombed churches and murdered integrationists are not funny. The irony springs from a vision of truth. Its perception depends, as Thompson says, on detachment, on the marshaling of knowledge and facts, on the awareness, for example, that the South is dominated by a Bible-thumping fundamentalism that alleges utter fidelity to the letter of Scripture. And yet many who so loudly proclaimed their Christianity failed to condemn the tossing of bombs. To perceive that, calls only for detached intelligence. To feel it, causes pain, which is only deepened by one's commitment to and radically different understanding of the Christianity claimed by the offenders. The irony strikes home with its fullest force to him who holds the truth prostituted in such a situation.

## Distinctive Marks of Irony

It is now time to come closer to defining irony, and I wish to distinguish it from some other terms denoting that which is close by irony. We have seen how the opposite ends of irony are in tragedy on the one side and comedy on the other. The categories are perhaps too narrow. We are not now considering fiction alone — using the word to mean literature made for its own sake, frequently dubbed " creative writing " — but of other kinds of literature as well.

Perhaps we need to distinguish irony from its near neighbors in several different ways. Let me suggest, then, that ironic tragedy is to be distinguished from nonironic tragedy, if there is such a thing, by observing whether or not the tragic circumstances are meaningful. Ironic tragedy postulates a meaningful universe, a moral universe, if you like, in which the tragic destiny involves the restoration of broken morality. Greek tragedy, on the whole, is ironic in that sense, for it is based by and large upon the *hybris* that represents an overstepping of moral bounds. Ironic tragedy, then, comprehends the tragic fate in terms of an assumption about the meaning of the world, on the basis, as I suggested before, of a vision of truth.

What of comedy? Clearly, there is both ironic and nonironic comedy. It has been suggested that irony has in it something of pain. Comic irony includes a hurt. Yet to be comic it cannot hurt too much. If it begins to hurt too much, it becomes either tragedy or denunciation. Once more, we must think of the vision of truth. Comedy, or humor, which is much more difficult to write about than tragedy, points out the grotesque and absurd, the laughable and ridiculous, in what we take for granted. But if it does not sting, it is not ironic but merely funny. Jack Benny is funny, but seldom ironic; Mort Sahl is ironic, but seldom merely funny. On the one side, humor moves beyond irony to the joke, which is a rather accidental combination of incongruities, such as the sign on a Volkswagen: "Help Stamp Out Cadillacs." On the other side, it moves beyond irony to what has been called "sick humor." [22] The one is content to accept incongruity and live with it; the other would prefer the whole sorry mess to be done away. Comic irony, in distinction from both, laughs to bring about amendment.

We must distinguish irony from another group of terms. One thinks, for example, of sarcasm, which is often equated with irony, in that it usually means the opposite of what it says. Sometimes the two can be distinguished only by the tone of voice used, and many writers do not bother to separate irony and sarcasm. Sarcasm will seldom attempt to hide its feelings, and its tone is ordinarily very heavy. Irony, on the other hand, uses a lighter tone and will therefore have a far more ambiguous effect. Paul's heavy-handed reference to "these superlative apostles" (II Cor. 12:11) is sarcastic, not ironic, and the same can be said of the

---

[22] Since "sick" is an accurate adjective, the text need not be cluttered with examples. The following may convey its character to any innocent thus far spared from it: "Mommy, what's a vampire?" "Shut up, and drink your blood!"

term " superpatriots " as applied to right-wing conservatives.

Invective is of the same order, though it seldom bothers with double meanings. It is simply denunciation. To those who already agree, it is purest truth; to those who disagree, darkest falsehood. Byron's reaction to a bad review of some poetry was, I think, invective:

> Still must I hear? — shall hoarse Fitzgerald bawl
> His creaking couplets in a tavern hall,
> And I not sing? [23]

Invective and sarcasm have in common the aim not only to wound but to destroy. I would distinguish them from irony, because I do not believe that irony, properly so called, is meant to destroy.[24] To be sure, it is criticism, and its criticism may be bitter in the extreme. But the basis of irony in a vision of truth means that irony aims at amendment of the incongruous rather than its annihilation.

Another term is " parody," a form of satire that imitates its object by exaggeration in order to ridicule it.[25] Parody uses the grand style on a trivial subject, such as the famous and ancient *Battle of Frogs and Mice* in the style of Homer, or it uses the bumbling prose of Dwight Eisenhower on a grand subject, as in a version of the Gettysburg Address.[26] There may be a certain irony in some parodies, but it is by no means constant, for parody is actually a form of sarcasm. Though it may produce a good

[23] " English Bards and Scotch Reviewers." The criticism was in *The Edinburgh Review*. Highet points out (*op. cit.*, p. 48) that Byron was imitating Juvenal, making the poem both invective and parody.

[24] David Worcester, *The Art of Satire* (Harvard University Press, 1940), p. 78, says, " When we dislike a writer's irony, we call it sarcasm." That may be psychologically sound, though it is hardly a definition. Perhaps Mr. Worcester was being sarcastic.

[25] See Highet, *op. cit.*, pp. 67–147.

[26] Oliver Jensen, " The Gettysburg Address in Eisenhowese," in Dwight Macdonald, ed., *Parodies: An Anthology from Chaucer to Beerbohm — and After* (Random House, Inc., 1960), pp. 447–448.

laugh, the laugh is always tinged with bitterness. A Democrat will laugh much harder at the "Eisenhowese" Gettysburg Address than will a Republican. Parody, like sarcasm, always produces a victim. The victim may be slaughtered, or he may only be a fraternity pledge up for hazing. But even fraternity hazing sometimes gets out of hand.

Satire, too, is not to be equated with irony. It may, of course, have irony in it, and no doubt some satires are almost pure irony. *The Praise of Folly* splendidly exemplifies ironic satire. There is little in the early sixteenth century that Folly does not satirize, and the sharpest barbs are aimed at the fattest and laziest sacred cows. But the barbs are always based on truth. Folly herself cries that only fools dare speak the truth:

With all their felicity, indeed, the princes of earth seem to me most unfortunate in this respect, that they have no one to tell them the truth, but are compelled to have toadies instead of friends. But, some one will say, the ears of princes have an antipathy to truth, and for this reason the princes shun wise counsellors, fearing that possibly one more free than the others will stand forth and dare to speak things true rather than pleasant. Yes, by and large, veracity is disliked by kings. And yet a remarkable thing happens in the experience of my fools: from them not only true things, but even sharp reproaches, will be listened to; so that a statement which, if it came from a wise man's mouth, might be a capital offense, coming from a fool gives rise to incredible delight. Veracity, you know, has a certain authentic power of giving pleasure, if nothing offensive goes with it; but this the gods have granted only to fools.[27]

If that is the power of fools, Folly possesses it to the extreme degree. But Folly is always dissimulating. As Erasmus remarks

---

[27] *The Praise of Folly*, pp. 49–50. Erasmus is speaking of those "fools," comparable to the "fools" in Shakespeare (e.g., in *King Lear*), who were looked upon as half mad, half idiot. The "fool" was viewed not as a comedian but as a simpleton.

to Thomas More in his dedicatory preface: " If there is anyone whom the work cannot please, he should at least remember this, that it is a fine thing to be slandered by Folly." [28] That, at any rate, is said ironically, and the irony that Folly should expose the ludicrous incongruities of the sixteenth century informs the whole declamation.[29]

That some satires are ironic does not mean that all satires are. Voltaire's *Candide,* in which he satirizes by example the contention of Leibniz that this is the best of all possible worlds, is finally not ironic. All Voltaire wants to do is to exhibit this piece of reasoning as fatuous nonsense. He has no positive purpose, presents no alternative to Leibniz. " The implicit purpose of the author is to deny that design in life exists." [30] Sheer denial is not of the character of irony, and we should have to call *Candide* a sarcastic satire. Must we not say the same for what is perhaps the best-known satire in English, Swift's *Gulliver's Travels?* Swift uses the medium of the travel and adventure story to explore his own society and its failings. And the effect of the satire is to exhibit the whole of human society as dismally debased, unredeemed and irredeemable, to make us look upon humanity with loathing and contempt. Swift's demonstration of incongruity does not point to truth. He does not want or expect amendment of the human condition; he wants us to bellow with rage.[31]

[28] *Ibid.,* p. 4.

[29] Professor Hudson suggests the same irony in his introductory essay, " The Folly of Erasmus," but argues that irony cannot explain the boisterous exuberance of the piece, its *festivitas* (pp. xxxiii, xxxvii). I am not certain that irony and exuberance are so far apart. Exuberance undirected by truth is mere energy. But that is not Folly's kind of exuberance. Truth may receive humorous statement, which, if the truth be genuinely held, always carries with it that " gusto, abandon, and joyous release " that Professor Hudson ascribes to Erasmus. The exuberance and the irony are not, I suggest, incompatible but complementary.

[30] Highet, *op. cit.,* p. 11.

[31] Some recent critics have interpreted Swift far more positively than this, pointing out that the portrait of the Portuguese ship captain proves that humanity is not irredeemable for Swift. The sympathy of the portrait is so mitigated, however, by expressions of loathing for humanity that it can scarcely bear

He would have felt himself admirably justified had he been able
to see Walt Disney's bowdlerization of *Gulliver's Travels*.

It is sometimes suggested that the Christian doctrine of original
sin lies behind Swift's conclusion. If so, we must see in Swift's
understanding a radically heterodox view of original sin. For
the Christian doctrine of sin, original or other, is based on its
doctrine of salvation, and Swift seems to have had no such doctrine.[32] If original sin is perceived only through salvation, then
it must be classed not as pessimism but as irony, involving the
awareness of a crucial incongruity between the " is " and the
" ought " of human existence, between the human self-perception
and the human reality. But the incongruity is stated not in order
to damn the reality but in order to redeem it.

We may now summarize the argument, attempting to lay
down guidelines for the identification of irony. We have seen
that irony is criticism, implicit or explicit, which perceives in
things as they are an incongruity. The incongruity is by no means
merely mean and contemptible, though it may be willful. Nor is
it only accidental, the work of fate, a matter of the way the ball
bounces or the cookie crumbles. The incongruity may be that of
ironic satire, between what is and what ought to be. It may be
an incongruity between what is actually so and what the object
of ironic criticism thinks to be so, as in the irony of tragedy, or
in the ironies we perceive in history.[33]

But irony is distinguished from other perceptions of incongruity

---

the weight put upon it. Much more compelling is the interpretation of my col-
league, W. B. Carnochan, " The Complexity of Swift: Gulliver's Fourth Voyage,"
*Studies in Philology*, Vol. 60 (1963), pp. 23–44, who argues that the self-irony
of Gulliver on his own disgust for mankind shows that Swift is not unambiguously convinced of his own denunciation. With all deference to the experts, I
still fail to see that Swift actually offers even a gleam of positive evaluation upon
man.

[32] Highet, *op. cit.*, p. 160.

[33] Cf. Reinhold Niebuhr's provocative book, *The Irony of American History*
(Charles Scribner's Sons, 1952).

by two characteristics. One is the means of statement, which we may describe as understatement or a method of suggestion rather than of plain statement. The other is a stance in truth from which the perception comes.

I have tried to illustrate the method of suggestion above. It may be the use of words with opposite or contrasting meanings. It may be the simple juxtaposition of the " is " and the " ought," leaving the moral to the reader's perceptiveness. It may use the techniques of double-edged speech, in which a character says one thing and his audience, with a wider context of knowledge, understands another. But the ironist's method forbids his coming right out and saying, " What you say or think is wrong; here is what is right." The ironic criticism requires of its hearers and readers the burden of recognition, the discovery of the relation between the ironist's " is " and his " ought." And to use the ironic method is to risk the failure of this recognition, the misunderstanding of the ironist's criticism.[34]

The other distinguishing mark of irony is its stance in truth. To be sure, this is truth as the ironist sees it, which means that he too may be subject to the deft barbs of irony. But the ironist's criticism comes from a more or less explicit " ought," or a more transcendent " is," which, if it is not an integral part of the ironic discourse, is an implicit background to it. The vision of truth prevents ironic criticism from being sarcastic or nihilistic.[35] It is

---

[34] Hudson, *op. cit.,* pp. xxxvi–xxxvii, refers to an amusing instance, in which a modern publisher took Erasmus' satire on churchmen as an attack on faith itself. " From the serene Citadel of Truth, armed with the weapons of reason and satire, Erasmus has in this work severely bombarded the strongholds of faith." To this Hudson replies, quite rightly, " But Erasmus, we may flatly say, was interested in defending and arming the strongholds of faith."

[35] I have puzzled over Aristophanes' caricature of Socrates in *The Clouds* in this regard. Is it ironic or sarcastic satire? On the one hand, though there may be some extenuating factors, Aristophanes appears to caricature Socrates in order to destroy his influence, and this is indignantly brought up in Plato's *Apology*. On the other hand, Aristophanes opposes Socrates from a stance in what he considers truth, perhaps something approaching a fifth-century B.C. Athenian John

not, therefore, mere opposition but is also protest, in the classic
sense of the term: testifying in favor of one thing as over against
another.[36]

Where these two factors are combined in the perception and
statement of incongruity, there, we may fairly say, we have irony.
Let it be repeated that the ironist depends on his hearer or reader
for recognition, and therefore he risks misunderstanding. The
misunderstanding may sometimes lie in a reader's recognition of
irony where the author did not intend it. No matter. The author's intentions do not mark off the limits within which we
read him. They cannot, of course, be overlooked. But we may
perceive an irony that even he did not perceive. What he says
may have an ironic effect on us, whether or not he worked for
that effect. This effect is not invalid. The work stands before
us, not as an antiquated object to which we apply analysis as to
a cadaver, but as a living voice whose accents we hear and with
which we enter conversation. What happens between us and a
book, then, is neither the imposition of our own thoughts upon
it, since its pages contain not our thoughts but another's, nor the
imposition of its author's thoughts upon us, since we read with

---

Birch Society — but that is probably unfair to Aristophanes, since the John Birch
Society shows no traces of a sense of humor, let alone a capacity for satire. Socrates is undermining what Aristophanes holds to be true, and the dramatist uses
the weapons of satire and caricature to show it. Yet we cannot easily slide Aristophanes into a pigeonhole. Perhaps it is as well; he is too mercurial a genius for
that.

[36] I disagree here with the conclusion to which A. R. Thompson comes (*op.
cit.*, p. 257): "Whenever an ironist acquires a genuine faith and a genuine
desire to establish it, he stops being an ironist and preaches." Again: "We conclude that spiritual ironists are sick souls, and that irony as a weapon is usually
a method of destruction. But the reason that the ironist's soul is sick is that he
has visions of a better world than the existing one, and the destruction of present evil gives opportunity for future good" (pp. 257–258). That may be a fair
judgment on the so-called "romantic irony," and, with some reservations, I
would accept the last sentence. But I think that Thompson has confused irony
and sarcasm. His term "sick" is far too strong, though he does not use it in the
sense referred to in note 22 above. Precisely the health of a vision of truth, "a
genuine faith," makes irony possible.

our minds, not his. What happens is a new relationship between reader and writer, a conversation (I would say " dialogue " had the word not lately been overused) in which each acts upon the other. The effect an author makes on us, whatever his intentions, is an aspect of our understanding his work. We are called on precisely to " understand " him, not simply to accept his ideas.

## THE IRONIC IN THE OLD TESTAMENT: SOME EXAMPLES

I propose finally to point to a few instances of irony in the Old Testament, indicating where I think the irony is, how it is expressed. My purpose is simply to illustrate the statement, implied by the existence of this book, that irony is present in the Old Testament.

We may begin by referring to an ironic touch in a narrative. In Judg., ch. 3, is the story of Ehud the judge and his murder of Eglon, the fat king of Moab. Eglon has subjugated Israel, and Ehud is taking him the tribute money (v. 15) as well as a concealed sword with two " edges " (Heb., *pēyôth;* literally, " mouths "). Having delivered the money, Ehud now informs Eglon that he has a " secret message " (*dābār,* "word "), at which Eglon admits him alone to the roof chamber. Ehud repeats, " I have a message from God for you," [37] at which he produces the sword and plunges it to the hilt in Eglon's obese belly. There are two pieces of irony here. One is Ehud's use of the manipulation of misunderstanding of his " message," Eglon understanding a spoken message, Ehud meaning the action of murder. The other is the advantage taken of the usual term " mouth " for the business edge of a sword in conjunction with Ehud's " message." We watch the scene with full knowledge of what will happen,

[37] Quotations from the Old Testament throughout the book, unless otherwise identified, are in my own translation. Should they correspond to any published translation, it is fortuitous.

and we listen to Ehud's cryptic words, double-edged like his
sword. The episode is unquestionably gruesome, the irony also
gruesome.[38]

Of a different kind is the irony in the first two chapters of
The Book of Amos. Whatever the origins and authenticity of
these oracles on the nations,[39] the final editor has an ironic standpoint. To see it, we need a map. With a map we can observe the
geographical progression of the oracles from the periphery to the
center, from northeast (Damascus) to southwest (Gaza), from
northwest (Tyre) to southeast (Edom), up the eastern border
(Ammon and Moab),[40] crossing to the direct south (Judah), and
finally, with the sudden plunge, bringing the judgment to the
center, to Israel itself. We can imagine the xenophobic listeners
nodding in happy agreement as the prophet's doom moves across
one enemy after another, the very piling up of oracles lulling
them to a doze until suddenly, with that characteristic prophetic
shock, they are jerked awake with "For three transgressions
of.—Israel, or for four . . ." The oracles are so adroitly arranged
as to appear haphazard, satisfying the hearers' desire for destruction on their enemies, while all the time the doom circles closer
and closer. The irony lies in the shock of the climax, which is
surely not intended to be noticed until too late.

A subtly ironic touch by means of a metaphor appears in
Hos. 6:3-4.

[38] Cf. the remark of Max Eastman, *The Enjoyment of Laughter* (Simon and
Schuster, Inc., 1936), p. 203, that the Greek dramatists sometimes "exchange
with the audience a gruesome wink at the expense of their doomed hero." Eastman goes on to suggest that this tragic reversal has almost the character of a
practical joke. That quality is more noticeable in the present instance than in
Greek tragedy.

[39] Most commentators feel that at least the oracle on Judah (ch. 2:4-5) and
probably those on Tyre (ch. 1:9-10) and Edom (vs. 11-12) are secondary. See,
e.g., T. H. Robinson, "Die zwölf kleinen Propheten," 2te Auflage (*HAT*,
J. C. B. Mohr, Tübingen, 1954), p. 76, who thinks that a redactor has brought
the oracles together.

[40] It would be nicer for the progression if these two had been reversed, but
their present order does not damage the point.

"So let us know, let us pursue knowing Yahweh;
Like dawn, his coming is certain,
And he will come to us like the showers,
Like the rain that waters the earth." [41]
What shall I do with you, Ephraim?
What shall I do with you, Judah? [42]
When your loyalty is like a morning cloud,
And like the dew, early to depart.

The " loyalty " (*chesed*), a mutual and enduring relationship expected to surmount any threat, is ironic, for it is a contradiction
in terms to speak of an enduring loyalty that evaporates like dew
on the grass. We note also the metaphorical relationships of the
two verses. The " dawn," to which Yahweh's coming is compared in v. 3, is balanced in v. 4 by the " morning " and " early."
The " showers " and " rain," metaphors of Yahweh's gracious
care for his people, are balanced by the " cloud " and " dew,"
metaphors of Israel's unfaithfulness. The assurance of Yahweh's
return to Israel is rendered ironic by the perception that Yahweh's
coming demands loyalty, but Israel's loyalty is a useless and non-
irrigating vapor.

We may return finally to another instance of irony in narrative,
the incident of David and Bathsheba (II Sam. 11:1 to 12:23),
which opens in the telling with an implied irony:

In the spring of the year, the time when kings go forth to war,
David sent off Joab and his retainers and all Israel. And they
despoiled the Ammonites and laid siege to Rabbah. But David re-
mained in Jerusalem. (Ch. 11:1.)

It is only a touch. One might miss it. A warrior king like David
stays home while his army is out on a campaign, at the time

[41] Reading *yarweh* for *yôreh*.
[42] Read " Israel "? The mention of Judah in the context is strange.

usual for kings to go out to battle. The palace roof in Jerusalem,
of course, provides a nice vantage point to observe the fetching
sight of Bathsheba at her bath (v. 2). We may hazard the guess
that Bathsheba may not have been unaware of David's whereabouts. He summons; she comes. One does not argue with a
king. And when a woman's husband is off to war, the king does
not wrestle long with his conscience. Of course the inevitable
happens: Bathsheba turns up pregnant.

It is now necessary that David clear himself, and he sends for
Uriah, the husband. If David can get Uriah to sleep with his
wife, the alibi will be sufficient. Uriah proves recalcitrant, un-
willing to enjoy himself while his comrades are suffering the
hardships of war. David tries everything he can think of to get
Uriah to his house, suggestion and gift (v. 8), drunkenness (v. 13).
Uriah remains stubbornly and inconveniently loyal to David.
We cannot miss the irony of this loyalty, prudish as Uriah may
be about it.[48] For precisely this spells Uriah's disaster. He is sent
back to battle, and instructions are given that he is not to return (v. 15). Joab asks no questions but does as he is told, sending David the news in quite casual fashion (v. 21). David's return message is strange: " Do not let this matter trouble you,
for the sword devours now this one, now that one " (v. 25). Is
he telling Joab not to be inquisitive? Or is he pacifying his own
conscience with a rationalization: " That's the way war is "? I
am inclined to the latter reading. David's conscience is bothering
him, and he is salving it with this pallid platitude.

At this point, David's respect for custom and tradition is in
marked contrast to his disrespect for it before. He carefully waits
for Bathsheba to finish her period of mourning before making
her an honest woman (vs. 26-27). It all looks fine, and everyone

---

[48] There is, of course, the fact that men at war were vowed to a ceremonial
purity that excluded sexual activities. This is doubtless in Uriah's mind, though
it does not bother David at all.

is happy — except Yahweh. We now have Nathan's famous parable about the poor man's little ewe, which the rich man heedlessly snatched from him (ch. 12:1-4). David, apparently thinking this is an actual case of injustice, becomes all righteously indignant (vs. 5-6). His devout care for just treatment of the poor man is an ironic contrast to the obvious subject of the parable. "You are the man!" (V. 7.) Now denunciation begins, and we need not follow through Nathan's oracle of reproof.

The irony of the episode is, I think, evident. The incongruity between "is" and "ought" is perceptible to any reader from the beginning, but ironically it is not perceptible to David until he is told in plain language. He stumbles blindly on, compounding the trespasses, piling Pelion on Ossa, always only one jump ahead of his conscience. Having committed adultery, he tries to cover his tracks by engineering Bathsheba's legitimate intercourse. That failing, he does what in spirit adds up to murder, as Nathan tells him: "You have struck Uriah the Hittite with the sword, . . . and you have slain him with the sword of the Ammonites" (ch. 12:9). Then David passes it off as the fortunes of war. Finally, confronted with an allegory of it all, he turns lawful.

There is a further ironic touch in the story. The child of the union dies, and David, on receiving the news, immediately puts off his penitence. The servants are surprised. David's reply is strange. He fasted, wept, and prayed while the child was alive on the chance that Yahweh would change his mind (v. 22). "But now he is dead. Why should I fast? Can I bring him back again?" (V. 23.) Are we not irresistibly reminded that Uriah too is dead and cannot be brought back? "The sword devours now this one, now that one." (Ch. 11:25.) With the illegitimate child, David had done all he could to keep him alive. With Uriah, he had done all he could, short of using his own weapon, to take his life. With injustice, then, David succeeded. With mercy, he failed.

These few examples should suffice to establish the presence of irony in the Old Testament and perhaps to suggest something of its flavor. Those familiar with the Old Testament will probably already have thought of other examples.

The following essays will attempt identification and interpretation of irony as it appears in certain books or portions of books. The six to be studied by no means exhaust the occurrences of irony in the Old Testament, as the examples already given demonstrate. They seem to me particularly strong and representative instances of the use and functions of irony, which pervades the Old Testament to a degree no scholar has yet penetrated. These essays may mark a small beginning on the comprehension of that pervasiveness.

# II

## JONAH:
## THE ABSURDITY OF GOD

Controversies over The Book of Jonah have apparently all but ceased. One's viewpoint on the historicity of the "great fish" (ch. 1:17 [Heb., ch. 2:1]) no longer determines his orthodoxy or heterodoxy, and reference to Matt. 12:40 does not provide conclusive proof of the matter. That theological battle has been finished. There is even a remarkable unanimity on the interpretation of the book among Old Testament scholars (a notably quarrelsome lot), which might seem suspicious were it not so welcome. It is agreed that the story is fictional and that the psalm in ch. 2:2-9 (Heb., ch. 2:3-10) is a later insertion. Most scholars date the writing of the book in the late fifth or early fourth century B.C., since its implied universalism best accords with a postexilic date and may be understood as a protest against a xenophobic mood in the somewhat self-righteous reforming zeal of those years.[1]

Some scholars have interpreted the book not merely as a piece of fiction but as an allegory, in which Jonah represents Israel, swallowed by Babylon (the fish) after the preexilic storms of in-

---

[1] Yehezkel Kaufmann, *The Religion of Israel,* tr. and abridged by Moshe Greenberg (The University of Chicago Press, 1960), p. 282, holds that the book was written in the eighth century and recounts stories early told (and perhaps partly historical) of the prophet referred to in II Kings 14:25. The prevailing view he calls "a tissue of errors," but he fails to substantiate that forthright judgment. It is, of course, true that we have very little objective evidence on which to base a dating.

ternational stress but then released to go reluctantly to the nations with the proclamation of the universal God. The allegory has been worked out to various levels of detail; George Adam Smith went so far as to identify the plant (ch. 4:6-7) with Zerubbabel, while other allegorizations were so general as scarcely to qualify as allegory in the strict sense at all. On the whole, the effort has been abandoned, for some pieces of the story will not fit into any allegorical mold.

Most commentators now call The Book of Jonah a parable, using the word more or less loosely to mean a story with a didactic point. That the book is a story rather than a collection of oracles, like all the other prophetic books, distinguishes it formally from the others. To be sure, third-person narratives occur within some of the other prophetic books (e.g., Isa., chs. 36 to 39; Jer. 26:1-19; chs. 28; 36 to 44; 52; Hos. 1:1-9; Amos 7:10-17). But either these stories are taken from other sources (Isa., chs. 36 to 39, and Jer., ch. 52, mainly from II Kings), or they are told principally for oracles incorporated in them. The stories in the first six chapters of The Book of Daniel might seem to provide an analogy to the tale of Jonah, though they can hardly be called parables, for their purpose is rather to exhort and encourage than to teach. The Books of Ruth and Esther are self-contained stories, but only Ruth could be called remotely didactic, and its point is made even more subtly than that of Jonah.

The Book of Ruth is like Jonah in that it is protest literature. Yet, unlike Jonah, the subject of its protestations does not appear in the book.[2] Indeed, the fact that the figure of Jonah represents all that the author of the book means to reject suggests that there

[2] With not many exceptions, the scholarly consensus is that Ruth was written, perhaps from traditional materials, at about the same time as Jonah, to oppose the reformers who sought to force Jewish men to divorce their non-Jewish wives. Cf. Ezra, ch. 10; Neh. 13:23-27. Note especially the reference in Neh. 13:23 to women of Moab, of whom Ruth is one. Still another voice protesting this climate of opinion may be heard in Mal. 2:13-16.

is a better term than the loose " parable " by which to identify his method. The Book of Jonah is a satire.[3] It portrays the prophet in order to ridicule him. To be sure, the author clarifies his position by playing the figure of Jonah off against God. Hence it can be said with some justice that God is the central actor in the story.[4] But our attention is directed primarily to the prophet, and his attitude is the focal point of the tale. The attitude of God — and of the author — highlights the attitude of Jonah in order to satirize it. And the satire is through and through ironic. Its basis is a perception of incongruity. It uses the " method of suggestion " to which I referred in the previous chapter; and it clearly takes its " stance in truth." To demonstrate the former must be the major purpose of this account of the book.[5]

The author has taken as his subject the prophet briefly referred to in II Kings 14:25, a native of Gath-hepher who prophesied about extending the borders of Israel in the time of Jeroboam II in the eighth century B.C. No other information about the prophet exists, though some have speculated that our author took some previously existing tales about him and wove them together to make his story. Since there is no evidence for this, we can as easily assume that he wrote the story out of his head. But why did he pick up this otherwise unknown prophet? Perhaps Jonah was so obscure a figure that a new story about him

[3] The only scholars I can find who use this term are Adolphe Lods, *The Prophets and the Rise of Judaism*, tr. by S. H. Hooke (Routledge & Kegan Paul, Ltd., London, 1937), pp. 15, 334, and W. F. Stinespring, "Irony and Satire," *IDB*, Vol. 2, p. 928. Stinespring also calls the stories in the early chapters of Daniel satires.

[4] So Artur Weiser, *Das Buch der zwölf kleinen Propheten*, Vol. I (ATD, Vandenhoeck & Ruprecht, Göttingen, 1949), p. 199.

[5] I have been unable to find a single commentator on The Book of Jonah who says that it makes its point by means of irony. B. Davie Napier comes closest to it in *Song of the Vineyard* (Harper & Brothers, 1962), pp. 366–368. Eduard Haller, "Die Erzählung von dem Propheten Jona" (*Theologische Existenz heute*, N.F. 65, Chr. Kaiser Verlag, München, 1958), p. 6, thinks that the author precisely holds back from irony.

would contradict nothing previously known. An analogous process took place with the figure of Enoch in the intertestamental
period. Or is the author making an ironic point with the very
name? It is surely not incidental to the author's purpose that
Jonah is the son of Amittai, and that the name Amittai is related to the noun *ᵉmeth,* " truth, faithfulness." The Hebrew
phrase " son of," moreover, frequently expresses category: " son
of valor " (*ben chayil*) in I Sam. 14:52 is a " valiant man "; " son
of iniquity " (*ben ᶜawᵉlāh*) in Ps. 89:22 (Heb., v. 23) is an " iniqui-
tous man." Jonah, by analogy, is a " son of faithfulness or truth,"
but he abandons his faithfulness at the first opportunity and
speaks truth only under duress, even then not understanding it.

The prophet is confronted by a divine command from nowhere:
" Get up, go to Nineveh, that great city, and proclaim against
it; for their wickedness has risen up to me " (ch. 1:2). Nineveh:
that name would raise a mingled fear and anticipation in the
heart of any prophet commanded to go there. The capital of Assyria, the very symbol of utter moral degradation: there a prophet
would be among savage wolves, but there, too, he could justly
proclaim doom upon indubitable wickedness. The denunciation
of Nineveh would be a real pleasure — the prophet Nahum, at
least, found it so.

But Jonah promptly " gets up " (the same verb as in Yahweh's
command, v. 2) and hurries to take ship in the opposite direction. Our author does not tell us why, though later he will put
a certain rationale in Jonah's mouth (ch. 4:2). He wants us now
to observe the incongruity of a prophet's unhesitating and total
abandonment of his prophetic task. Jonah sets off by ship for
Tarshish, " fleeing," as the author tells us twice, " from the presence of Yahweh." [6]

[6] What place is designated by Tarshish, or whether any specific place is
meant by it, remains uncertain, but it seems clear that the author assumes it to
be about as far west as one can go. T. H. Robinson, *loc. cit.,* p. 121, calls it the
" ultima Thule " of the Old Testament. Haller, *loc. cit.,* p. 16, says that it means

The Old Testament tells the story of only one other sea voyage, the one taken by Noah. The sea to the Israelites was a fearful and threatening realm, the habitation of monsters of chaos (cf. Isa. 27:1), and so inimical to God that he had set explicit boundaries to it (Jer. 5:22; Job 38:8-11). In the psalms, the sea's roaring suggests Yahweh's enemies (cf. Ps. 46:3; 65:7; 93:4). In Daniel's vision, the four monstrous beasts, symbolic of Yahweh's national foes, come up out of the tumult of the " great sea " (Dan. 7:2-3). Only once do we have reference to seafaring occupations by worshipers of Yahweh (Ps. 107:23-32). Indeed, when Solomon wanted to institute ocean trade, he apparently had to charter Phoenician ships and sailors to do it for him (I Kings 9:26-28). And when John, the author of the book of The Revelation, describes the " new heaven and new earth " to be awaited by the faithful, one of its characteristics is that " the sea was no more " (Rev. 21:1).[7]

God curbs and controls the sea (cf. Ps. 89:10), and Jonah's effort to escape God's presence on the sea is an ironically perceived impossibility.[8] For the storm, which Yahweh " hurls " upon the sea, is, as so often in the Old Testament, the sign not of the divine absence but of his presence.[9] The pagan sailors give thought to their gods first of all in the storm, even before they

---

" the end of the world." The author's meaning is certainly not different from that of the poet in Ps. 139:9.

[7] There is, of course, the molten " sea " before the Temple (I Kings 7:23-26), probably a Canaanite symbol. Such terms as $t^e h \hat{o} m$, " the deep, abyss," and $mayim$ $rabb\hat{i}m$, " many, or great, waters," convey the chaotic character of the sea. Cf. H. G. May, " Some Cosmic Connotations of Mayim Rabbîm, ' Many Waters,' " JBL, Vol. 74 (1955), pp. 9–21.

[8] T. H. Robinson, loc. cit., p. 121, thinks that the expression $wayyitt\bar{e}n$ $s^e k\bar{a}r\bar{a}h$, " and he paid the fare " (v. 3), means that Jonah chartered the whole ship to himself. That would add to the portrait of a man desperately eager to escape, and no mention is made of other passengers. But the author had no reason to speak of other passengers, since he wanted our attention focused on Jonah.

[9] Passages illustrating this are numerous. To take examples only from psalmodic literature, cf. Ps. 29; 77:16 ff.; 97:2-5; 107:23 ff.; 148:7-8; Hab. ch. 3.

begin to lighten ship. Jonah, on the other hand, is down in the
hold fast asleep.[10] Is he so certain that he has escaped? Or is he
simply ignorant of storms at sea? The sailors are not ignorant,
and, aware of their own frailty, make application to the higher
powers. "*In Sturm und Wetter ist Gott unser Ritter*."[11] That,
at least, is in the captain's mind, and his exhortation to Jonah
awakens ironic echoes of the divine commission to the prophet:
"What's with you, sleeping? Get up, cry to your God. Perhaps
that god will give us a thought, and we will not perish" (Jonah
1:6). Clearly the resources are almost exhausted, and the aid of
one more god might tip the balance. But there is no indication
whatever that Jonah prayed. He was, it would seem, well beyond
all that.

Someone, however, was responsible for the storm. To the ancient mind, storms were not the products of impersonal meteoro-
logical forces but were directed to specific ends by specific wills.
The sailors want to know "on whose account this evil has come
to us."[12] Someone is to blame, and if the blame can be placed,
the danger may pass. To identify the guilty party, they do the
ancient equivalent of tossing coins or throwing dice. As we knew
it would, the thrown lot singles out Jonah. Now, for the first
time, the sailors show some interest in this strange character,
and — must it not strike us as wildly incongruous? — in the
midst of the howling storm, request of Jonah a thumbnail auto-
biography. "Tell us, please, what is your business, and whence

10 The verb *rādam* denotes a very sound sleep; cf. *tardēmāh*, "deep sleep,"
in Gen. 2:21. We must notice the parallel between this incident and the episode
of the stilling of the sea in Mark 4:35-41 and parallels in Matt. 8:23-27; Luke
8:22-25.

11 Friedrich Nötscher, *Zwölfprophetenbuch* (Echter-Bibel, Echter-Verlag,
Würzburg, 1954), p. 83. The rhyme cannot be reproduced in English; literally,
"In storm and tempest God is our deliverer."

12 Nötscher, *op. cit.*, translates the phrase in a way that we could interpret (he
does not) as irony: "*Wem wir dies Unglück verdanken*": "To whom we are
indebted for this misfortune."

have you come? What is your country, and from what people are you? " (V. 8.) [13]

Jonah's answer touches only part of their question and partly a question they have not asked: " I am a Hebrew, and I fear Yahweh the God of heaven, who made the sea and the land " (v. 9).[14] Jonah's theology is unexceptionable, but, like so much theology, it seems to make no difference to his action. We are certainly intended to perceive the incongruity between the prophet's confession of Yahweh as creator of the sea and his attempt to escape on the sea. Jonah, moreover, does not perceive it, and we are unquestionably supposed to notice that also. Perhaps the author intends that we see, too, that Jonah uses the verb " to fear " in the very weakened sense of " to nod liturgically toward."

What, now, is to be done to save the ship? In notable contrast to his erstwhile unwillingness to proclaim the word to Nineveh, Jonah offers himself as a sacrifice: " Pick me up and hurl me into the sea " (v. 12). A touch of sympathetic magic may be implied there. If Jonah be " hurled to the sea " (*hētíl el hayyām*), it may offset and nullify the storm, which Yahweh had " hurled to the sea " (*hētíl el hayyām,* v. 4). On the other hand, perhaps we must see Jonah's offer not as a sudden burst of generosity but as his perception that death might yet be a way out of his frightful mission.[15] Jonah will express the same thought again (ch. 4:3, 8).

The crew first struggles to avoid this solution, to save the prophet alive (ch. 1:13). Failing in that, they take the precaution of declaring their innocence before throwing Jonah overboard. " Do not hold against us innocent blood." (V. 14.) That means,

[13] Most commentators excise the phrase *bāᵃsher lᵉmí hārāʾāh hazzôth lānû* in v. 8 with important manuscripts of LXX. It does seem obtuse of the sailors to ask again " on whose account this evil has come to us," since Jonah's selection by lot clearly demonstrates that he is the culprit.

[14] Almost all commentators agree that v. 10b is a gloss, incomprehensible in view of the sailor's questions to Jonah in v. 8.

[15] So, persuasively, Haller, *loc. cit.,* p. 24.

" Do not blame us for murder if this man is not guilty; we know only what we are told, and he has told us that he is guilty." Upon Jonah's departure into the sea, the storm ceases, and the sailors are greatly afraid, as they were before (vs. 5, 10), so afraid indeed that they sacrifice to Yahweh.

Their fear is different, however, from the " fear " that Jonah confessed (v. 9). We are perhaps to see the last act of these erstwhile pagan sailors as genuine conversion. And we, who generally look upon fear as something to be avoided (hence we often trivialize it into mere " anxiety "), ought also to notice that, although the sailors were " afraid " at the onset of the storm (v. 5), their fear is far greater at their rescue from it. We will see more in this strange tale of the fearful grace of God, a grace that is fearful because it so stoutly refuses to be limited by Jonah's — or our — theological categories.

Jonah, meanwhile, has been dealt with by the famous fish. The text has, of course, a " big fish " (*dāg gādôl*), not specifically a whale, for which we might expect such a term as *tannîn,* " sea monster." It could be argued that the Hebrews, landlubbers that they were, would not know the difference, that the fact that whales are properly not fishes but mammals is of very recent discovery. There are sperm whales in the Mediterranean, after all, and only a sperm whale among the cetaceans would have a gullet large enough to swallow a human being. Further, the LXX translates *dāg* in this passage and no other by *kētos,* the etymological source of the name Cetacea, and that may mean that already a tradition of interpretation had pointed to the whale as the culprit. The question is of less than burning significance. The author is emphasizing Jonah's humiliation in being transported back to his proper element inside the belly of a fish and then being summarily spat out on dry land (or perhaps, more picturesquely and if anything more humiliating, " vomited "). It is a touch both of the miraculous and of the ludicrous, and it bespeaks a writer of extraordinary literary gifts. Not only the sea itself but also its very denizens are in conspiracy, under Yahweh, to disabuse the prophet of his escapism. How silly Jonah must have felt in the eyes of God, or of anyone else looking on, as he was vomited head over heels across the dunes! It is enough to take the ego out of any man.

Once more with patience (" for the second time," ch. 3:1) comes the command. Subtly, our author has emphasized Jonah's new subordination by the new phrasing of the order: " Get up, go to Nineveh, that great city, and proclaim to it the proclamation that I am telling you " (v. 2). No reason is given this time; the proclamation is quite simply to be delivered. Jonah is no longer the collaborator, a party to deliberations. He is now an underling, who takes orders and raises no questions. Nor does the author waste his time or ours telling us where Jonah was or by what route he traveled to Nineveh. The essentials are stated, and no more. The command has been given, and now Jonah " gets up and goes" in the right direction. We might speculate, on the basis of his later reactions, that he grumbled the whole journey through, but even that does not occupy our narrator. " So Jonah got up and went to Nineveh, as Yahweh had told him." (V. 3.) There is a subtle touch in that sentence. In the first episode, " Jonah got up *to flee*" (*librō<sup>a</sup>ch,* with the infinitive, ch. 1:3); here, " Jonah got up *and went*" (*wayyēlek,* with the coordinate finite verb). It gives the last flick of retrospective irony to the tale of the voyage. Given the command to go, Jonah's intention " to flee" could not come to maturity (ch. 1). God's intention that he go was the only ultimate possibility, and Jonah's tardy but inevitable acquiescence is deftly conveyed by the use of the coordinate verb in ch. 3:3.

" Now Nineveh was a great city, even to God, three days' journey across." (Ch. 3:3b.) According to Herodotus, a day's march for an army was about 150 stadia, roughly seventeen miles, which

would make a "three days' journey" something like fifty miles!
It has been argued that the three days' journey refers not to the
diameter of the city but to its circumference, which would approximate the figures of Diodorus Siculus, who reported the circumference of Nineveh as about 480 stadia, a little over fifty miles.
Diodorus apparently assumed the city to have been a walled
rectangle of 150 by 90 stadia, or approximately 17 by 10 miles.
In point of fact, Diodorus, living five centuries after Nineveh had
ceased to exist, exaggerated the matter, though less than our
author did, for the city turned out, on being excavated, to have
a circumference of about $7\frac{1}{2}$ miles and a breadth at its widest
part of about 3 miles.[16] All of this is to say that the author of
The Book of Jonah was talking about an imaginary city, which
he had never seen but which had a huge and evil reputation in
the ancient world. The size of the city is exaggerated to imply
the magnitude of the prophet's task. Nineveh represents that
ruthless, utterly depraved, tyrannical nation which had deprived
Israel of ten of its twelve tribes. In the author's mind, Nineveh
is not a quantity but a quality, not a mere metropolis but an
immorality. He takes the symbol of the ancient world's most
impressive evil, magnifies and intensifies it by mass, and sends
his timorous prophet into the middle of it.

We should say, not quite to the middle. It takes but one day's
journey for the prophet's message to be heard. " Yet forty days,"
he cries, " and Nineveh will be turned upside down." (V. 4b.)
The threat as we read it now has a double meaning. It can mean
what Jonah intends it to mean, that the city is doomed, that it
will be overthrown as Sodom and Gomorrah were overthrown.[17]
But the verb (*hāphak*) can also mean " to be changed " in a

16 The data, including quotations from Diodorus Siculus, are given by
J. A. Bewer, *A Critical and Exegetical Commentary on the Book of Jonah* (ICC,
T. & T. Clark, Edinburgh, 1912), pp. 50–52.

17 The verb *hāphak*, used here, is that used in Gen. 19:25, 29. Cf. also Amos
4:11; Isa. 1:7 (emending *zārîm* to *sedôm*, with most scholars).

positive sense, from something bad to something good.[18] The latter is certainly not in the prophet's mind, but, given the response of the populace, may we not say that it is in the author's mind? "Forty days hence, Nineveh will be a different place." So it will: "The men of Nineveh turned faithful [yā'ªmînû] to God." [19] Like a dry haystack meeting a pine-knot torch, Nineveh explodes into repentance (v. 5).

No preacher has ever been confronted with such astounding success. Sackcloth becomes the uniform of all, both young and old. The king himself hears the word, as it seems, at second hand: "The matter reached the king." Immediately he forsakes his throne and his royal robes to grovel in the dust. His edict (vs. 7-9), duly drawn, witnessed, and signed by royalty and nobility alike, requires fasting, wearing sackcloth, prayer, and repentance even of the animals. Perhaps St. Francis preached to the birds, but only Jonah brought about the prayer and repentance of cattle!

Of course this is exaggeration, just as the city has been exaggerated. Everything about Nineveh is exaggerated, by the author's design. He intends the overwhelming success of the reluctant prophet to surprise everyone, Jonah included. This is a satire, and the author deliberately overdraws his scene to highlight the irony of the peevish prophet's totally unexpected suc-

[18] Cf., in the Qal, Zeph. 3:9; I Sam. 10:9; Jer. 31:13; Neh. 13:2; in the Niph., which we have in Jonah 3:4, cf. Hos. 11:8; Ex. 14:5; Esth. 9:22.

[19] Practically all commentators transpose ch. 4:5 from its present position, where it seems to confuse the narrative, to a position after ch. 3:4, assuming that the prophet went out to his lean-to east of the city to wait out the forty-day period before knowing the response of the Ninevites. Bewer, *op. cit.*, p. 52, and J. D. Smart, "Jonah," *IB*, Vol. 6 (Abingdon Press, 1956), p. 889, accept the LXX reading, "three days," in ch. 3:4, as the original text, instead of the forty days of MT, and retain ch. 4:5 in its present place. Bewer views v. 5b as a gloss. I see no compelling reason to alter the number, and I would confine the gloss in v. 5b to the words, "and he made himself a lean-to there and sat under it in the shade," with Smart, *loc. cit.*, p. 892. The problem with lightheartedly transposing this verse from one chapter to another is that one must account for its earlier movement to its present position. No scholars have done so, and I find myself therefore not overwhelmed by their reasoning.

cess. We are supposed to laugh at the ludicrous picture, precisely because Jonah becomes so upset.

We are also, I think, supposed to notice that the king's edict contains a piece of rather sophisticated theology. " Who knows — God may repent and have pity, and turn from his burning anger, and we may not perish." (V. 9; cf. Joel 2:14.) The Ninevites are not repenting in order to force God to call off the catastrophe. Their penitence is not magical. The author wants us to perceive that the Ninevites appear to understand more about the divine grace than Jonah does.[20] The irony of that need hardly be underlined.

But when Yahweh actually does " repent " (nācham, Niph.), the irony of the whole story comes swiftly to a head. Jonah is thoroughly vexed with God. " Really now, Yahweh! Is this not what I said while I was still in my own country? " (Ch. 4:2.) That is the first we have heard of any such expostulation. The author has purposely left it out before this, for only now can we comprehend the prophet's viewpoint. " That is why I hurried to flee to Tarshish: namely, that I knew that you are a God gracious and merciful, slow to anger and great of grace, and one who repents of evil." It would be possible to miss the author's satiric purpose here. He puts into the prophet's mouth a formula that occurs almost verbatim six other times in the Old Testament: Ex. 34:6; Ps. 86:15; 103:8; 145:8; Joel 2:13; Neh. 9:17; and it is echoed in Ps. 111:4; 112:4; Neh. 9:31; II Chron. 30:9. Jonah is mouthing — not for the first time — a liturgical cliché, a rote theology. He had spouted another such phrase to the sailors (Jonah 1:9).

He speaks the pious and well-worn words, but he thoroughly disapproves of their being true. " That is why I hurried to flee to Tarshish." No danger that this absurdly gracious God would

---

[20] So Smart, loc. cit., p. 890: "The whole is a model of how men should respond to God's word of judgment upon them." Cf. also Weiser, op. cit., p. 197.

bother me there! "So now, Yahweh, take my life from me, for it is better that I die than live." (Ch. 4:3.) Is the prophet thinking of his reputation? He had predicted doom, and now he will be made to look silly.[21] Yet Jonah's problem is not that he has been proved a liar, but that he is the agent of an unreasonable God. What business has a God of justice turning on the mercy act at *Nineveh?*

Jonah's request for death is a subtle piece of ironic satire. It is phrased in words very similar to those spoken by Elijah: "Enough now, Yahweh! Take my life, for I am not better than my fathers." (I Kings 19:4.) But where Elijah is in genuine despair over his failure to turn the hearts of idolatrous Israel, Jonah's despair rises out of vexation at God's acceptance of pagan Nineveh. And his sullen death wish is surely a parody of Elijah's profound discouragement.

Yahweh's response is freighted with irony: "Do you do well to be angry?" (v. 4). The prophet does not favor the deity with an answer but proceeds out of the city to take up his vigil, "until he should see what would happen in the city" (v. 5). Will Yahweh change his mind? Perhaps Jonah hopes he will. Or might the Ninevites change theirs? The forty days are not yet over. There may be time for the people to weary of piety and fall back into their previous evil ways.

The last lesson is yet to be learned. Now, as with the "great fish" (ch. 1:17), Yahweh "appoints" a plant to let the prophet sit in comfort. What kind of plant a *qîqāyôn* may be is uncertain. Most commentators identify it with the ricinus, the castor-oil tree, on the basis of Egyptian *kiki* and Talmudic Hebrew *qîq*. The LXX and Syriac versions seem to have thought of the bottle gourd, Symmachus and Jerome of ivy. It does not matter, and

---

[21] So Weiser, *op cit.*, p. 198. See also the hilarious and perceptive one-act play on Jonah, "It Should Happen to a Dog," by Wolf Mankowitz, in *Religious Drama 3*, ed. by Marvin Halverson (Meridian Books, 1959), pp. 121-135.

we would as soon get satisfaction by trying to identify the variety of Jack's beanstalk. The plant is merely miraculous, growing to shade proportions "in a night" (v. 10). At last the peevish prophet has something to cheer about: "And Jonah rejoiced greatly over the plant" (v. 6).

But Yahweh is not finished "appointing." This time it is a worm which, just at dawn, attacks the plant, so that it withers. Jonah has enjoyed the shade for only one day, and now Yahweh "appoints" the hot east wind to blow on Jonah. The east wind in Palestine comes immediately off the desert with unrelieved heat. Since our author had probably never been to upper Mesopotamia, since he was writing for Palestinians, and since he obviously does not labor over geographical verisimilitude, we need not inquire after the effect of an east wind at Nineveh. In Palestine, it is the sirocco, the absolutely dry, furnacelike blast of heat that parches the body by evaporating its perspiration. The wind and the heat of the sun, which "beat upon Jonah's head" with the force of heavy blows, combine to bring the prophet, quite understandably, to the verge of prostration. Once again he cries out for death: "Better I die than live" (v. 8b). What is there to live for? The prophetic message has gone awry, the shade that made waiting at least bearable is gone, and the maintenance of life is just too much trouble. How can a man function with a God like this, who favors his enemies but who, as soon as he has given one little thought to his servant's comfort, promptly makes life miserable for him again?

Yahweh repeats his earlier question: "Do you do well to be angry over the plant?" And the silly prophet's pleasure and displeasure come to their climax in his petulant and incautious reply: "Yes, I do well to be angry, angry enough to die!" (v. 9). Everything has gone wrong. Jonah has had to deal with an absurd God who insists on being what he says he will be. If living must involve living with a God like that, death is preferable.

At last, the author gives us — and Jonah — the full force of the divine irony. " You feel sorry for the plant, though you neither toiled over it nor grew it, though it came up in a night and perished in a night. But I, I am not to feel sorry for Nineveh, that great city, in which are more than 120,000 persons who do not know the difference between right and left, and many beasts as well! " (Vs. 10-11.) Yahweh has finally, as Artur Weiser says, " gotten him [Jonah] where he wants him." [22] For the first time, Jonah has committed himself to something. His verbal commitments to God earlier in the story were, as we have seen, a mere spouting of rote phrases with no relation to Jonah's real feelings. Now Jonah is willing to die for a castor-oil plant. Could any satirist have drawn his portrait more deftly? " The most profound issue of modern life," said Abraham J. Heschel, disagreeing with Albert Camus, " is not suicide; it is martyrdom. The question is, 'For what are you willing to die?'" [23] Jonah was willing to die earlier for the sake of escaping his prophetic commission (ch. 1:12), and the coincidence of rescuing a shipload of sailors did not affect him. But when it comes to Nineveh, " that great city," his vexation at the divine absurdity overcomes his humanity.

With ironic patience, Yahweh's final speech lays bare the absurdity of Jonah's position. The plant means nothing to Jonah except shade from the sun. It is sheer luxury. He has had neither responsibility for nor governance over it. " You feel sorry. . . . But I, I am not to feel sorry." Jonah, unable to take seriously either of his confessions of Yahweh, " the God who made the sea and the dry land " (ch. 1:9), " a God gracious and merciful, slow to anger and great of grace, and one who repents of evil " (ch. 4:2), is the personification of that arrogant isolationism

[22] Weiser, *op. cit.*, p. 199.
[23] I can claim for these words no more than paraphrase. They were spoken in a lecture at Stanford University in May, 1963.

which holds the God of heaven and earth in its pocket, all the while making pious noises about his universal reign and the breadth of his compassion. But the author of The Book of Jonah challenges this isolationism to consider the implications of such a reign and such a compassion. In that sense, we may see Jonah as representative of Israel. Such an untenable understanding of God's ways with man as that held by Jonah was a persistent notion in Israel. Jesus was battling the same pattern of belief when he said to the chief priests and elders, " The tax collectors and the harlots go into the kingdom of God before you " (Matt. 21:31).

From this final vantage point, we may perceive an ironic effect also in the interpolated psalm (Jonah 2:2-9 [Heb., ch. 2:3-10]). The psalm is a prayer of thanksgiving for deliverance from trouble, and the image of drowning (cf. especially vs. 3 and 5) gives it a superficial justification for being inserted. The deliverance from trouble preserves the psalmist's life from the equivalent of death (cf. " Sheol " in v. 2, " the Pit " in v. 6). His prayer is a memory of and dependence on God in the midst of the worst imaginable adversity, and he congratulates himself that it is no idol to whom he prays (v. 9), for idolatry would be the abandonment of covenantal loyalty (*chesed*, v. 8). Yet that loyalty is precisely what Jonah subsequently abandons, for he has no concept except a rhetorical one that " salvation belongs to Yahweh " (v. 9). The irony of the psalm was certainly not intended by its author, nor by the glossator who interpolated it. Set against the irony of the entire satire, however, it is surely perceptible.

We would be mistaken if we sought to spell out the positive theology of our author in too much detail. His purpose was not to propose some theological statements for our consideration, but to expose absurdity by the irony of satire.[24] Like all ironists, he

24 I would even say that he is not proposing a specifically "missionary" function for Israel in the terms in which we usually think of that function. I am

took his stand upon an ultimately serious truth. The alternative to Jonah's absurdity is the absurdity of God. If the author's readers are not prepared to settle for the former, he offers no recourse but to the latter. And the mystery of grace is no less absurd than the mystery of justice.

------

not sure that I would go as far in arguing a missionary point to Jonah as the very subtle and well-stated position of Haller, *loc. cit.*, pp. 50–54, who avoids all the traps that this very elusive subject often holds for the unwary.

# III

---

## SAUL:

## THE TRAGEDY OF GREATNESS

An ENIGMATIC FIGURE, Saul has always been overshadowed by his successor, David, and shadowed over by his own strange, private war with David. That David was the greatest of Israel's kings and that Saul not only opposed him but attempted his murder have always conspired to reduce Saul's appeal to readers of the Old Testament. Our more modern times, however, have conspired to recognize again Saul's essential greatness.

Recent commentators say all but unanimously that Saul is a tragic figure. "Israel never again brought forth a poetic characterization which in many details came so close to the spirit of Greek tragedy." [1] Saul's life was "full of tragic greatness." [2] The question is, What makes Saul tragic? Here the commentators are not unanimous. Is it that Saul attempted the impossible — to unite two incompatible concepts of kingship? [3] Is it the psychic degeneration brought on by Saul's knowledge of his rejection by

---

[1] Gerhard von Rad, *Theologie des Alten Testaments*, Vol. I (Chr. Kaiser Verlag, München, 1957), p. 323. My only quarrel with the statement lies with the term "poetic." I should prefer some such word as "artistic," and perhaps that is what von Rad means.

[2] Hans Wilhelm Hertzberg, *I & II Samuel, A Commentary*, tr. by J. S. Bowden (The Old Testament Library, The Westminster Press, 1965), p. 234.

[3] So Walther Eichrodt, *Theology of the Old Testament*, Vol. I, tr. by J. A. Baker (The Westminster Press, 1961), pp. 443–445. The two aspects are the charismatic quality derived from judgeship and the necessary institutionalization and regularization of monarchy.

SAUL: THE TRAGEDY OF GREATNESS

Yahweh?[4] Perhaps the tragedy lies in a fatal flaw, the unde-
pendability of his will,[5] or in the gloomy inevitability of David's
good fortune and Saul's bad.[6] Is Saul's tragedy his personal
alienation from Samuel on the one hand and David on the
other?[7] Did a disordered and unstable personality and the political forces of the time conspire to make him incapable of coping
with his task?[8] There may be other ways of delineating Saul's
tragedy; those quoted illustrate the variety of viewpoints on it.

This variety exists because, in one way or another, all who
state the problem are concerned to explain Saul's *historical* position. They look for the circumstances of the period, for the evi-
dences of Saul's actions and personality, for the historical interplay
of persons upon one another and of personalities and events.
What was Saul like? How did he and Samuel get along? What
were the facts of Saul's election as king? What were the extant
views of the kingship? These questions are foremost in the minds
of those whose views I have too briefly encapsulated above. They
are not the questions that were foremost in the narrator's mind.

I propose to investigate the tragedy of Saul as a *literary* problem.
I am not particularly concerned that the narratives betray the
existence, in the eleventh century or later, of more than one view
of the nature of kingship. I am not particularly concerned about
the apparent multiplicity of sources, the analysis of which has

[4] B. Davie Napier, *Song of the Vineyard*, p. 151. Cf. also his *From Faith to Faith* (Harper & Brothers, 1955), pp. 114, 116–117.

[5] I assume that that is what is meant by Fleming James, *Personalities of the Old Testament* (Charles Scribner's Sons, 1951), pp. 113–114. At the beginning of his essay on Saul (p. 96), James calls him a " tragic figure " but does not elaborate further on the term.

[6] N. K. Gottwald, *A Light to the Nations* (Harper & Brothers, 1959), pp. 187–188. Gottwald is perhaps too critical of David and too concerned to re-habilitate Saul. One can be sympathetic to Saul, as the narrator is, and still recognize his fatal fault.

[7] B. W. Anderson, *Understanding the Old Testament* (Prentice-Hall, Inc., 1957), p. 125.

[8] John Bright, *A History of Israel* (The Westminster Press, 1959), pp. 170–171.

occupied a great deal of attention.[9] I am not even particularly concerned with the " Saul of history." I am interested in the story, which bears its own integrity. We do not need to reject the viewpoint of the narrator in order to perceive the tragedy of Saul. Quite to the contrary, the views of that narrator or final editor are the material of the investigation. We are looking not for the historical facts of the matter but for the indications of how the author wanted us to read and understand the story. This aspect of literary criticism, the very center of any study of litera-ture, Old Testament scholars have too readily neglected.[10]

The story of Saul, with its prologue, the career of Samuel, is very carefully constructed to present the narrator's view of the matter. It is put together far more like a novel than like a piece of modern historiography. The theme is the theological ambiguity of the establishment of a monarchy and Saul's failure to fill the bill. The historian has in mind, of course, that David's reign was normative in the history of kingship. Saul, therefore, *cannot* be too successful. It is remarkable, in view of that assumption, that Saul is presented in as sympathetic a light as he appears. But our author had doubts about the propriety of establishing a king-ship at all, and he has presented Saul's failure as a tragic and therefore ambiguous failure. In a sense, he has told the story of a man not fitted for a job that should not have been opened. Yet

[9] Perhaps the fullest account of the source analyses is in O. Eissfeldt, *Einleitung in das Alte Testament*, 2te Auflage (J. C. B. Mohr, Tübingen, 1956), pp. 323–338. Good briefer accounts are to be found in S. Szikszai, " Samuel, I and II," *IDB*, Vol. 4, pp. 204–209; N. H. Snaith, " The Historical Books," in *The Old Testament and Modern Study*, ed. by H. H. Rowley (Oxford University Press, Oxford, 1951), pp. 97–102. Let it be clear that I am not rejecting the en-terprises of source analysis or of form or tradition criticism.

[10] We have scarcely begun analyzing the material when we have dissected it into sources and redactional layers and pointed out crudities and historical im-possibilities. The effect of doing nothing more than that is given, e.g., by G. B. Caird, " I and II Samuel," *IB*, Vol. 2 (Abingdon Press, 1953), and by Eiss-feldt, *op. cit.* Regardless of what these scholars *thought* they were doing, that is the *impression* they give.

Saul came close enough to being great that he emerges as tragic. And the story revolves around those dramatic ironies in which Saul's genuine greatness is played off against his fatal weakness, and in which kingship's demands for greatness are played off against the ambiguity of kingship.

## The Ambiguous Kingship

We may take I Sam., ch. 8, as the prologue not alone to the Saul story but to the entire unfolding of kingship. This chapter represents a point of view hostile to the kingship, perhaps on the very good grounds of subsequent sad experience with kings, possibly Solomon and Manasseh in particular.[11] Certainly Samuel's descriptive response to the request by the elders of Israel for a king is too circumstantial to be accepted as predictive.

This will be the procedure [*mishpāt*] of the king who reigns over you: he will take your sons and put them in his chariotry and cavalry, and they will run before his chariot. And he will appoint captains of regiments and captains of companies, and some to plow his land and some to reap his harvest and some to make his weapons and the fittings of his chariot. And he will take your daughters to be perfumers and cooks and bakers. And he will take your best fields and vineyards and olive orchards and give them to his retainers. And he will tax your grain and grape products ten percent, and give it to his officers and his retainers. And he will take your male and female slaves and the best of your cattle [12] and your asses, and put them to his own work. He will tax your flocks ten percent, and you will become his slaves. And you will cry aloud in that day about your king, whom you chose

[11] Bright, *op. cit.*, p. 207, specifies Solomon. Most scholars hold, with Martin Noth, *Überlieferungsgeschichtliche Studien* (Max Niemeyer Verlag, Tübingen, 1957), pp. 54–57, that the chapter owes its present form to the Deuteronomist.

[12] Reading *beqarkem* with LXX instead of MT *bachūrēkem*, " your young men."

for yourselves, but Yahweh will not answer you in that day.
(Vs. 11-18.)

It is easy enough to point out that this chapter, along with
chs. 10:17-27 and 12, represents a strand hostile to the kingship
contrasted with the other strand, chs. 9:1 to 10:16 and 11, which
seems favorable to kingship. But we must note the placement of
the incident and take seriously the historian's purpose in order-
ing the matter as he did. This episode begins the tale of the kingship, incorporates the first mention of a king in this part of the
Deuteronomic history, and it immediately sets the entire kingship tradition in the light of apostasy. The elders present weak
reasons for having a king: " Look, you are old, and your sons
are not following your example. Now make us a king to rule
us, like the nations " (v. 5). The fact of incompetent incumbents
is no reason to throw over the whole institution of judgeship.
Samuel himself had succeeded the immoral family of Eli (cf. chs.
2:12-17, 27-36; 3:11-14). The remark about being " like the nations " is certainly reported ironically by the narrator. The purpose
of Israel is precisely not to be " like the nations," and when this
reasoning is reiterated (ch. 8:19-20), the historian shows his ironic
evaluation of the people's desire for a king.

The popular reasoning is shown to be unsound also by what
precedes it in the story. The career of Samuel shows that the
judgeship, properly related to Yahweh's sovereignty, is entirely
sufficient for Israel. Samuel, born as a result of a mother's promise
of his services (ch. 1 [13]), taken to the priestly center and initiated

[13] It is often noticed that the story of Samuel's birth contains several wordplays between the child's name and the verb *shā'al*, "to ask" (vs. 20, 27, 28).
This verb has no relationship to the name Samuel, but it is cognate to the name
Saul (*shā'ûl*; the form occurs in v. 28). Clearly the story began as that of the
birth of Saul, not of Samuel. Equally clearly, the narrator could find no place
in his tale for the birth story of Saul, who must be presented as already prepared
for the kingship (ch. 9). The birth of Samuel, on the other hand, could be used
to good effect as the prologue to Samuel's rise to power. That the alteration of

into the offices (chs. 2:11 to 3:18), present as priest, prophet, and judge at the crucial time of the loss and recovery of the Ark (chs. 3:19 to 7:4), presiding over Israel at the definitive defeat of the Philistines (ch. 7:5-12), has, as the summary passage puts it, secured safety from the Philistines and all the other inimical neighbors (vs. 13-17). Hence, immediately preceding the people's request for a king, we are informed that no external circumstances require the introduction of kingship. And the internal circumstances alleged by the elders have also been shown by Samuel's career to be irrelevant.

By the way he leads up to the episode of ch. 8, and by the way he reports the request, the narrator demonstrates the undesirability, therefore the irony, of the people's decision. Faced with two very good reasons for not having a king: (1) that he will burden them with grievous injustice and (2) that Yahweh is opposed to the move, they insist on having one. Yahweh's response to Samuel emphasizes the irony of the request:

Listen to the people's voice, to all they say to you. For it is not you they are rejecting; it is I they are rejecting from reigning over them. Now they are treating you just as they have treated me from the day I brought them up out of Egypt until today: they have abandoned me and served other gods. (Ch. 8:7-8; cf. v. 22.)

It is now time to be introduced to the chosen man (ch. 9). Saul is presented from the first in a favorable light, as a handsome and gigantic man (v. 2), going about his normal affairs. His lost asses and his convenient arrival at Ramah present a suggestive dramatic irony in the difference between what Saul knows and what we know. At Samuel's cryptic remark: " And for whom

---

the story was the work of the final " author " can only be uncertain. It would not have been unworthy of him.

is all Israel's desire? Is it not for you and your family? " (v. 20),
Saul is baffled: "Why do you talk to me like this? " (v. 21).
Samuel's question itself carries a double meaning in the light
of ch. 8. Israel desires a king, and Saul is the man. He is, therefore, straightforwardly the object of Israel's desire. But we have
seen that Israel's desire (*chemdāh*) amounts to a rejection of
Yahweh, and the term is sometimes used of an idolatrous and
wicked desire.[14] Not only is Samuel's question opaque to Saul,
though not to us; it is also ironically dual in meaning. Samuel's
comment about the food set aside for Saul (ch. 9:24) conveys
the same enigmatic quality to Saul, and again we know its import where he does not.

With the secret anointment of Saul (ch. 10:1), the matter
finally comes clear. But then comes the very strange scene of
Saul's involvement with the *n<sup>e</sup>bî'îm* (vs. 9-13). Why is that episode
there? Is it to show a connection between kingship and the
prophetic office? Is it to emphasize Saul's seizure by the Spirit (vs.
6, 10) ? No, clearly the scene is there in order to state its " punch
line": "Is Saul too among the prophets? " This became a
proverb, we are told, which is explained by a different incident
in ch. 19:23-24. But it is an ironic proverb, suggesting someone
very seriously out of place. And the ironic, if not sarcastic, response
of the bystander is essential to the meaning of the incident:
" And who is their father? " The expression " sons of the prophets," a frequent designation of such prophetic bands as the one
found in this episode, is not seen here, but the question certainly
brings it to mind. "And who is their father? " seems to imply
either that the prophets have no recognizable " father," and
hence are symbolically called illegitimate, or that whoever is to
be recognized as their " father " is well known to and rejected
by all, meaning, in effect, " And everyone knows who *their* father

[14] Cf. Dan. 11:37; the cognate, *chemed*, in Isa. 32:12; Amos 5:11; forms of
the verb *chāmad* in Ex. 20:17; Deut. 5:18; 7:25; Isa. 1:29; 44:9.

is! " The scene, then, picks up the ambiguities of kingship once again, suggesting the illegitimacy of the monarchy by the involvement of Saul with the " illegitimate " prophets.

The irony is now heightened by the interchange between Saul and his uncle (ch. 10:14-16). I do not think that we are to infer that the uncle somehow knows about Saul's anointment. There, indeed, is the irony. We know, and Saul knows, but the uncle does not. He comes close to discovery, and there is a long moment of suspense before Saul turns the question aside with his partial answer. Why is Saul silent? He has not been told to conceal the matter. Are we to assume that the anointment is not to be made known until the public ratification at Mizpah? Or is this Saul's personal modesty? From the present context, we do not know. But it fits a pattern which we shall see in due course.

The people now gather at Mizpah for the election of a king (vs. 17-27). Samuel's speech reiterates the apostasy of establishing a kingship. The rehearsal of the exodus tradition points up the irony of the people's decision to have a king, by the emphatic use of the personal pronouns: " Thus says Yahweh, God of Israel: I ['ānôkî] brought Israel up out of Egypt (v. 18). . . . But you ['attem] have today rejected your God " (v. 19). The whole process of selection, therefore, stands under the accusation of the people's self-willed rejection of Yahweh. When the lot has fallen on Saul, and he is nowhere to be found, we have an instant of mingled suspense and comedy. The climactic moment has come, but the man of the hour is " hidden among the baggage " (v. 22). This detail makes no sense except in the light of the previous episode with Samuel, when Saul is told he will be king.[15] But

[15] If we ascribe ch. 10:17-27 to the so-called Late Source with ch. 8, while ascribing chs. 9:1 to 10:16 to the Early Source, we must assume that the Late Source had some such story as the latter in order to account for this detail. Moreover, ch. 10:18-19 presupposes ch. 8, but v. 23 presupposes ch. 9:2. To suggest that ch. 10:17-19 is from the Late Source and vs. 20-27 from the Early Source would be to deprive the Late Source of any anointment scene, which will

the incident suggests even more strongly than the previous one that Saul does not want to be king and must, as it were, be dragged out of hiding for it. Samuel indulges in a demagogic *ecce homo:* " There is none like him among the whole people! " (v. 24). Must that not strike us ironically, in the light both of what has gone before and of what will shortly happen? Saul's reluctance and Samuel's rhetoric surely underline the dubiety of the choice of Saul. At this point, only the *b^enē b^eliyya'al*[16] articulate it: " How will this save us? " (v. 27).[17] That touch has its own irony.

In the exploit at Jabesh-gilead (ch. 11:1-11), Saul shows his military mettle for the first time. When, after the victory, the people demand the heads of the previous doubters (v. 12), the episode emerges as an implicit answer to the ironic question of ch. 10:27. It may have originated as an independent tradition of Saul's elevation to the monarchy, as the form critics and source analysts tell us. But at present it serves the purpose of consolidating Saul's position. His refusal to do away with the former malcontents (v. 13) ingratiates him with them, and the " renewal " of the kingship at Gilgal, while somewhat puzzling, may have something to do historically with a plurality of central shrines.[18]

---

hardly do. The simplest solution to the dilemma seems to me to be to give proper respect to the editor as having constructed his own narrative — out of previously existing materials, of course — and having made it into a remarkably consistent unity, which cannot so simply be analyzed into self-consistent sources.

[16] A difficult term to translate. RSV's " worthless fellows " is not very helpful. It will serve for the uses of the term in Deut. 13:13; Judg. 19:22; I Sam. 2:12; Prov. 16:27; II Sam. 23:6; I Sam. 25:17; and perhaps in II Sam. 16:7; I Kings 21:13. But in I Sam. 30:22, the term seems to imply not a moral but a social judgment, meaning, perhaps, social outcasts, freebooters, soldiers of fortune. The similar term *bath b^eliyya'al* (I Sam. 1:16) may suggest the same thing. I am inclined to see it in that meaning in the present passage.

[17] The term *zeh*, usually taken to mean " this man," Saul, may refer only to the act of king-making.

[18] The problem of the amphictyonic sanctuary remains obscure, despite much recent work on it. I do not think it is solved by appeal to separate sources. Ch. 10:17-27 takes place at Mizpah, ch. 11:15 at Gilgal. Similarly, in Judg. 20:1,

It is sometimes suggested that in v. 14 the Deuteronomist has harmonized the differing accounts of Saul's accession to the throne by altering an original *neqaddēsh*, " let us sanctify," to the present *nechaddēsh*, " let us renew." If so, we must stand in awe of his ingenuity. Not everyone could bring two different stories into harmony by altering a single consonant!

The stage is set for Samuel's temporary eclipse. His valedictory speech (ch. 12:1-17), aimed once again at the people's apostasy, is extremely truculent and ungracious. We might expect that of a man who has been thrown out of public office by popular demand. Petulantly, Samuel extorts agreement from the people that he is morally blameless (vs. 1-5), thus exploding again their first reason for having a king (ch. 8:5). Rehearsing the history of Israel with Yahweh since the descent into Egypt (ch. 12:6-12), he now emphasizes the Jabesh-gilead incident as the rationale for having a king.[19] There, at least, was an external threat. But the exploits of earlier judges in more critical situations have rendered even that an insufficient reason. Samuel's entire speech undermines the now irrevocable decision to have a king, and his stringent exhortations to obedience reveal Israel's parlous condition before God. By insistently hammering at obedience by " you and your king " (vs. 14, 15, 25), Samuel emphasizes

_____

the people assemble at Mizpah to decide what to do about Benjamin, and in v. 18 they go to Bethel to receive marching orders from Yahweh. Albrecht Alt has argued in " Die Wallfahrt von Sichem nach Bethel," *Kleine Schriften*, Vol. I (C. H. Beck'sche Verlagsbuchhandlung, München, 1953), pp. 79–88, that in Gen., ch. 35, we may have reference to a change of sanctuaries from Shechem to Bethel. It is possible, however, that at any given time, there were two "central sanctuaries " in the nation, perhaps designated for different kinds of gatherings, as all three of these passages could imply. Note also that Solomon is privately anointed at Gihon (I Kings 1:38-39) but subsequently goes to sacrifice at " the great high place " in Gibeon (ch. 3:4), raising the question whether both are in some sense coronation episodes.

[19] That again raises the problem of assigning I Sam., ch. 11, to the Early Source and ch. 12 to the Late Source, unless the Late Source be viewed as a supplementary rather than an alternative account. The supplementation hypothesis, however, is not in favor.

the rebellion of the king-making and, incidentally and ironically,
points forward (as we shall see) to the grounds on which Saul
will be rejected. The miraculous rain at wheat-harvest time finally
brings the people to admit their fault (v. 19).

Everything in these chapters, therefore, points up the ambiguity
of the monarchy, even when the ostensible mood is one of appro-
bation of monarchy. The thematic antinomies carry the thread of
irony in the narrative. The kingship is born in rebellion (chs. 8;
10:19; 12), but it requires obedience (ch. 12). Its incumbent is
the most impressive figure in Israel (chs. 9:2; 10:23; 11:1-11) but
the most reluctant (chs. 9:21; 10:14-16, 21-22). The people move
from defiant insistence (ch. 8) through wild joy (ch. 11) to
trembling penitence (ch. 12), at the same time that Saul moves
from taciturn silence (chs. 9:1 to 10:16) through hesitance (ch.
10:21-22) to initiative and confidence (ch. 11).

## SAUL AND THE PEOPLE

We now begin the story of Saul's reign, and our sense of its
irony must be heightened by the observation that somewhere
along the line of transmission even the bare chronology of the
reign has been mutilated (ch. 13:1).

War with the Philistines is again imminent. Even a temporary
victory at Geba cannot stave it off (v. 3), for reprisals are quick
in coming, and Israel is in bad condition (cf. vs. 4, 6-7). At Gilgal,
Saul's army is slipping away from him across the Jordan, and
the situation is fast becoming critical. Saul has obeyed Samuel's
command to wait seven days (cf. ch. 10:8), but Samuel has not
arrived. Saul, therefore, takes it on himself to offer the requisite
sacrifices (ch. 13:8-9). Naturally, no sooner has he done so than
the tardy prophet arrives (v. 10), irked at being disobeyed. Saul
pleads military necessity, but, in a feeble rationalization, he adds,
"I forced myself and made the offerings" (v. 12). In reply,

Samuel tells Saul that he has been rejected.

It is very strange that, although the seven days' waiting period has been mentioned before (ch. 10:8), there is no direct indication here, as in the subsequent rejection story (ch. 15:11), that Samuel is speaking Yahweh's word. It is also anomalous that, according to ch. 13:8, Saul has in fact obeyed Samuel's command, proceeding with the sacrifice only when military considerations absolutely demanded it. Have we here a subtle indication that Samuel's message is represented by the narrator as being not Yahweh's but Samuel's own? This rejection is not mentioned subsequently. Saul's action must be read as an effort to preserve the army for the coming battle. He is prepared to fly in the prophet's face rather than lose his army, though he is not prepared, even so, to tell Samuel to stop talking like a blithering idiot.

The odds in the battle that is to come are all against Israel. Saul has only six hundred men (v. 15), with perhaps as many as a thousand with Jonathan at Geba (cf. vs. 2-3), whereas the Philistines are alleged to have a vast army (v. 5). The Israelite army is ill-equipped, Saul and Jonathan alone having swords and spears, because the Philistines hold a monopoly on iron products (vs. 19-22). The details are doubtless exaggerated in the interests of glorifying the coming victory by magnifying the odds against Saul.

Jonathan's valor provides the victory (ch. 14:1-45). Is that an ironic touch? We are reminded of a later victory over the Philistines in which Saul will depend on another to fight the decisive action single-handed (ch. 17). Saul is sitting under his pomegranate tree (ch. 14:2), unaware of Jonathan's plan until a lookout reports strange activity in the Philistine camp (v. 16). Saul pauses for divination (as a result of Samuel's rebuke in ch. 13?), but before it is finished, his presence and that of his army are clearly required (vs. 18-20). The Philistines have been

thrown into utter confusion by Jonathan's exploit and are killing
each other (v. 20).

At this point, Saul gives an order that provides a double irony
to the incident. Presumably to prevent the people's leaving the
chase to gather loot, he orders no one to eat until evening when
the battle is over (v. 24). Jonathan, the architect of the day's
victory, fails to hear the command and eats some honey (v. 27).
Informed of the order, he cavalierly dismisses it: " My father
has brought trouble on the land " (v. 29). Saul is prepared to
continue the battle by night, and now he must be persuaded to
the divination (v. 36). No answer is forthcoming. Something has
gone wrong. We know what it is: Jonathan has disobeyed the
oath. Saul does not know. When he asks the people what has
happened, they do not answer (v. 39). The next divination singles
out Saul and Jonathan as the source of the trouble (v. 41), and
the next, Jonathan alone (v. 42).

Saul had sworn that the culprit would die (v. 39). Ironically,
Jonathan, to whom the victory is due and who has publicly accused Saul of " bringing trouble on the land," stands condemned.
Saul is prepared to carry out his sentence, but now the people
intervene. And once more, with the second level of irony, Saul
follows the policy that stands him in good stead with the people.
To Saul's solemn oath (v. 39) is opposed the people's equally
solemn oath (v. 45), both taken on the name of Yahweh. And
Saul's oath falls by the wayside.

We have seen, therefore, two incidents based on Saul's relationship to the people. In the first, he accepted the charge of disobedience in an action designed to keep the people with him. In
the second, he abandoned an oath in the face of pressure from the
people. Saul is not exactly fulfilling the portrait of a king as absolute tyrant drawn by Samuel in ch. 8.

## REJECTION

Chapter 15 is the psychological center of the Saul story. What has gone before has been leading up to it, and from it flows what follows after. To this point Saul has been effective if reluctant; from this point he is declining in effectiveness if not in reluctance.

The issue turns once again on obedience. That, we recall, was the central issue of Samuel's valedictory speech in ch. 12, and it was the ostensible issue in the rejection story in ch. 13. Here it comes to the climax. The obedience is underlined by Samuel's first words to Saul, words that will echo in the crucial context: "Yahweh sent me to anoint you king over his people Israel. Now, therefore, listen to the words of Yahweh" (v. 1). The order is unambiguous: exterminate the Amalekites to the last chicken (v. 3). We are not required to approve the command in order to understand the incident. The fact that nothing could bring most of us to approve it may cause a certain barrier to our understanding. But the fact that, in the event, the Amalekites are exterminated only to the next-to-last person and to the last scrawny chicken must not give us a higher appreciation for Saul's moral sensitivity than it warrants. "Saul and the people" take Agag, the king, prisoner and preserve the best of the livestock, destroying the poorer specimens (v. 9).

It does not escape the divine knowledge (vs. 10-11). "I repent that I made Saul king." Now the rejection of Saul appears on Yahweh's lips. Perhaps we are too suspicious of Samuel in pointing out that in ch. 13 we have only Samuel's word for it. But why, in response to Yahweh's decision, does Samuel become angry (v. 11b)? His motivation is not at all clear. Obviously, it has something to do with Yahweh's words. Equally obviously, the narrator expects us to understand, since he does not tell us. Is Samuel thinking of the extra trouble this causes him? Is he wondering why Yahweh has taken so long? Is Samuel angry

merely because Saul has again disobeyed? In that case, there
would be no reason for him to stay up all night crying in anger
to Yahweh. Is he interceding for Saul? If so, why is he " angry "
about it? Or is he attempting to change Yahweh's mind? [20]
Yet surely Samuel is not opposed to Yahweh's rejecting Saul.
Samuel is clearly angry with Yahweh, and I see no explanation
for this anger except that Samuel feels that he has already accomplished Saul's rejection (ch. 13) and is furious with Yahweh
for not letting it go at that. Samuel's anger here is the best support for the argument that the earlier rejection was illegitimate,
was understood by the narrator as Samuel's rejection of Saul, but
not Yahweh's.

Samuel meets Saul at Gilgal. The place is not unimportant. At
Gilgal, Saul was finally established in the kingship (ch. 11:15). At
Gilgal, Saul is finally rejected. We know this, though Saul does
not, and we hear Saul's cheery greeting to Samuel ironically:
" I have performed Yahweh's word " (ch. 15:13). Samuel's reply
is profoundly ironic: " And what is this sound of bleating in my
ears, and the lowing of cattle that I hear? " (v. 14). Saul promptly
puts the onus on the people. " They brought them from the
Amalekites, the best of whose flocks and cattle the people spared
in order to sacrifice them to Yahweh your God. But the rest we
destroyed." (V. 15.) The pronouns are the most eloquent parts
of this extraordinary speech. " They " brought them; the sacrifice
is to Yahweh " your " God; but the rest " we " destroyed. Saul
includes himself only in the act which he was commanded to
perform.

Now Samuel pins Saul to the wall with an observation the
force of which seems completely to have escaped commentators
on Saul, and which, in my opinion, forms the psychological center of the entire Saul story. " Though you are little in your own
eyes, are you not in fact the chief of the tribes of Israel? " (V. 17.)

[20] Cf. Hertzberg, *op. cit.*, p. 126.

The irony is twofold. On the one hand, twice we have been told that Saul stands head and shoulders above the rest of the people (chs. 9:2; 10:23). He is literally large in everyone else's eyes, but little in his own. On the other hand, the greatest fact of Saul's life, his kingship, ought to, but does not, override his self-deprecation.

Moreover, this penetrating psychological observation now brings to expression what has lurked just below the surface all along. The first time we meet Saul and he converses with Samuel, we hear an echo of these words in Saul's own mouth (ch. 9:21). He refuses to talk about his anointment (ch. 10:14-16). He hides when the election takes place (vs. 21-22). He holds his peace at the grumblings of his opponents (v. 27), but ingratiates himself with them after the battle at Jabesh-gilead (ch. 11:13). When military necessity leads him to proceed with his job against Samuel's wishes, he accepts the prophet's threat (ch. 13:11-14) in order to keep the people with him. When Jonathan lightheartedly disobeys his rather dubious order, and it appears that Saul will have to kill him, the people intervene and Saul submits to them (ch. 14:45). Whether he has been dealing with Samuel or with the people, Saul has been " little in his own eyes."

Now, true to form, he has acted with more than one eye on the popular reaction. He has taken Agag prisoner instead of killing him. Why? It is hard to see any reason except that he wants to display Agag, and therefore to prove the exploit, before the populace. He has allowed the people to keep the best livestock. Why? Is it really " to sacrifice them to Yahweh your God in Gilgal " (ch. 15:21)? Perhaps it is, or perhaps that is a dodge. In any case, the great booty of fine animals brought from the Amalek campaign will impress the people, whether they sacrifice them or take them home for other purposes. What Saul has neglected, it seems, is that he is king by Yahweh's anointment. Not even the excuse of piety can serve to cover disobedience.

Certainly that is the burden of the profound poem in vs. 22-23. But Saul's apparent motivation does not even rise to the level of piety. He has cared more for his "public image" than for his royal responsibility.[21]

The sequel illustrates the same point. Saul agrees that he is in the wrong because he "feared the people and listened to their voice" (v. 24). His request for pardon is summarily denied (clearly Samuel was not crying to Yahweh the night before, v. 11, to intercede for Saul), and Samuel refuses to go with him for worship (v. 26). Samuel takes dramatic, if slightly illogical, opportunity from the torn robe to give the oracle of rejection and the choice of a successor (vs. 27-29). But Saul is still thinking about his status with the people: "I have sinned; yet now, please honor me before the elders of my people and before Israel. And return with me, and I will worship Yahweh your God" (v. 30). The rejection, it is quite clear, is privately conveyed. The people know nothing of it.[22] Saul has nothing left but keeping up appearances with the people, and that is still at the front of his mind. This provides the thematic irony of the entire story. For Saul neglects his responsibilities to Yahweh in favor of public relations. And his personal insecurity prevents his actuating the greatness that he has in him and that his office requires.

## SUCCESSOR AND DEGENERATION

The dramatic moment to introduce the successor has come. As Saul was secretly anointed before being publicly elected, so

[21] It is perhaps worth pointing out that, if Saul's fault is that he is not king enough, Solomon's is that he is king too much. Certainly a good bit of the antimonarchic sentiment in the preexilic period stemmed from the nation's unhappy experience with Solomon. In addition, there was probably an ideological opposition to monarchy, which doubtless appeared very early, perhaps earlier than Saul.

[22] It is sometimes stated that Saul's rejection was public. Yet if it had been, his almost frantic plea to Samuel to honor him before the elders and the people would be senseless. Cf., e.g., Napier, *Song of the Vineyard*, p. 151.

now David appears as the secret object of Yahweh's choice. The successor is explicitly and ironically contrasted with Saul. When Eliab comes into sight, Samuel is told, " Do not consider his appearance or the height of his stature, for I have rejected him; for God does not see as man sees, for man looks only to the eyes, but Yahweh looks to the heart " (ch. 16:7; cf. chs. 9:2; 10:23). David, the youngest of Jesse's sons, is chosen. He too is appealing to the eye (ch. 16:12), and, ironically enough, that is all we are told of him.

The irony of this secret choice is extended by the two accounts of David's introduction to Saul's court. Saul is tormented by an evil spirit (vs. 14-15), and music is considered an effective antidote. The successor enters Saul's court for the purpose of healing him. And the irony is deepened by the narrator's comment: " And he loved him greatly, and he became his armor-bearer " (v. 21b). To sort out the antecedents of the pronouns is somewhat troublesome. David is the subject of the verbs in v. 21a, as well as of the last clause, " and he became his armor-bearer." But who is the subject, and who the object, of " And he loved him "? It would lend even more depth to the irony if Saul were the subject and David the object, as RSV has it, but I do not think we can allow it. The most obvious reading of " He loved him greatly " in the context is, " David loved Saul greatly." In the light of what will shortly transpire, there is enough irony in that statement.

The alternative account of David's introduction to Saul (if the David-Goliath story, ch. 17, is that [28]) contains the same or

[28] The incoherences between ch. 16:14-23 and ch. 17 are considerable and evident. It has been noted that Codex Vaticanus (B) of the LXX removes most of them by omitting chs. 17:12-31, 41, 50, 55 to 18:5. These very verses are the grounds for recognizing ch. 17 as a separate source (see, e.g., Szikszai, *loc. cit.*, p. 207). LXX could have followed a Hebrew text, since Hebrew fragments of I Samuel found at Qumran support LXX readings against MT, showing variant early textual traditions. The omissions could, however, have been made in the interests of harmonization. Certainly we cannot accept the LXX version merely because we would like to remove the incoherences, for we would then have to

a supplementary irony. David, the successor, fights Saul's battle
for him. That reminds us of Jonathan's earlier exploit at Mich-
mash (ch. 14), and it is one side of the irony. The other side
reminds us of the difference between Saul's choice and David's
(ch. 16:7). The little boy with the slingshot and the absolute
assurance does against the Philistine giant what the mighty Saul,
taller than any man in the country but "little in his own eyes,"
cannot do. The successor has already begun to succeed.

Thus is set the military theme that dominates the relationship
between Saul and David in the following chapters. The theme
is firmly established with ch. 18:5, where David has been made
an officer. He is entirely successful in all that he does, and "this
was good in the eyes of all the people." Even the victory
chants of the women pick up the theme, and there the trouble
begins.

> Saul has slain his thousands,
> And David his ten thousands.
> (V. 7.)

Saul's reaction could almost be predicted. "And what more
can he have but the kingdom?" (V. 8.) It is consistent with what
we have seen. Saul is afraid of this fantastically successful stripling
who threatens to displace him in the eyes of the people. Saul's
"littleness in his own eyes" requires that he be bolstered by
public regard, but even that seems now to be slipping away from
him. Dubious of his own qualities, he grasps the more desperately
at his status. "What more can he have but the kingdom?" It
is the remark of a man who is not sure that he wants the king-

---

account for their later insertion, which is very difficult to do, as S. R. Driver
points out in *Notes on the Hebrew Text of the Books of Samuel* (Clarendon
Press, Oxford, 1913), pp. 149–151. Only one thing can be said with certainty,
though it is not terribly helpful: the double accounts of David's entry into Saul's
court did not bother the editor.

dom but cannot endure any threat of its loss, one "little in his own eyes" and therefore fearful of nothing more than displacement from high position. "From a psychological point of view," says Hertzberg, "Saul is seeing ghosts." [24] That is the one irony in the statement — the irony of Saul's insecurity. The other irony, of course, is the more obvious one: Saul is unaware that he is speaking precise truth, as we know from ch. 16.

We need not rehearse the dreary details of Saul's pursuit of David through the subsequent chapters. The high point has passed, and the direction now is downward. Detail is piled on detail, incident on incident, to draw the portrait and to underline its tragic irony. Saul swings from overt attempts at murder (chs. 18:10-11; 19:8-10, 11-17) to more subtle, indirect means of securing David's death (ch. 18:20-29). He wants David out of the way, for only so can he maintain his status. Ironically, the implication of the very slogan that aroused Saul's jealousy does not occur to him, for he does not consider the possible reaction, by those who sang the victory chants, if he were to succeed in killing David. He is quite simply obsessed with removing this threat to his position.

He alienates his own family in the effort to alienate them from David. Michal helps David to escape, as does Jonathan (chs. 19:1-7, 11-17; 20). In his rage, Saul tries to kill Jonathan, arguing that Jonathan's devotion to David will prevent his ever having the kingship for himself (ch. 20:31). Saul senses, then, that David is "the neighbor of yours who is better than you" (ch. 15:28) to whom the kingship is to be given. Jonathan can even say that Saul "knows" David will be king (ch. 23:17). I do not think, however, that the narrator means Saul's knowledge is the same as ours, since we know of David's anointment. Saul suspects that David is the appointed successor, but he does not know it in the full sense. We do know it, however, and that knowledge renders

[24] *I & II Samuel*, p. 157.

deeply ironic Saul's efforts to overcome David, which cannot succeed.

The matter becomes public, it appears, after David has received help from the priests at Nob (ch. 21:1-9). He conceals from Ahimelech that he is in flight from Saul, pretending that he is on a secret mission (v. 2). The brief flight to the Philistines is of no use, since they suspect him, though their information is bad. " Is not this David, king of the land? " (V. 11 [Heb., v. 12].) The remark carries the irony of being true even though false. Gathering a band of malcontents around him (ch. 22:1-2) and depositing his parents safely in Moab (vs. 3-5), David returns to Judah. Now Saul brings the clash into the open. He turns on the members of his court and, apparently out of a clear sky, accuses them of conspiracy (vs. 7-8). His suspicion has mounted to the point where he has lost faith in the people. When his own servants will not lift a hand against the priests of Nob (v. 17), he feels quite alone.

Now the obsession grows wilder. We get the impression that Saul lets the business of the kingdom fall apart while he is running over the hills in pursuit of David. Whether or not that was the case, that is what our narrator means us to think. Saul must be called back from one expedition because of a sudden Philistine raid (ch. 23:27-28). But in the light of Saul's suspicion of the people, we must note the irony of the fact that wherever David goes, someone informs Saul. David cannot stay in Keilah, because the people will surrender him to Saul (ch. 23:6-13). When he is at Horesh, in the Wilderness of Ziph, the Ziphites tell Saul his whereabouts (vs. 19-24), and someone tells Saul when David is at En-gedi (ch. 24:1). This is the first of two incidents (the other in ch. 26) where David spares Saul's life, and here Saul does state that David will become king (ch. 24:20). Once more the loyalist Ziphites inform Saul of David's encampment at Hachilah (ch. 26:1), and Saul musters his whole army. Again

David makes an example of Saul by refusing to kill him. There is almost a cat-and-mouse aspect to this series of forays, though it is difficult to know sometimes which of the antagonists is the cat and which the mouse. David finally flees to Achish at Gath, thinking that there he is out of danger. But now, ironically, Achish expects David to fight against Israel (ch. 28:1-2). After David's deceptive claims to Achish that he has been raiding Judean towns (ch. 27:10-12), he could surely expect nothing else.

The suspense created by Achish's command to David to fight in the coming battle, with its extremely ironic potentiality, is intensified by the narrator's interpolation of the story of Saul and the witch of En-dor (ch. 28:3-25). The story is a symbolic return to the beginning. Saul's obsession with David has prevented his trusting any man, even though his subjects have demonstrated their loyalty many times. He must now break his own edict against necromancers, as he broke his oath in ch. 14. He can turn only to Samuel, now dead, for Samuel, so far as he knew, always told Saul the truth, terrible though it was. To get to En-dor from his bivouac on Mt. Gilboa, Saul must even take a careful detour around the Philistine encampment at Shunem. The danger involved suggests the straits to which Saul has come. He must get one final word from Samuel, and he can do so only through a necromancer.

It does not help. Samuel is petulant at being disturbed (v. 15), and he now makes explicit to Saul for the first time that the kingdom is given to David (v. 17). Saul had already surmised that, but Samuel's word makes it certain. Samuel then refers back to the incident with Amalek, in which we saw the decisive insight into Saul's character (ch. 15). Nothing but disaster is in sight for Saul. He failed to trust Yahweh to make him king in fact as well as in name, and hence he has lost his trust in the people, in whom he had put the greater store. The reintroduction of Samuel at this point in the narrative is of great significance. With

Samuel, Saul is forced back to brutal reality, away from brutal illusion. He has been battling David all this time, as he thought, but in reality he has been battling Yahweh.

With the recovery of reality, Saul achieves at last something like clarity. His cause is hopeless, and his death at his own hand in battle reveals for the last time his concern for his "image." His lack of confidence in himself and in Yahweh to make him king has led him to the tragic illusion that he has lost his stature among the people. He bids the armor-bearer kill him — is mention of the armor-bearer, a position David once held (ch. 16:21), an accidental or deliberate irony? — "lest these uncircumcised ones come and make sport of me" (ch. 31:4).[25] To avoid the mockery of being captured — like Agag — he falls on his own sword, his act of suicide a final failure of nerve.

Two remaining episodes in the tragic story highlight the irony of the whole. Saul's recourse to Samuel's ghost demonstrated his feeling that the people were no longer with him. But the starkly heroic act of the men of Jabesh-gilead (ch. 31:11-13), the site of Saul's first triumph (ch. 11), shows the lasting respect, loyalty, and affection that he had in fact acquired. The other piece of tragic irony is the moving lament uttered by David over Saul (II Sam. 1:19-27). We cannot imagine that David wanted to fight against Saul, but only because the Philistine officers felt him a poor security risk (I Sam., ch. 29) did he escape this very command in the battle of Mt. Gilboa. He was considered by others Saul's most faithful servant (ch. 22:14). When he could easily have done so, he would not kill Saul (chs. 24:4 ff.; 26:9 ff.).[26]

---

[25] Omitting ûdeqārûnî with I Chron. 10:4.

[26] I do not mean to suggest that David was thinking only of Saul. He was a shrewd politician and an ambitious one, and he certainly had one eye on his standing with the people, an attitude unquestionably present in II Sam., ch. 1. There may also be implied a certain superstitious fear of touching "Yahweh's anointed." But we cannot ascribe to David hatred of Saul; that is simply not to be found in the story.

" He loved him greatly." (Ch. 16:21) Saul's obsession with David was the construct of his own mind, and David's response to Saul's death demonstrates to us how tragically needless it was. Saul's genuine greatness — his stature before the people, and the affection in which he was held, as shown by the deed of the men of Jabesh-gilead — could have had full, free play in the monarchy. He could have been the kind of ruler to turn the kingship's intrinsic ambiguity to the proper ends. But he was not the man. He was " little in his own eyes," and he found it impossible to conceive that obedience to Yahweh might override his own self-perceived shortcomings.

There is, then, as von Rad has observed, something in the Saul story very close to the spirit of Greek tragedy. He adds, however, that there is this difference, that " Saul did not stand under any dark power of fate, and did not reach out beyond himself in *hybris*." [27] Yet there is a kind of nemesis hovering above Saul, the certainty that David will succeed and Saul will not. There is what can be called *hybris* in Saul's decisive choice for what will raise him in the people's estimation rather than for what he has been divinely commanded in the Amalek incident. It might be argued that that is not *hybris,* a " reaching out beyond himself," an extension of greatness too far, since Saul chose the lesser authority rather than the greater. Yet it is a choice of a *different* authority from that under which Saul stands. It is a decision against the divine, and such a decision always implicitly elevates the decider above the divine.

The tragic irony of the Saul story, as our narrator wished us to see it, lies in the disparities between the demand on Saul and Saul's capacity to meet it, and between what Saul understood of his role and what by divine oracle we are given to understand of it. It lies in the difference between his perception of himself

[27] *Theologie des Alten Testaments,* Vol. I, p. 324.

and others' perception of him. The narrator judges Saul adversely. That is the way with Old Testament narrators; they are never content merely to state facts. But the narrator conveys by the way he constructs the story that Saul could have achieved a positive judgment. When that possibility had passed, decline and failure were inexorable.

To be sure, we have looked at the story *as story,* not as historical reportage. The facts of the matter are not our concern here. We have in the Saul story a masterpiece of structure, dramatic order and suspense, and tragic irony. Someday, someone will turn the story of Saul into a great tragedy for the stage. He will have to fill in characters and dialogue, and he will have to make explicit in speech and action much that the narrator has left implicit. But he will not have to alter a single episode. Then perhaps Saul will be recognized as a tragic figure of the same stature as Oedipus or Othello.

# IV

## GENESIS:
## THE IRONY OF ISRAEL

An essay on irony in the book of Genesis should probably be of book length. Such an essay, thoroughly done, would approximate a commentary, which would necessitate attention to many subjects that must here be passed by. I cannot consider in any detail the problems of the composition of the book of Genesis, whether they be solved by documentary analysis, by traditio-historical criticism, by form criticism, or by any other method. I will not, therefore, weary the reader with J, E, D, and P, as the study of irony in Genesis does not necessitate either a positive or a negative decision regarding the documentary hypothesis. Whatever account of the composition of the book of Genesis is accepted, the book achieved that final form in which we now read it. This study will consider the book as it now stands. If it can be shown that failure to analyze documents has seriously distorted the perception of irony in the text, I will then be prepared to mend my ways.

### Eden to Babel: Variations on an Ironic Theme

Irony in narrative may take several forms. It may be a *punctual* irony, the use of words and expressions of ironic intention at particular, more or less isolated, "points." It may be *episodic* irony, the perception of an entire episode with an ironic aim or content. It may be *thematic* irony, the conjunction of a number of episodes all of which point to an ironic theme or motif. These three types of narrative irony may be interrelated. An episode may, for example, take its ironic flavor from a number of ironic expressions and words in it, and punctual irony may therefore establish episodic irony. On the other hand, the irony of a particular episode may arise from its conjunction with one or more themes of the wider context. Again, thematic irony may be recognized by a continuum of several episodes with ironic content. In the first eleven chapters of Genesis, we have this sort of thematic irony. The various myths of man's origins, taken separately, are filled with irony. At the same time, the common ironic theme of these episodes is set against the background of another theme that lends depth to the irony.

The ironic theme in these chapters is that of man's failure to live up to the aim of his creation.[1] Whatever the process through which the separate stories were combined into one, the passage is finally intended to have a thematic unity. The final editor (or editors) was far more than a mere compiler, but was in a true sense an " author." [2] Hence, the theory that the episode of Gen., ch. 3, belongs to the J document, while the creation story of chs. 1:1 to 2:4a belongs to the P document, though perhaps true, does not prevent our recognizing a thematic effect of the latter story upon the former, which, moreover, is surely intended by the " author " who brought them together.

[1] I would refer the reader also to my discussion of these passages in *You Shall Be My People: The Books of Covenant and Law* (The Westminster Press, 1959), pp. 78–84.

[2] Cf. the perspicacious remark of F. van Trigt, made in another connection, in " La significance de la lutte de Jacob près du Yabboq, Gen. xxxii 23-33," in *Oudtestamentische Studiën,* deel XII, " Studies on the Book of Genesis " (E. J. Brill, Leiden, 1958), p. 302: " *En effet, à moins de fermer entièrement les yeux sur la composition exceptionelle de l'ensemble des récits, nous y découvrons des ' auteurs' qui sont bien plus que des compilateurs des données d'une vieille tradition."*

The creation motif, indeed, is the backdrop to all that occurs in these chapters. The drama of failure is played out against the creation of man and the earth, the motif of sin against the "very good" creation (*tôb me'ôd*, ch. 1:31). Divinely ordained as ruler of earth (ch. 1:28) and as "servant of the soil" (cf. *le'obdāh*, ch. 2:15), man misrules and denies his servitude. Disregarding his limitations (ch. 2:17), he reaches for the divine knowledge. The theme of sin and failure, therefore, is ironic in part because it is juxtaposed to the theme of the good creation.

At the same time, the myths of sin are ironic in content. The myth of the primal fall (ch. 3) betrays its irony in several ways. There is, first of all, the play on words in the primal couple's "nakedness" (*'arummîn*, ch. 2:25) and the serpent's "subtlety" (*'ārûm*, ch. 3:1), suggesting that the subtle serpent exerts an uncanny power over the naked and defenseless human beings.[8] The serpent's speech itself is an ironic overstatement: "Did God really say that you may not eat from any trees of the garden?" (v. 1). When the woman hastens to God's defense, remembering

[8] I suggested, without documentation, in *You Shall Be My People*, p. 79, that nakedness (*'ērôm*) connotes helplessness. Cf. the uses of *'ērôm* in Ezek. 18:7, 16, in parallel with "hungry"; in ch. 16:7, 22, 39, of the personified young Jerusalem in her helplessness without God; in ch. 23:29 of Oholibah in her deliverance to those whom she hates; in Deut. 28:48, where nakedness, hunger, thirst, and want are the conditions under which Israel will serve her enemies, i.e., that nothing is of any help against those conditions. The cognate *'ārôm*, used in Gen. 2:25, is found in Hos. 2:5 in a context very much like that of Ezek., ch. 16; in Micah 1:8, perhaps of a symbolic act of the prophet somewhat like that of Isa., ch. 20, which also uses the word; in Amos 2:16 of the flight of ignominiously defeated warriors; in Isa. 58:7 in the same sense as in Ezek. 18:7, 16; in Job 22:6 of the weakness of the poor before the mighty; in Job 24:7, 10 of the sad state of men whom God ignores; in Job 26:6 of the openness of Sheol before God; and in Job 1:21 of man's condition before God at birth and death alike. Taken together, these passages suggest to me that the connotation of *'ērôm* and *'ārôm* is not sexual but situational, nakedness as the absence of defense against threatening powers. For other opinions of the symbolic connotations of nakedness in Gen., ch. 3, see Robert Gordis, "The Knowledge of Good and Evil in the Old Testament and the Qumran Scrolls," *JBL*, Vol. 76 (1957), pp. 123–138, and literature cited there; Walter Zimmerli, *1. Mose 1–11: Die Urgeschichte*, 2te Auflage (Prophezei, Zwingli Verlag, Zürich, 1957), p. 147.

at the same time the one tree that has been forbidden, the serpent
scoffs. God is "holding out" on the human beings, for that one
forbidden tree is the one important source of power. "God knows
that in the day that you eat of it, your eyes will be opened, and
you will become like God, knowing good and evil." (V. 5.) And
so she eats, and he as well. "It is not good that man should be
alone." (Ch. 2:18.) With the eating of the fruit, half of the serpent's promise comes true: their eyes are opened. The other half
is ironically reversed: "And they saw that they were—naked"
(ch. 3:7). The fruit, touted as the source of divine power, produces not the Godlike knowledge of good and evil but only the
perception of helplessness. Having grasped after the divine knowledge, man now ludicrously hides from the God he sought to displace (v. 8). With the alteration of man's relationship with God,
extending even to the ironic blaming of God for the whole situation ("the woman *whom you gave to be with me,*" v. 12), all of
man's relationships are now changed. As soon as man's created
oneness is a solidarity in sin, it splits apart. Woman is subordinated to man (v. 16),[4] and man loses the cooperation of the soil
(*ᵃdāmāh*) of whose stuff he (*'ādām*) was made (vs. 17-18). Man's
function in the creation has been fundamentally changed. He remains, as he must, "the servant of the soil" (v. 23), but the soil
that has formed him represents now the frightful finis of his
sojourn. "You are dust." That would have stated only fact before,
but now, seen against man's pretense to divinity, it is an ironic
judgment. "And to dust you shall return." If man insists on
trying to achieve higher than human status, his destiny is to be
less than man. Grasping for everything, Adam and Eve lose
everything.

In the Cain and Abel myth, the irony is slightly different. Cain,

---

[4] Is it not surprising that, in a culture where the subordination of woman
to man was a virtually unquestioned social principle, the etiology of the subordination should be in the context of man's primal sin? Perhaps woman's subordination was not unquestioned in Israel.

like Adam, is the "servant of the soil" (ch. 4:2), but Yahweh's failure to accept his offering (v. 5) raises Cain's ire. Yet Yahweh disarmingly requires only "doing well," or else sin will wait in ambush.[5] But Cain's action brings out the irony in both the promise and the threat of Yahweh. He takes the course of ambush, falling upon Abel in the field. He who has been exhorted to "do well" does, on the contrary, evil. When Yahweh asks, "Where is Abel your brother?" (v. 9), Cain's famous answer carries a double irony. On the one hand, Cain does not admit that he is his "brother's keeper," and the question implies his own ironic perception of the idea. On the other hand, the obvious answer to Cain's question is affirmative, uncovering Cain's ironic failure to perceive his true relationship to his brother. There may even be a third level of irony in Cain's use of the term "keeper" (shômēr), perhaps alluding to Abel's vocation as shepherd, as the term is used several times of "keeping" sheep (cf. Gen. 30:31; I Sam. 17:20; Jer. 31:10).

With Yahweh's curse, Cain, like Adam before him, loses his vocation, and the soil, which he was to serve but which has given evidence against him (Gen. 4:10), now turns uncooperative (v. 12), and Cain must become a nomad. His outcry reflects his fear that the fate he meted out to Abel will now be his (hārag, "slay"; cf. the same verb in v. 8). Ironically, Cain is not permitted to pay off his debt so easily. On the contrary, having taken vengeance, he is now the agent by whom vengeance is to be multiplied in the world. The tragedy of vengeance comes to its savage extension with the Song of Lamech (vs. 23-24), where Lamech claims the privilege of seventy-sevenfold vengeance for very slight

---

[5] This remark is closely related to the curse on the woman in ch. 3:16. Here, "its [sin's] desire [teshûqāh] is centered on you, but you must master [māshal] it"; there, "your desire [teshûqāh] is centered on your husband, but he must master [māshal] you." Cain's relationship to sin ought to be like man's relationship to woman. The statement rings loud with irony, in both itself and the context of the Eden myth. Cf. Zimmerli, op. cit., p. 212.

provocation. Here, then, is the pass brought on by one rupture of brotherly responsibility, the tragically ironic expansion of vengeance in a world where vengeance has no proper place, except as it belongs to God (v. 15). Once more man claims the divine prerogative and sounds strangely beastly as he does so.

The curious little myth in ch. 6:1-4, with its drastic perception of " total depravity " (v. 5), is very difficult to penetrate. Clearly the narrator views the marriages between the " sons of God " and the " daughters of men " as illegitimate if not incongruous, since these unions occasion the divine limitation on the length of human life. The limitation seems required because human beings continue to grasp after more than is good for them, and, if the sequence (v. 5) is the narrator's comment on the story, human aspiration to what is more than human produces nothing but evil, an ironic perception not different from that of ch. 3. Meanwhile, however, we have the enigmatic reference to the Nephilim, the heroes and famous men of old (v. 4). Clearly they are connected to the illicit marriages of vs. 1 and 2. We must certainly assume that the ancient editor saw as well as we do that the name Nephilim suggests an etymology from the verb *nāphal,* "to fall." [6] The references to " heroes " and " famous men " in the context of the illicit divine-human marriages and in relationship to the name Nephilim falls, then, into line with the theme of human self-elevation noticeable throughout these chapters. Human power and fame carry an ironically illegitimate air. They are the " fallen " issue of an unnatural conjunction of powers.

Now we are confronted by the statement of utter human evil (v. 5), and the whole creation is cast in the ironic light of failure. Man has " increased " as he was told to do (cf. *r$^e$bû,* ch. 1:28, and *rôb,* ch. 6:1), but what he has actually " increased " is evil (cf.

---

[6] Not until the Ethiopic Enoch in the second century B.C. is this myth, rather than that of Adam and Eve, used as the primal myth of the Fall. Cf. I Enoch, chs. 6 to 8.

*rabbāh* in ch. 6:5). The goodness of creation has gone wrong, and it is time to begin again.[7] The waters of the flood are a return to the waters of chaos, an ironic conclusion to the first act of the creation. In addition, the rain as the source of the flood in the J strand (ch. 7:4) represents an advance on man's cosmic experience, since the J creation story begins by noting that " Yahweh God had not yet made it rain on the earth " (ch. 2:5).[8] The flood is at once a retrogression, the return of the chaos from which creation came, and a progression, the introduction of a new experience, rain. In the context of the flood, however, progress is ironically undesirable.

With the conclusion of the flood, Noah attempts a return to normalcy. But the occasion of his trouble is once more the soil. Noah becomes an *'ish hā'ᵃdāmāh,* plants a vineyard, and gets stupidly drunk on its produce (ch. 9:20-21). Now, the son may — and does — sarcastically lord it over the father, and the curse is again present in the earth (vs. 22-27).[9] The irony is twofold. On the one hand, the sphere of the fertility cults with their looking upon nakedness [10] and their drunkenness is the condition into which Noah, the righteous and perfect man (cf. ch. 6:9), falls. On the other hand, Noah curses Canaan, who bespeaks precisely that fertility realm, forbidden to the Israelite, into which he himself has fallen.

Noah's sons now proceed to populate the earth, thus leading

[7] To be sure, the " goodness " of creation is a theme of the P creation story, and ch. 6:5-8 is normally analyzed as J. Nonetheless, we cannot ignore the fact that the " sources " have been combined into a unity, and it is illegitimate to avoid the conjunctions of images and themes in what is now a single story.

[8] Cf. U. Cassuto's reading of ch. 2:5 in *A Commentary on the Book of Genesis, Part One: From Adam to Noah* (Magnes Press, Jerusalem, 1961), pp. 102–104.

[9] The curse was certainly originally on Ham, but was transferred to Canaan because Canaan was Israel's immediate religious problem. Von Rad, *Genesis,* tr. by John H. Marks (The Westminster Press, 1961), pp. 131–132, argues, however, that " Ham the father of " in vs. 18 and 22 is a harmonizing gloss.

[10] Also a mark of the fertility cult. Cf., e.g., Ex. 20:26. See also the remarks above, note 3, on the nakedness motif in Gen., ch. 3.

to the dangerous unity of the tower-building (ch. 11:1-9). The tower, indeed, is built at Shinar in the territory of Nimrod, Ham's grandson (ch. 10:10), suggesting again that Ham is the source of trouble. But the irony of the story of the Tower of Babel lies principally in its completing and rounding out the theme of man's exclusion from Eden. Here men attempt an anti-Eden, a humanly constructed paradise from which God is to be excluded.[11] The tower (*migdāl*) is defensive security against God, that man may be free to pursue his technologically assured salvation. But man's unity is ruptured by the humorously economical means of the confusion of language. We might expect Yahweh to fling people and bricks about the landscape with a mighty arm. The narrators give us a more subtle and, I believe, ironic perception of the Deity's workings. The breaking of man's linguistic unity produces precisely what the entire project was designed to prevent, the scattering of man over the earth (ch. 11:8). The narrator has capped the irony by identifying the tower with Babylon, the location of Judah's exile (v. 9), and by sardonically connecting the name Babel with the verb *bālal*, "to confuse." This type of ironic humor is to be found in every underground movement, and perhaps it implies a sixth-century B.C. "demythologization" of the story.

The ironic theme in these chapters is the perception of incongruity between the purpose of man's creation and how he actually acts, between the "is" and the "ought." It is expressed through the piling up of ironic episodes in which man, reaching beyond the Creator's limitations, is hurled down below his proper place, in which he causes his own downfall by attempting his own

---

[11] I owe this interpretation to remarks in a lecture by Prof. A. J. Heschel at Stanford in May, 1963. A rather similar interpretation is proposed by Walter Zimmerli, *op. cit.*, pp. 399–404, but on pp. 405–407 Zimmerli seems to me to confuse the point by referring to the Tower of Babel as the Marduk temple in Babylon. The point of the tower is that it is a defense tower, not that it is a pagan temple.

elevation. Another thread of an ironic theme running through these chapters is the juncture of *'ādām* and *'ªdāmāh,* man's relationship to the soil. Somehow, whenever man acts in his appointed role as " servant of the soil," trouble ensues, for Adam, for Cain, for Noah. The irony of this theme may imply the danger of man's dependence on the soil for his life, because of the powerful impetus to fertility-centered worship. Or it might simply convey the fact that man, even engaged in his appointed pursuits, finds a way to try to lift himself toward divinity. Whatever the precise meaning of the theme, a careful look both at the details of the section and at their effect emphasizes a fundamentally ironic portrayal of man.

## ABRAHAM: THE IRONIES OF PROMISE

The thematic unity of the Abraham story is woven about the thread of promise. The continued narrowing of the genealogical tables in chs. 10 and 11, until finally, at ch. 11:26-32, we have settled down with Abraham, suggests that Abraham represents the solution to the ironic theme of man as sinner set in chs. 1 to 11. But with Abraham the solution remains provisional, not yet achieved but a promise for the future.

The promise has two interconnected aspects, both implied in Abraham's vocation (ch. 12:1-2): " Go out from your land, from your relatives, and from your family, to the land I will show you. And I will make of you a great nation, and I will bless you and will give you a great name." The two themes are the promise of the land, which becomes a definite promise of possession only in v. 7, and the assurance that Abraham's descendants will be a great nation. With the former, we have in prospect the solution to man's homelessness, vividly related in the expulsion from Eden (ch. 3:23-24), the curse on Cain (ch. 4:16), the dispersion of Noah's sons (ch. 10), and the scattering of men from the Tower

of Babel (ch. 11:8). With the promise of descendants, the centrif-
ugal movement of man is to be arrested, for around the Abra-
hamic nation will gather the blessedness of mankind ("all the
clans of the soil" [*'ᵃdāmāh*]). Hence, Abraham's "great name"
sets the legitimate counterpoise to the illegitimate "name" sought
by the tower builders (ch. 11:4), for this power and identity are
not grasped by man for himself with the object of excluding God
but are presented to man by God.

But here is promise, not actuality. The land will be given to
Abraham's descendants (ch. 12:7), not to Abraham, who journeys through and within it. Yet Abraham's greatness of name
begins to pay off even in Egypt (vs. 10-20), where, for all his
timidity, Pharaoh treats him with respect both before and after
the near-disaster over Sarah's temporary sojourn as his wife.[12]
As he finds himself once again in Canaanite territory, his wealth
might make us think the promise has already come. His pos-
sessions and Lot's are so vast that "the land could not support
them both together" (ch. 13:6). In their times of trouble, the
hearers of that remark ironically compared their own tenuous
hold of the land with Abraham's power, as Ezekiel tells us from
the Babylonian exile: "Son of man, the dwellers in these wastes
on Israel's soil are saying, 'Abraham was but one man, and he
possessed the land, whereas we are many. We should be given
possession of the land'" (Ezek. 33:24).

Yet the very prosperity of Abraham and Lot causes them to
separate, Abraham to the barren hills, Lot to the fertile Jordan
valley. But Lot's country retains the problems that plagued man
in the beginning. "The people of Sodom were very wicked and
sinful against Yahweh." (Gen. 13:13.) In the interest of his comfort, Lot has regressed, passing his life among those who represent mankind before Abraham. Abraham, however, receives the

---

[12] The story has its ironic potential, best realized in the second version, ch.
20:1-18. Discussion will be postponed for that version. The same story, of course,
is told of Isaac in ch. 26:6-11.

reiteration of the double promise, that the land will be given to his descendants and of these there will be many (vs. 15-17). Yet the blessing remains Yahweh's; the earth's families have not yet bestowed it.

In the next episode, a glimmering of the universal blessing appears (ch. 14). Some of earth's families are bent on displacing the heir to the land, though they come only as far as poor, hapless Lot. But from Salem comes the blessing of Melchizedek (vs. 19-20). The story has given exegetes a great deal of difficulty. Not only does it not fit into any of the Pentateuchal strata; it is also enigmatic in language and background. In the context, the story reflects the ambiguity of Lot's decision in ch. 13, which will come to its climax in ch. 19, and it also reflects the beginnings of the actualization of the promise to Abraham. From Salem the blessing comes, and hearers of the story would have made the same connection between Salem and Jerusalem that we make. They knew perfectly well that Jerusalem became an Israelite city only with David (II Sam. 5:6-10). The blessing comes also from Melchizedek, a name that we may suppose they would understand to mean "My king is righteous." The episode conveys, then, both the eschatological universality of blessing on Abraham from the earth's families and the certainty of Israel's establishment in the land, where Jerusalem will be the seat of the righteous kingship. The promise begins to have its fulfillment, then, even with Abraham himself.

But the promise remains unfulfilled, for Abraham cannot possess the land without decendants. It is all very well for Yahweh to promise Abraham that his " reward is great indeed " (ch. 15:1). Abraham protests with more than a hint of irony: " O Lord Yahweh, what are you going to give me? I am still childless " (v. 2).[13] The promise is repeated, the number of Abraham's

[13] V. 2b is in a hopeless textual state. It appears to say that Abraham will be forced to adopt a slave in order to have an heir. V. 3 is not very much help. RSV has interpolated " slave," which may be the sense of it, though the expres-

descendants being compared to the stars (v. 5) — previously they were compared to the grains of dust (ch. 13:16). The covenant ceremony seals the promise (ch. 15:7-21).

We must continue to await its fulfillment, however. The birth of Ishmael (ch. 16:1-16) and the vexation he causes Sarah (ch. 21:9-21) provide an ironic suspense to the promise of descendants. The fact that the custom of giving a maid to a man to provide heirs is attested elsewhere in the Old Testament (cf. its practice in ch. 30:3-13) and in the ancient Near East does not efface the fact that Ishmael is clearly not the promised heir, any more than the children of Bilhah and Zilpah in ch. 30 are on an equality with the children of Leah and, finally, Rachel. The struggle between Hagar and Sarah underscores the relative — though not absolute — illegitimacy of Ishmael. Hagar's arrogance too lends irony to Ishmael's position, for however sympathetic we are intended to be to Hagar in her two excursions into the desert (chs. 16:7-14; 21:14-21), the narrator intends us to remain convinced that Ishmael's birth is an interlude between promise and fulfillment. There is in addition a certain etiological irony, similar to that on Moab and Ammon (ch. 19:30-38), that Ishmael, while blessed as the son of Abraham and circumcised covenantally with him, passes to his Ishmaelite descendants the relative illegitimacy that he received through his mother.

But the fulfillment of the promise still awaits its actuality. The heir will not be born until ch. 21, and we have barely reached ch. 17. The continued promise in the priestly circumcision-covenant narrative retains its irony in the explanation of Abraham's

---

sion *ben bēthî,* " son of my house," is not clear. L. A. Snijders, " Genesis XV. The Covenant with Abraham," in *Oudtestamentische Studiën,* deel XII, pp. 269–270, has suggested the reading *ben mashshāq* for *ben mesheq* in v. 2a, meaning " the attacker, he who forces himself on one " (cf. Isa. 33:4). The gloss, " that is, Damascus " (*dammesheq*), is a deliberate pun, according to Snijders. The idea is by no means impossible, but the syntax remains obscure, and I am not convinced.

new name, "father of a multitude" (v. 5), since Abraham is not
as yet father of anyone. The promise of a son moves Abraham
at last to laughter: "Shall a son be born to a centenarian? And
can Sarah — can a ninety-year-old woman — give birth?" (v. 17).
The idea, of course, is ridiculous. But God will have the last laugh.
"You shall call him Isaac" (*yitschāq*, "he laughs"). (V. 19.)
One wonders how anyone could say, as Alfred North Whitehead
commented, that there is no humor in the Old Testament.[14] The
laughter rings out again in ch. 18 when Sarah, eavesdropping on
the conversation between Yahweh and Abraham, laughs to herself (v. 12): "After I am decrepit, do I get some pleasure? And
with an elderly husband?" Not often in the Old Testament do
human beings laugh at Yahweh, and Sarah hastily denies having
laughed (v. 15). Certainly, however, the rhetorical questions expressing the incongruity of old folks' bearing babies are ironic.[15]

But when, having been told Yahweh's intention to wipe out
Sodom and Gomorrah, Abraham begins to argue, the irony is far
different. Clearly he intends an escape clause for Lot, as he bar-
gains Yahweh down from fifty to ten righteous people as sufficient to avert the catastrophe. The ground of the argument,
however, is a moral one: "Are you really going to destroy the
righteous along with the wicked? . . . Far be it from you to do
such a thing, to kill the righteous along with the wicked, the
same thing happening to both. Far be it from you! Should not the
whole world's judge do justice?" (vs. 23, 25). The final question
contains an ironic wordplay: "Should not the *shôphēṭ* of the

---

[14] *Dialogues of Alfred North Whitehead*, edited by Lucien Price (The New
American Library of World Literature, Inc., 1956 [originally published by Little,
Brown and Company, 1954]), p. 163.

[15] In the Canaanite story of Aqhat, Dan'el, the prospective father, also laughs
at the news, but his laughter is that of sheer pleasure: "He parted his jaws and
laughed" (AQHT A.ii.10; cf. *ANET*, p. 150). In a brief note, "Abraham and
the Aqhat Legend," *JBL*, Vol. 77 (1958), pp. 72–73, I argued for a connection in
tradition between the Aqhat story and the continuum of episodes leading up to
the birth of Isaac.

whole world do *mishpāṭ*? " Yahweh's function as " judge " implies his pursuit of " justice." Abraham pleads not for the evil cities or even primarily for his nephew but for the divine consistency. The proposal to wipe out the righteous with the wicked seems to him an incongruity, and he is prepared even to tackle Yahweh with its irony.[16]

With the imminent destruction of Sodom and Gomorrah, Lot's ludicrous delay is comically ironic (ch. 19:16-22). Lot does not want to leave Sodom. He " dawdles " (*yithmah*e*māh,* v. 16) and must be coerced out of the city. Told to flee to the hills, he protests that he is as much afraid of the hills as of the city (v. 19). Here we are, waiting for the fire and brimstone to strike the city to ashes, and Lot stands around arguing about the escape route! " That city over there is nearer to flee to." (V. 20.) Lot even wants as easy a journey as possible, not considering that proximity to Sodom is, to say the least, unhealthy. Furthermore, that city over there is " a little one," presumably beneath the notice of fire and brimstone. It must nevertheless be specifically exempted by the angel from the destruction, and we receive the impression that the exemption is granted in irritated desperation and haste (vs. 21-22).

Before Abraham's promised child comes, another episode builds up the suspense when, for the second time, Abraham almost gives away Sarah on whom the promise of the heir depends (ch. 20:1-18).[17] Abimelech is completely taken in, believing everything

[16] Cf. von Rad, *Genesis,* pp. 206–210, who fails to mark the irony of the question. I have often wondered whether the narrator intended a certain irony in the fact that Abraham ceases his bargaining with ten. As it turns out, there are only four righteous in Sodom (ch. 19:15). Is the narrator saying, with extreme subtlety, that if Abraham had carried his boldness far enough — say, to four — Sodom might have been spared? Perhaps the point rests on silence, which cannot establish it.

[17] The story is told again of Isaac (ch. 26:6-11), and the contention of Noth, *Überlieferungsgeschichte des Pentateuch* (W. Kohlhammer Verlag, Stuttgart, 1948), pp. 115–116, that the tale originated with Isaac, is probably correct.

he is told in utter innocence (vs. 4-5). Confronted with his perfidy, Abraham has his own rationalization. He feared the pagans (v. 11), and anyway, there is a sense — a very tenuous sense, to be sure — in which Sarah is his sister, since she is the daughter of his father though not of his mother (v. 12).[18] There is no other reference to this fact, and it seems quite possible that the writer intends it as pure fabrication on Abraham's part. Nor can we miss the irony in Abraham's remark that he asked Sarah to report him as her brother out of " loyalty " (*chesed,* v. 13). That is the " loyalty " of wife for husband! In this version of the story, Abimelech adds his own subtle touch of irony. He gives Abraham the rights of the countryside. " And to Sarah he said, ' See, I have given a thousand pieces of silver to your — brother.' " (V. 16.)

The laughter to which we have alluded before now comes to its fruition, with the birth of the child who will be a living and walking laugh. Yet no sooner has the promised child been born than the trail of threats to the actualization of the promise comes to its climax. " Take your son, your only son, whom you love, Isaac, and go to the land of Moriah, and offer him there as a burnt offering on one of the mountains which I will designate." (Ch. 22:2.) The command piles up the terms of endearment in a concentrated tragic irony, capped by the mention of the boy's name, with its echo of the laughter that greeted the promise and the actuality of his birth. When they reach the mountain, Abraham's response to Isaac's question about the offering is profoundly ironic: " God will see to the offering, my son " (v. 8). The answer satisfies the boy, intensifying the irony of its double meaning. We may also note the possible connection of the name Moriah with the verb that Abraham uses here (*yir'eh*) and the name that is finally given the mountain in v. 14: *Yahweh yir'eh,* " Yah-

---

[18] It has often been noted that the remark presupposes a matrilineal system, for a man marrying the daughter of his father would avoid incest only on the assumption that the blood-line passes through the mother.

weh will see." This is even clearer in the reading of the Samaritan Pentateuch, *môrā'āh* for *môriyyāh* in v. 2, reflected in the LXX reading (*optasias*) and the Vulgate (*visionis*). Vision, the seeing that produces understanding, is a central theme in the story, but, in the shadow of the all but unbearable beginning, Abraham is blind to it until the surprising end.

At the same time, we must connect the passage to the larger theme of the Abraham story, the provision of an heir to the covenantal promise. Lot, the first potential candidate, separated himself from Abraham and fell from consideration. Abraham apparently considered adopting Eliezer the slave. The birth of Ishmael was only an apparent solution to the problem of Sarah's sterility, for with Isaac's birth, Ishmael and his mother had been cast out. Everything then rests on Isaac's shoulders. Immediately comes the command to sacrifice the child of the promise, whose coming has seemed so dubious for so long. In the structure of the Abraham story, this episode is the culmination of the continual frustration of Yahweh's plans for Abraham, up to the point (v. 11) where the angel of Yahweh calls him.[19] The suspense, creating almost unbearable tension, could have approached the character of *The Perils of Pauline,* save for the sober restraint of the narrator. And the episode's irony finds its depth from the context, which at the same time gives the passage its meaning.

The problem of descendants solved, half of Yahweh's promise to Abraham (ch. 12:1-2) bears the likelihood of actualization. But the other half of the theme, the promise of possession of the land, which has been subordinated for several chapters, casts an ironic reflection on an otherwise rather isolated episode, the purchase of the cave of Machpelah (ch. 23:1-20). At first glance, the purchase of land for a tomb is not promising material for irony. Yet the story possesses not only irony but also humor, in what may be taken as a mild satire on commercial bargaining customs (vs.

---

[19] Note the expression *mal'ak yhwh* in an allegedly E passage.

3-16).[20] Who would haggle over a price at a time like this? Abraham would (by implication, perhaps, his descendants as well), and so would the Hittites. And the studied casualness with which Ephron, having urged Abraham to take the land for nothing and knowing that he would not, mentions the value of the plot (v. 15) is certainly humorous. The irony of the episode arises out of the theme of God's promise of the land to Abraham. The first time Abraham arrives in Canaan, the promise is given (ch. 12:7), and it is reiterated when he and Lot separate (ch. 13:14-17), in the covenant ceremony (ch. 15:7, 16, 18-21), and in the promise related to the circumcision (ch. 17:8). The land is Abraham's by promise. Yet he must bargain with a Hittite over the purchase of a piece of it for a burial ground.[21] " I am an alien and a sojourner among you." (Ch. 23:4.) It is the irony inherent in the promise that remains only promise. And when the servant must be sent off to Abraham's relatives in Mesopotamia to find a wife for Isaac (ch. 24), the irony is deepened. For all the promise, Abraham remains an alien in the land that is his.

The Abraham story is a tightly structured whole, carrying its double theme of the promised heir and the promised land by the constant contrast of promise and ironic actuality. Indeed, that irony is finally intrinsic to the theme of promise in the Abraham tradition. Wherever the promise is not and cannot be actualized, those who await its fulfillment are inevitably entangled in the ironic incongruity between what is and what will be.

## Jacob: The Irony of Brotherhood

It is surprising that God appears so rarely in the Jacob story, as compared to his almost constant confrontation of Abraham.

[20] So also von Rad, *Genesis,* p. 242. The humor is in a passage universally analyzed as P. The Priestly writers are not ordinarily singled out as purveyors of the comic.

[21] R. de Vaux, O.P., *La Genèse* (BJ, Les Éditions du Cerf, Paris, 1962), p. 109, makes the connection of this story with the theme of promise but fails to mark its irony.

To be sure, the points of the divine interjection are crucial: the oracle to Rebekah about her sons (ch. 25:23); the vision at Bethel (ch. 28:11-17); the intervention on behalf of Leah (chs. 29:31 to 30:24); the meeting and wrestling with Jacob at the Jabbok (ch. 32:1-2, 22-32); Jacob's movement from Shechem to Bethel (ch. 35:1-15). It has been argued that the second and fourth of these episodes afford the theological grounds for the understanding of the entire Jacob story.[22] In the one (ch. 28:11-17) he receives the covenantal promise of the land; in the other (ch. 32:22-32), the covenantal name, Israel. We should not miss the irony of the fact that in the former episode, Jacob receives the promise of the land at just the moment that he is hotfooting it away from the land. Nor should we overlook the irony that the name Israel, whose meaning is disputed but which perhaps signifies something like " he strives with God," is given at just the moment that Jacob, in abject terror, is about to meet his estranged brother Esau.

It is equally noticeable, however, that those two episodes stand structurally between the two major groups of stories in which Jacob is central. Chapter 28:11-17 is the episode of transition between the first set of Jacob-Esau stories and the Jacob-Laban cycle; ch. 32:22-32 is the transition from the Jacob-Laban cycle to the second part of the Jacob-Esau cycle. We have, therefore, to do with Jacob's actions with Esau on the one hand and with Laban on the other. In these contexts the Jacob tradition must be understood. And the narrator, by judicious placement of the revelations to Jacob, has set the human interactions in the context of the divine action.

The Jacob-Esau conflict begins before the twins' birth. The oracle to Rebekah expresses an ironic reversal of normal inheritance pattern; the younger will dominate the older (ch. 25:23).[23]

[22] Cf. Napier, *From Faith to Faith*, pp. 85–87.

[23] The pattern occurs so often that perhaps it is virtually normal. Note the younger sons in the Old Testament who attain preeminence: Isaac, Jacob, Joseph, Ephraim (Gen. 48:14), Othniel (Judg. 3:9), David, Solomon.

That theme brings the relation between Jacob and Esau to its focus. The conflict of the brothers is foreshadowed in the comment, rich in ironic potential, of ch. 25:28: " And Isaac loved Esau because of the meat in his [Isaac's] mouth; but Rebekah loved Jacob." We have already seen the reason for Rebekah's preference for Jacob: he is destined for primacy. Rebekah looks to the future; Isaac thinks only of his stomach.

Esau too thinks only of his stomach. The caustic gibe cast at the Edomites by referring to their descendance from Esau (v. 30) in the context of his stupid abandonment of his inheritance for a bowl of lentil soup perhaps reflects the late exilic or early postexilic enmity between Israel and Edom. Jacob's mulcting Esau of his birthright (vs. 29-34) shows how easy is the supplanting, adumbrated in the oracle to Rebekah and in the birth narrative (v. 26). Esau has only to be momentarily hungry to "despise" his inheritance rights.

From the private transaction, we move to the more nearly public one (ch. 27). Isaac is prepared to pass the blessing to Esau, the rightful heir. We know, from the previous episode, that Esau has forfeited his right to the blessing. Yet ironically, Jacob must resort to deception to gain the blessing. Rebekah presumably knows nothing of the bartered birthright. She knows only the oracle given her, and she now takes into her own hands the assurance of its fulfillment. She has everything well in hand, including Jacob's fearful anxieties that the scheme may not succeed (ch. 27:5-17).

The dialogue between Jacob and Isaac (vs. 18-29) is filled with dramatic ironies. Isaac is very suspicious. "Who are you, my son? " (V. 18.) "How is this? You have been so quick to find [game], my son." (V. 20.) "Come here and let me feel you, my son. Are you really he, my son Esau, or not? " (V. 21.) "The voice is Jacob's, but the hands are Esau's." (V. 22.) Finally, almost the last gasp of suspicion: "Are you really he, my son

Esau? " (v. 24).[24] Isaac seems satisfied, and yet, after the meal, he must check once again. " Come here and kiss me, my son." (V. 26.) Isaac wants to smell his son, and that leads into the opening metaphor of the blessing. The poem, conveying the irretrievable blessing and inheritance, is thoroughly ironic, intended as it is to apply to Esau and metaphorically inapplicable to Jacob:

> See, my son's smell
> Is like the field's smell,
> Which Yahweh has blessed.
> May God give you the heaven's dew
> And the ground's fat things,
> Much of grain and of wine.
> Peoples shall serve you,
> Nations bow to you.
> Be master over your brothers,[25]
> And may your mother's sons bow to you.
> Cursed be those who curse you,
> But blessed those who bless you.
>                                    (Vs. 27-29.)

Dramatic irony is enhanced by the timing of the ensuing action: " As Isaac had finished blessing Jacob, and just as Jacob had gone out from Isaac his father, Esau his brother came in with his game " (v. 30). Isaac's bad news arouses Esau's bitterly ironic criticism of Jacob. " Is his name not properly Jacob [supplanter]? He has supplanted me twice: he took my inheritance right, and now he has taken my blessing." (V. 36.) The bitter play on the name, *ya'ᵃqôb*, with the verbal form, *wayya'q*ᵉ*bēnî*, takes us back to the boys' birth and to the oracle to Rebekah (ch. 25:23). All

---

[24] Reading, with Samaritan Pentateuch, *ha'attāh*. Only with the interrogative prefix would we expect Jacob to answer as he does, "I am."

[25] LXX and Targum Onkelos read the singular, "your brother," an ironic reference to Jacob. The counterpart, spoken to Esau in v. 37, is in the singular, suggesting the propriety of the singular here. It requires only repointing from *'acheḵā* to *'achîḵᵃ.*

Isaac has left for Esau is the curse, the very reverse of what he has given Jacob (ch. 27:39-40).

The parental preference, then, has deepened the ironies of the brothers' relationships. Isaac's preference for Esau has perhaps made both of them careless. Rebekah's fondness for Jacob leads to her underhanded machinations on his behalf, which are not yet complete. She manages to get Isaac not only to approve but to suggest Jacob's disappearance before Esau can kill him (chs. 27:46 to 28:2).

The sojourn in Padan-aram, which occupies the next chapters, sets out the conflict between Jacob and Laban. Here is presented, with an almost Aristophanic gusto, the comic confrontation of *eirōn* with *alazōn* (cf. Chapter I), of the ironical man with the impostor. The stories are told from the Israelite bias, of course, and Jacob therefore finally triumphs over his sometimes dense but occasionally too shrewd kinsman.

The first episode, at least, is Laban's triumph (ch. 29:15-30). Jacob, desiring to marry Rachel, contracts to do so, but Laban slips Leah into the tent in the dark. Jacob is furious, Laban bland. "It simply is not done around here, to marry off the younger daughter before the elder." (V. 26.) Undoubtedly Laban sees Leah's chances of a good match to be inferior to Rachel's, since Leah has poor eyesight (v. 17). But Jacob must swallow defeat and work seven years more for nothing. The *alazōn* has won the first round, and Jacob has learned the hard lesson: *caveat emptor*. In the second, Yahweh enters the action. "Now Yahweh saw that Leah was hated, and he opened up her womb; but Rachel was barren." (V. 31.) The trick is hard on Rachel, but, we sense, hardly easier for Leah. Her pathetic explanations of the naming of each child underline her awareness that she is not loved (cf. chs. 29:32-35; 30:11, 13, 18, 20). At the last, Rachel finally is able to bear a son, which caps the perception of Yahweh's ironic preference for the underdog.

Jacob now wants to leave for home (ch. 30:26), and he asks for severance pay. Laban is ostensibly generous but has some trickery up his own sleeve. When Jacob offers to take only the speckled and spotted sheep and goats and the black lambs, Laban's agreement is accompanied by the removal of all those animals from Jacob's ken (vs. 32-36). But the *eirōn* has profited from his experience, and pulls the breeding trick that enriches him and impoverishes Laban (vs. 37-43). Any animal husbandman will testify that the trick is impossible, though it reflects old wives' tales that are still abroad. Yet the very comic improbability of the action provides the irony. Laban seems to have won again, certainly thinks he has won, but Jacob outsmarts him. The narrator's comment (ch. 31:2) is a masterpiece of ironic understatement: " And Jacob perceived in Laban's face the fact that he was not, as before, on his side." [26] A convenient order from Yahweh (v. 3) is an excuse to get under way, but Jacob wins his wives to his side with a rather demagogic speech, designed to set them against their father (vs. 5-13). The response is as indignant as he had hoped: " Have we still any portion or inheritance in our father's family? Does he not consider us foreigners? For he sold us, and now he is using up our money. All the wealth that God has taken from our father is ours and our children's. So now, do whatever God has told you " (vs. 14-16). They are thoroughly in Jacob's camp, and Rachel even spirits away Laban's *terāphîm*, which will anger him more than anything else.

The chase is on, and when Laban overtakes them and launches his furious accusation, Jacob replies — for him — quite calmly: he knows nothing about Laban's *terāphîm*, and encourages Laban to look for them. Rachel having hidden them under the camel saddle pleads that she cannot get up " for the way of women is upon me " (v. 35). Laban, rummaging through the tent — we

[26] That is a paraphrase. The sentence reads literally: " And Jacob saw the face of Laban, and behold, he was not with him as previously."

have the unforgettable picture of the old man flinging goods and chattels in all directions — fails, ironically, to find them. It is another feather in the cap of *eirōneia*. Now Jacob in his turn lambastes Laban with real indignation (vs. 36-42). But we must sense the narrator's irony: Jacob has not been so single-mindedly occupied with Laban's welfare rather than his own as he avers. The ensuing covenant is at best a truculent one. The famous Mizpah benediction (vs. 49-50) is an ironic warning, in which Laban's concern for his daughters' welfare is very different from the attitude they had perceived (vs. 14-16).

We now move back to the Jacob-Esau cycle (chs. 32-33). As Jacob left Canaan in fear of Esau, he returns in fear. This is clear from his reaction to the news that Esau is coming to meet him and his careful refusal to go anywhere with his brother. Why, then, does he send messengers to Esau (ch. 32:3)? I think we must find the meaning in the connection between the otherwise strange naming of Mahanaim in vs. 1-2 and the sending of the messengers in vs. 3-5. At first blush, vs. 1-2 looks like a simple etiology. However, those who meet Jacob are " God's messengers, angels " (*mal'akē 'elōhîm*), and Jacob exclaims, on seeing them, " This is God's army " (*mach°neh*). In v. 3, Jacob sends his own " messengers " (*mal'ākîm*) to Esau. He is certainly not requesting a reunion. The message says only that Jacob has amassed considerable wealth and power, and he tells this to Esau in order " to find favor " in his sight. Jacob is bluffing. His wealth and the presence of " God's army " give him a sense of security, and he sends his *mal'ākîm* to Esau as God sent *mal'ākîm* to him. The otherwise odd passage, vs. 1-2, provides a partial motivation for Jacob's bluff.

Ironically, as soon as the bluff is called, or Jacob thinks it is called, his security leaves him. The reply brought by the messengers is artfully casual: " We came to your brother Esau, and he too is coming to meet you — and four hundred men with him " (v. 6). Jacob is now really frightened, and divides his forces into two " companies " (*mach<sup>a</sup>nôth*, recalling the *mach<sup>a</sup>neh* of v. 2). This, however, is for purely defensive reasons. The rather pitiful prayer (vs. 9-12) must strike us as " foxhole piety." In the following verses (vs. 13-23) [27] the very confusing account of the movements of companies, flocks, herds, persons, and Jacob himself is perhaps deliberately intended to convey Jacob's terrified fluttering over this unexpected catastrophe.

Clearly, Jacob expected to move unhindered into Canaan, the Land of Promise, as his message to Esau would suggest. When he misunderstands Esau's response — as we see from ch. 33:4 — the realization of the promise seems hopeless. He even goes so far as to arrange things so that his vaunted wealth may conceivably fall into Esau's hand in the interest of his own survival (cf. ch. 32:8, 11, 20). But before he can meet Esau, he must face an even greater challenge, the night-long battle on the bank of the Jabbok (vs. 22-32). The passage is crucial to the structure of the entire Jacob tradition, and it has received a great deal of attention in terms of questions with which we cannot here be concerned. Has it an ironic effect or content? I think it does. On the one hand, Jacob, in mortal dread of confronting Esau, finds himself instead wrestling with God.[28] The fulfillment of the promise to Jacob rests finally not with his success over against Esau and Laban but with his success with God. " You have battled with God and with men, and you have overcome." (V. 28.) On the other hand, however, Jacob does not emerge unscathed; he limps (v. 31).

But when, barely surviving the crucial fight with God, he now

[27] Cf. John L. McKenzie, S.J., "Jacob at Peniel: Gn 32, 24-32," *CBQ*, Vol. 25 (1963), pp. 71–76, for an account of efforts to sort out the confusion by source analysis.

[28] I speak of the story in its present form. Its origins and developments do not concern me here. For a thorough and penetrating consideration of the entire passage, cf. F. van Trigt, *loc. cit.*, pp. 280–309.

has immediately¹ to face Esau, his fright has not abated, though his nerve has abated no less. The brothers weep on meeting (ch. 33:4), and the suggestion that, where Esau's weeping is that of joy, Jacob's is the weeping of sheer relief, has much to commend it.²⁹ Jacob, making a vastly obsequious and overstated speech (vs. 10-11), practically forces Esau to take the gift he has given. When Esau offers to journey on to Edom with him (vs. 12-14), Jacob protests his necessary and inconvenient slowness. Jacob wants no part of Edom! Finally, he refuses Esau's offer of a bodyguard (v. 15). Once more, the *eirōn* is at work, pretending to Esau that he is coming south with him, letting Esau's assumption to that effect go unchallenged. Note also the ironic word that describes Jacob's arrival at Shechem, back in Canaan: " And Jacob arrived healthy (*shālēm*) at the city of Shechem " (v. 18). At last, like Abraham, the father of promise, Jacob must purchase a plot of land in the country promised him on which to pitch his tent (v. 19; cf. ch. 23).

Having withstood forces against him outside the land, Jacob must now withstand the foolishness of his sons. The episode at Shechem (ch. 34:1-31) has at least that thematic irony to it. It has, further, two bits of punctual irony. The men of Shechem are to be circumcised so that Dinah, Jacob's daughter, will be free to marry young Shechem. But where that reason will satisfy Hamor and his son Shechem, it will by no means satisfy the populace. Another reason must be given: " Their flocks, their goods, their cattle — will they not be ours? " (v. 23). Appeal to economic gain is more persuasive to the men of the city than the desires of a love-struck young prince. But the irony of the question rests both on its incompatibility with the intentions of the brothers (v. 13) and on the ensuing slaughter, which takes place when all the men are still in pain from being circumcised and hence are unable to fight (v. 25). Jacob has at least the grace to

²⁹ Napier, *From Faith to Faith,* p. 90.

castigate Simeon and Levi for this indiscretion, and it provides
some motivation for the move from Shechem to Bethel.

The irony in the Jacob story, as we have seen it, is for the most
part a comic irony, involving the triumph of Jacob over his adversaries. Where Jacob regards Esau as having the upper hand
and works to wrest it from him, he regards Laban with a certain
amount of contempt. The story is, of course, related to the nation-
alistic pleasure of Israel at the discomfiture of its foes, Aram and
Edom, and it is by no means unlikely that the national enmity
with those nations has helped to shape the story. At the same
time, Laban and Esau are not the only objects of irony. Jacob
too — and with him, Israel — receives the ironic treatment at several places in the story, in relation both to Esau and to Laban.
Insofar as the Jacob story contains the reflections of the national
mind upon itself vis-à-vis its inimical neighbors, we must recognize Israel's capacity to laugh at its own pretensions.

## JOSEPH: THE IRONY OF PROVIDENCE

In the complexes of tradition about Abraham and Jacob the
irony was primarily perceptible within the episodes themselves,
and secondarily in the relation of episodes to themes. In the Joseph
story we have to do with an overarching ironic theme which is
reflected to a lesser degree in the individual episodes. That is not
to say that we have neither punctual nor episodic irony in the
Joseph story. We do have both. But the lesser ironies do not really
add up to the greater. We need, nevertheless, to consider these
instances of irony, postponing the thematic irony for the present.

The reaction of the brothers and Jacob to Joseph's recounting
of his magniloquent dreams is at least ironic and probably sarcastic, greeting Joseph's prophecy of his dominion with what
comes to "Oh, is that so!" (ch. 37:8, 10). The same sarcasm
occurs later in the chapter, when Joseph comes with his father's

message to Dothan: "Look, here comes that master dreamer [ba'al hach°lômôth]" (v. 19). They propose to kill him then and there, "so we can see what comes of his dreams" (v. 20). But when, having paused to eat before disposing of Joseph, and seeing the Ishmaelite caravan coming along, the brothers decide instead to sell the boy into slavery, it appears that the Midianites beat them to it (vs. 25-28).[30] The brothers, then, receive no profit at all from their underhanded plot, unless their satisfaction at having the troublesome and arrogant youth disposed of is sufficient. Jacob's complete acceptance of the trumped-up story bears the dramatic irony of the difference between what Jacob is told and what the brothers know, as well as between what Jacob knows and what we know.

The ironic episode of Judah and Tamar is probably not integral to the Joseph legend.[31] It provides a sort of "meanwhile, back at the ranch" interlude while Joseph gets to Egypt, when the story line can be picked up once more. The incident revolves around the custom of levirate marriage, legislated in Deut. 25:5-6. When Tamar's first two husbands, Judah's elder sons, have died, Judah is reluctant to give her his youngest son, Shelah, perhaps feeling that Tamar is bad medicine. He promises Shelah to Tamar when he comes of age, and Tamar goes home to her father. The position of the young, childless widow in the ancient world was a precarious one, and it is important for Tamar that the promised marriage be carried through. When she finds that Shelah has come of age, but Judah has not suggested the promised marriage (Gen. 38:14), she takes the matter into her own hands. That Tamar perpetrates virtual blackmail on Judah is certainly condoned by narrator and hearers alike, for Judah has treated her

[30] The confusion between v. 27, which seems to mean that the brothers actually sold Joseph to the Ishmaelites, and v. 28, where passing Midianites do the job, has often been used to distinguish sources. I do not see the necessity of that conclusion.

[31] Cf. von Rad, *Genesis*, p. 351.

badly. His readiness to go to a roadside prostitute increases the comic irony, as does her insistence on a pledge of payment, which prepares us for the conclusion. We must also perceive the irony of the fact that two words for " prostitute " are used in the story: *zônāh*, the ordinary type, and *qᵉdēshāh*, a cultic prostitute. Along the road (v. 15), the narrator uses *zônāh*, and when, in v. 24, Judah is told of Tamar's indiscretion, we have the verb *zānāh*, " to engage in prostitution," and the noun *zᵉnûnîm*, " acts of prostitution." When, however, Judah sends his friend the Adullamite to Enaim to make his payment, he asks after a *qᵉdēshāh* (v. 20). Certainly the alternation of terms is not accidental. Judah is not about to inform strangers that he runs around after ordinary prostitutes, while anyone would assume perfect respectability in the search for a cultic prostitute. Ironically, had Judah's friend inquired for a *zônāh*, the men of Enaim might have recalled Tamar. When Tamar turns out to be pregnant, Judah is furiously indignant: " Bring her out and have her burned " (v. 24). Tamar is far ahead of him, however, producing with devastating irony Judah's property. Judah must accept the humiliation he was so eager to avoid. " She is righteous rather than I, since I did not give her to my son Shelah." (V. 26.)

As we pick up the Joseph story again, we must perceive a certain irony in the incident with Potiphar's wife (ch. 39:6b-23), where the innocent and guileless lad is thrown into prison on the word of a perjuring nymphomaniac. An ironic, if macabre, wordplay occurs in Joseph's interpretations of his fellow prisoners' dreams. To the butler, he says, " Within three days, Pharaoh will lift up your head " (*nāsāʾ rôsh*, " will take you back," ch. 40:13). To the baker, he says, " Within three days, Pharaoh will lift your head too — from your shoulders " (v. 19). We may even perceive a tiny piece of irony, perhaps unintended, in the list of presents that Jacob has the brothers take to the great man in Egypt (ch. 43:11), which includes some of the same materials that were being carried by the Ishmaelite caravan with whom Joseph went to Egypt in slavery (ch. 37:25). There is a hint of the ironic in Joseph's careful advice to his kinsmen not to tell Pharaoh that they are shepherds, since shepherds are disliked by Egyptians (ch. 46:33-34).[32] But when the family chooses the course of honesty with Pharaoh (ch. 47:3), the explosion Joseph apparently expected does not come.

We have, finally, some irony, both obvious and subtle, in the " Blessing of Jacob," ch. 49:2-27. The passage is difficult, full as it is of metaphors and allusions whose precise connotations escape us. Some of the blessings on the individual tribes probably refer to specific historical incidents which we no longer know; this would seem to be the case in the blessings on Gad (v. 19), Asher (v. 20), Naphtali (v. 21), and Benjamin (v. 27). Though the blessing on Issachar (vs. 14-15) may also allude to some now unknown incident, we can recognize some irony in it. We were told earlier that Issachar's name has to do with *śākār,* wages (ch. 30:18). For the sake of comfort, however, Issachar turns his " hired labor " into abject slavery. In addition, the poet describes Issachar with the image of the " castrated ass," the fruitless beast of burden.[33] With the blessing on Gad (v. 19), we have, as with several of the other blessings, a virtuoso play on the sound of the name: *gād gᵉdûd yᵉgûdennû, wᵉhû' yāgûd 'āqēb.* In the oracle on Dan (vs. 16-18)[34] is also a wordplay on the name in " Dan shall judge " (*dān yādîn*), but the sudden shift to an animal metaphor, of which this set of blessings has several (cf. vs. 9, 14, 21, 27), that of the snake, seems to suggest an ironic reversal of Dan's judicial function.[35] Certainly the implication of the snake's

[32] In view of v. 34, the phrase " the men are shepherds " (v. 32) is probably to be excised as a gloss from some uncomprehending reader.

[33] For this interpretation of a difficult text, cf. Samuel I. Feigen, " Ḥamôr Gārîm, ' Castrated Ass,' " *JNES,* Vol. 5 (1946), pp. 230–233.

[34] V. 18 is probably a gloss.

[35] The connection between vs. 16 and 17 is otherwise extremely tenuous. Cf. von Rad, *Genesis,* p. 422, who dismisses v. 17 as a later gloss.

ambush on the horse is a shift in tone from the previously implied, straightforward confrontation in the courts. If the two
images are not simply to be regarded as clumsily juxtaposed materials from diverse sources, their coherence would appear to lie
in irony.

Finally, the first three blessings, those on Reuben, on Simeon
and Levi, and on Judah, reflect an ironic perception of incidents
involving those persons. The blessing on Reuben (vs. 3-4) plays
on double meanings and refers as well to an earlier incident. Reuben is the " eldest," and therefore he has a certain " primacy "
(*yether*, v. 3), which is not, however, constant (v. 4a: *'al tôthār*).
*Yether* can also carry the connotation of " excess," and v. 3c could
be translated: " excessive of pride, excessive of might." The first-
born, of course, participates in a special way in the virile power
of the father; hence Reuben can be called " my strength and the
beginning of my power " (v. 3b: *kôchî weⁿrēshîth 'ônî*). Yet *'ôn,*
" power," can also have another meaning: " sorrow " (cf. *ben-
'ônî,* " son of my sorrow," ch. 35:18). And that very portion in
the father's virile power is the source of Reuben's downfall: " You
went up to your father's bed; then you defiled it — going up to
my couch " (v. 4b-c). The reference is to the barely mentioned
incident in ch. 35:22, where Reuben had slept with Bilhah, Jacob's
concubine.

The blessing on Simeon and Levi (ch. 49:5-7) is actually a
curse, denouncing their action at Shechem (ch. 34). In that it
implies a virtual disinheritance of these two tribes (and in the
later settlement neither tribe possessed independent territory),
we might perceive a kind of thematic irony in the passage that is
not made explicit in ironic language. With the blessing on Judah,
however (ch. 49:8-12), we have a devastating irony by means of
very subtle allusions and metaphors.[36] Wordplay appears again in

[36] I have argued the case at greater length in "The 'Blessing' on Judah,
Gen. 49:8-12," *JBL*, Vol. 82 (1963), pp. 427–432.

Judah ($y^e h \hat{u} d \bar{a} h$) and " praise " ($y \hat{o} d \hat{u}$), with an additional sound-play in " your hand " ($y \bar{a} d^e k \bar{a}$). The metaphor of the lion suggests the part Judah played in the deception of Jacob over Joseph's departure for Egypt in ch. 37:31 f. This is also the source of the allusion to dipping the garment in wine (note " blood of grapes," ch. 49:11). But vs. 10-11b and 12 make sense only when read as ironically symbolic allusions to the incident with Tamar (ch. 38). The scepter and judges' rod suggest the staff that Judah gave the " harlot " as collateral, the expression " between his feet " is certainly a euphemism for the sexual organs, reflecting the intercourse between them, and the enigmatic *shîlôh* of MT v. 10c is best read *shēlāh,* the name of the boy promised to Tamar as husband. We note further the connection of the term *śôrēqāh* " choice vine " (v. 11a) with the Valley of Soreq, near Timnah, the place to which Judah was going to shear his sheep on that occasion. And the foolishness of tying an ass to a vine, particularly to a fine vine like a *śôrēqāh,* reflects the irony of Judah's act with Tamar. Finally, the reference in v. 12 to the redness (?) of his " eyes " (*'ēnaim*) recalls the name of the town where the encounter between Judah and Tamar took place: Enaim. Viewed as a group of very subtle allusions to two earlier misdeeds of Judah, one with Joseph and the other with Tamar, the entire oracle masks a biting irony behind what looks like strong praise and high expectation.

The thematic irony of the Joseph legend does not depend on the punctual or episodic irony within it, nor does it emerge as the sum of the lesser ironies. We must now turn to the overarching irony of providence that provides the theme of the entire story. Modern psychologists did not invent " sibling rivalry." Jacob loves Joseph too well, a theme that we saw also behind the irony of his own career. But the father's too evident preference for the young boy quite naturally causes the other sons to hate him. All of this is succinctly put in ch. 37:3-4. And on this ironic incongruity — that love should produce hate — the entire story depends.

For the desire of the brothers to rid themselves of the young pest comes both out of their own hatred for him and out of their assumption that to get rid of him will reinstate them in Jacob's affections. Their spontaneous scheme is successful — though it would appear that someone else collects the cash (v. 28). But Joseph seems able to turn all he touches to gold. His expert interpretation of dreams in prison (ch. 40) makes possible his interpretation of the Pharaoh's dream (ch. 41:1-36), and the rags-to-riches theme of his success comes to its astounding climax (vs. 37-45). That much in itself would have been enough to establish the ironic theme of the Joseph story. When, however, the storyteller weaves the family back into the story in conjunction with the famine (ch. 42:1-5), the irony deepens still further. The boy, disposed of into slavery, now can dispose of his brother's destinies. Where his own dreams brought him to grief with his brothers before, now his interpretation of others' dreams have brought him to Pharaoh's favor and therefore to his position over the brothers. Their ignorance of his identity adds to the irony hanging over their abject request to buy food (ch. 42:6-38). We have, therefore, the dramatic irony of the difference between the character's perception of his situation — that he is dealing with an evil and tightfisted Egyptian — and the reality of the situation — that he is dealing with his little brother. But this is simply the underlying irony of the whole, which is finally explicated in two different but related ways:

But now, do not be dismayed or displeased with yourselves, having sold me here. To maintain life, God sent me on before you. For these two years, famine has been in the land, and for five years more there will be neither plowing nor harvesting. But God sent me before you to make you a remnant in the land, and to maintain your life for great survival. So now, it was not you who sent me here but God, and he has made me like a father to Pharaoh and a lord to his whole household and a ruler in all the land of Egypt. (Ch. 45:5-8.)

After Jacob's death, attempting to forestall any grudge Joseph might have borne them, the brothers concoct a message from Jacob requiring Joseph to forgive them for their previous misdeed. Joseph's reply is the epitome of magnanimity, and it also expresses the fundamental irony of the entire story:

Do not be afraid. For am I in God's place? You planned evil for me; God planned it for good, in order to make sure the survival of a numerous people as on this day. (Ch. 50:19-20.)

The ascription of ultimate causality to God caps the ironic theme of the story. To that point, we note some curiously twisted circumstances. When the divine intention is made explicit, however, the circumstances become something far more profound. Human beings do not finally override the divine purpose. " Surely the wrath of men shall praise thee." (Ps. 76:10.) Man's evil intentions may produce good; conversely, man's good intentions may produce evil. We have both in the Joseph story. Jacob's intentions of love give him only grief over Joseph. The brothers' intentions of hatred produce their survival in the famine. The providence of God rules and overrules the plans of men. Even the Pharaoh of Egypt cooperates with the God of Israel, more urbanely in this story than a subsequent Pharaoh does in the later events of the exodus. That Pharaoh, to be sure, " did not know Joseph " (Ex. 1:8).[37]

[37] In *You Shall Be My People*, pp. 69–70, I used this notice, together with Joseph's marriage to a daughter of the priest of On (Gen. 41:45), to date the descent of the Joseph tribes into Egypt in the Amarna period. I am now very dubious about using this material for that purpose, since I would see the Joseph story as fiction, written much too late to reflect accurate memory of Egyptian events and politics in pre-Mosaic times. As Noth points out (*Überlieferungs-*

The book of Genesis might stand as an exhibit of the different kinds and uses of irony in narrative. We have seen small points of irony, unrelated to larger context; we have seen ironic episodes, humorous or critical; we have seen the large canvases of ironic themes. We might be surprised at the amount of irony here, since the book of Genesis is occupied with the great themes of Israel's creation and election, with the covenant faith and the providential activity of God. Yet Israel's ironic vision comes to the fore precisely in conjunction with those august and solemn themes. In the final analysis the book is perhaps not ironic about God, though it proposes more than once that God is ironic about Israel. Equally, Israel is ironic about itself. Something about Israel's faith opens out to the free play of irony.

---

*geschichte des Pentateuch,* p. 226), the literary function of the Joseph story is to make the transition from the patriarchs of the promise to the exodus, to get Jacob and his family into Egypt in order that Yahweh may then get them out again. I do not therefore believe that the Joseph story has any historical basis. The notice of Ex. 1:8 serves the purpose of motivating the Egyptian persecution of the Israelites.

# V

## ISAIAH:
## FAITH ON THE BRINK

THE BOOK OF ISAIAH has been called, with an indelicate but jocose wit, "the garbage can of prophecy." Several scholarly generations have given their energies to sorting out the more or less miscellaneous prophetic materials in this book. It is now well agreed that chs. 1 to 39 are to be distinguished from the rest, and that chs. 40 to 55 are probably to be distinguished from chs. 56 to 66.[1] Within chs. 1 to 39 also are layers upon layers of material from many centuries. The whole of chs. 36 to 39, indeed, is lifted bodily (with a few alterations) from II Kings 18:13 to 20:19.[2]

The following passages within chs. 1 to 35, I consider genuinely Isaiah's: chs. 1:2-31 (with some doubts of vs. 27-31); 2:6-22; 3:1-9, 12-17, 24-26; 4:1; 5:1-12, 15-16 (?), 18-25a (to "for all this"), 26-30; 6:1-13 (omitting "The holy seed is its stump"); 7:1-8a, 9-25; 8:1-22; 9:1-21 (I will not argue long against those who dismiss vs. 1-7); 10:1-11, 13-18, 20-23, 27b-34; 11:1-5 (with the same questions as for ch. 9:1-7); 14:24-32; 17:1-11 (are

---

[1] Some will object to the distinction of Second from Third Isaiah. The problems and theories are set forth lucidly and fairly in the Introduction to the commentary on Isaiah, chs. 40 to 66, by James Muilenburg, IB, Vol. 5; cf. especially pp. 383–384.

[2] For discussion of this problem in detail, cf. R. B. Y. Scott's introduction to his commentary on Isaiah, chs. 1 to 39, in IB, Vol. 5, pp. 155–157.

vs. 7-9 a gloss?); 18:1-7; 19:1-15 (I am quite uncertain about this); 20:1-6; 22:1-5, 7-25; 28:1-4, 7-29; 29:1-16; 30:1-17, 27-28 (?); 31:1-9; 32:9:14. I will deal largely with the irony in these passages. Later writers, glossators, marginal commentators, and others also lay claim to our attention, however, and I will return in the last section to passages not listed.

## ISAIAH'S IRONIC TECHNIQUES

Isaiah uses many ways of expressing irony in poetry, and I desire here to illustrate the variety of his ironic expression. Probably most extensively he uses ironic *metaphor*. When, in ch. 7, Isaiah goes out to talk with Ahaz, he gives the king a metaphorical description of his adversaries: " Do not be timid of heart because of these two smoldering tails of firebrands " (v. 4). The metaphor ironically expresses the progressive extinguishing of Samaria and Damascus. With continued irony, Isaiah proceeds to an oracle:

> Thus says the Lord Yahweh:
> It shall not stand, nor shall it happen.
> For Aram's head is Damascus,
> And Damascus' head is Rezin.
> And Ephraim's head is Samaria,
> And Samaria's head is the son of Remaliah.
> (Vs. 7-9a.) [3]

The " head " metaphor is an ironic contrast to the " tails " of v. 4, but it is also an ironic praise in view of the clear meaning of v. 7b, that these fine " heads " are as nothing compared to Yahweh who disposes of them.

In the next chapter, castigating Judah for its faithlessness, the prophet predicts catastrophe with a metaphor of water:

[3] Omitting, with all commentators, v. 8b as an intrusive gloss.

>Because this people
>Has despised
>The waters of Shiloah,
>Which flow gently,
>Melting away [4] at Rezin
>And the son of Remaliah,
>Therefore, behold, the Lord
>Brings upon them
>The waters of the river,
>Strong and many,[5]
>And it will rise over all its channels
>And flow over all its banks.
>And it will sweep into Judah,
>Flooding and covering,
>Reaching up to the neck,
>And it will be outspread wings
>Filling the breadth of your land —
>O Immanuel!
>
>(Ch. 8:6-8.)

The ironic contrast between the gentle, life-giving water of Shiloah, Jerusalem's water-supply conduit, and the devastating flood of the Euphrates (" the river," v. 7) refers to Yahweh and Assyria respectively. Judah despises Yahweh's support, which would have provided life and safety, in favor of Assyria's aid, which will turn out destructively. The metaphor is extended in v. 8 with the introduction of the correlative metaphor of " outspread wings," a grim description of the flood waters spreading out across the country.

The prophet applies the rod and staff metaphor to Assyria in ch. 10:5 ff.:

[4] Read *māśós* for MT *meśóś*, " rejoicing." Perhaps a homophonic play on words is involved. Note also the wordplay with *mā'as*, " despised."

[5] Omitting the gloss following: " The king of Assyria and all his glory," which, though heavy-footed, is a correct interpretation.

Ho, Assyria,
Rod of my anger,
Staff of my fury!
(V. 5.) [6]

The irony is not evident until the oracle has described Assyria's
arrogant self-praise (e.g., v. 13). Then we observe how very precise the metaphor of rod and staff is. Assyria is a tool, possessing
no autonomy but ironically claiming independence. Assyria's
boast employs its own ironic simile of the nations:

And like a nest, my hand has found
The wealth of the peoples;
Like gathering eggs left behind,
I have gathered the whole earth.
Not a wing fluttered,
Not a beak opened or chirped. [7]
(V. 14.)

To conquer the world is as easy as to pluck eggs from the nest
of a docile chicken. Immediately the poet turns the irony back
on Assyria by returning to the tools:

Does the ax vaunt itself
Over him who hews with it?
Does the saw magnify itself
Over him who wields it?
In the same way,[8] a rod wields him who lifts it; [9]
In the same way a staff lifts what is not wood.
(V. 15.)

[6] The opening "Ho!" (*hôy*) is ordinarily used as an equivalent of "Woe!"
Commentators generally feel that its use here is not simply denunciatory (but cf.
Scott, *loc. cit.*, p. 240) but exclamatory. In the last line, I omit MT *hû' b*e*yādām*,
with most commentators, in the interests of the poetic parallelism.

[7] There is no way to reproduce the complex onomatopoetic play on sounds
in the Hebrew of this line: *ûphôtseh peh ûm*e*tsaphtsēph*.

[8] The Hebrew reads simply "as."

[9] Reading *m*e*rîmô* with several MSS. for the plural in MT, *m*e*rîmāw*.

The vivid irony of these rhetorical questions explicates the meaning of tools. The last two lines, phrased now not as questions but as statements reiterating the opening metaphor of the poem, compound the irony of Assyria's braggadocio. The ax vaunts itself over its user in the same way that a rod wields the man who lifts it: not at all. The metaphor dominates the whole oracle, opens and closes it,[10] puts all that the oracle conveys under the shadow of its ironic implications.

Another way of expressing irony is by *attribution,* the ironic quotation of words or ascription of thoughts to others.[11] One example, quoted above, is the double irony of the words ascribed to the king of Assyria in ch. 10:14. Another example, compounded with a metaphor, is found in ch. 5:19, where we read of those

> Who say, " Let it speed!
> Let his work hurry
> So that we can see! ,
> Let it draw near and come —
> This counsel of the Holy One
> Of Israel — that we may know." [12]

[10] I do not agree with scholars who analyze v. 16, or even vs. 17–19, as part of this oracle. See, e.g., Scott, *loc. cit.,* pp. 240, 243; Kissane, *The Book of Isaiah* (Brown and Nolan, Ltd., Dublin, 1941), Vol. I, pp. 122–129; Skinner, *The Book of the Prophet Isaiah, Chapters I–XXXIX* (CB, Cambridge University Press, Cambridge, 1915), p. 93. It is worth noting that Duhm rejected v. 15 on account of its " prolixity," and Gray, *The Book of Isaiah* (ICC, T. & T. Clark, Edinburgh, 1912), p. 199, adds that the thought is " awkwardly expressed." I see in the verse neither prolixity nor awkward expression.

[11] I am greatly indebted to Prof. Sheldon H. Blank of Hebrew Union College, Cincinnati, for his courtesy in sending me a copy of his unpublished paper, "Irony by Way of Attribution," read at the 1962 meeting of the Society of Biblical Literature and Exegesis. Several of the examples I take, though not all, were first suggested by Professor Blank, and I do him what I believe he will take to be honor by disagreeing with some of his interpretations.

[12] The presence of the last two lines of what seems a caesura is troublesome, since the principle of parallelism in Hebrew poetry would seem to rule out caesura. Nevertheless, one apparently finds it now and again; cf., e.g., Isa. 17:3: *ûsheʾar ʾārām kikebôd / benê yisrāʾēl yiheyû* ("And the remnant of Aram like the glory of / Israel's sons shall become "). The lines may be prose, not poetry, but no commentator has suggested that they are.

The speakers are sarcastically mocking the prophet, who babbles about a deed of God that never occurs. But the mockery is made more ironic by its link with the preceding metaphor:

> Woe to those who drag iniquity along
> With ox harness,[13]
> And sin with cart ropes — [14]
>
> (V. 18.)

Those very mockers (v. 19), who laboriously "drag" their iniquity like dumb oxen, sarcastically call on Yahweh to "hurry" his work. Of course, the prophet understands that what they will "see" and "know" when the counsel of Yahweh comes about will be very different from what they jeeringly suppose.

A different kind of quotation is found in ch. 28:15:

> Because you say,
> "We made a covenant with Death,
> With Sheol we made an agreement.
> The flooding scourge, when it passes,
> Will not come to us,
> For we have made lies our refuge,
> And in falsity we are sheltered."

The "flooding scourge" suggests the flood metaphor used of Assyria in ch. 8:7-8. The prophet parodies the communiqué from Judah's state department about a mutual assistance pact with Egypt, which might have said: "We have made a covenant [treaty] with Egypt, with Pharaoh we made an agreement. Assyria's invasion therefore will not trouble us, for we have protection with Egypt and security with Pharaoh." By substituting words, the prophet ironically criticizes the treaty-making, as he

[13] Reading *hashshôr* for MT *hashshāw*.
[14] Reading *ba'ǎbóth* for MT *ka'ǎbóth*.

frequently does with Judah's political ties with Egypt (cf. chs. 19:1-15 [if that be authentic]; 30:1-5, 7; 31:1-3).[15]

A third major technique of ironic expression is *wordplay* or *paronomasia*. This takes several different forms. The first is the juxtaposition of two uses of the same word with ironic implications, for example, the two occurrences of the verb *nāphal*, " fall," in ch. 9:8-10 (Heb., vs. 7-9):

> The Lord has sent a word to Jacob,
> And it has *fallen* upon Israel.
> And all the people shall know,
> Ephraim and Samaria's citizens,
> Who say in pride and arrogance of heart,
> " Bricks have *fallen,*
> So we will build with dressed stone.
> Sycamores have been cut down,
> So we will substitute cedar for them."

The prophet connects the word that has " fallen " in judgment upon Israel with the " fallen " bricks, and ironically portrays the people's utter misconception of their own plight.

A second type of wordplay is the juxtaposition of two forms of the same verb or root with different meanings, for example, the paronomastic oracle to Ahaz in ch. 7:9b, with its almost unreproduceable soundplay: *'im lô' ta'ᵃmînû kî lô' tē'āmēnû* (" If you will not stand firm, you will not be confirmed ").[16] Another example is in ch. 22:1-2, 5, describing the city's celebration after the lifting of Sennacherib's siege:

[15] This interpretation depends on Blank's paper, p. 3.

[16] I do not agree with those who would either excise the epigram as a marginal gloss, or, omitting the second half as a doublet, attach it to the invitation to Ahaz to ask a sign (v. 11). Cf. Blank, *Prophetic Faith in Isaiah* (Adam & Charles Black, Ltd., London, 1958), pp. 18–19 and note 12, p. 212. Many have been the efforts to reproduce in English even the pale similitude of this striking wordplay. Perhaps the most successful (if dubiously accurate) is George Adam Smith's " No faith, no staith! "

> What is all this,
> That all of you have
> Gone up on the rooftops?
> Full of noise,
> Turbulent city,
> Celebrating town!

After expressing his negatively ironic opinion of the celebration, he proceeds, in v. 5:

> For a day of turbulence,
> Of conquest and confusion
> Has the Lord Yahweh of hosts.

The two "turbulences" (v. 2, *hômiyyāh;* v. 5, *mᵉhûmāh*) are related but very different. The "turbulence of conquest and confusion"[17] will render the "turbulent" gaiety ironic in its own turn.

A third type of wordplay is the use of double meanings. A very subtle example is Isaiah's only reference to his son *Shᵉᵃr Yāshûb,* "A remnant shall turn," who is mentioned only in ch. 7:3, when Isaiah takes him along when he goes to speak with Ahaz. The child does nothing, is not mentioned again, simply stands in the background. But we must keep in mind that he is there all the while, a walking oracle. His presence, with its ambiguous meaning, casts the shadow of double-edged irony over the whole encounter. "A remnant shall turn": it is certainly a promise (cf. ch. 10:21), and the conversation between Isaiah and the king includes promises. But the name is also a threat: "A *remnant* shall turn," and the conversation also includes threats. The very presence of *Shᵉᵃr Yāshûb* suggests the duality

---

[17] The lines have some interesting rhymes and alliterations as well: *kî yôm mᵉhûmāh ûmᵉbûsāh ûmᵉbûkāh.*

of threat and promise in the episode.[18] In the same chapter another child is named: *'immānû'ēl,* "God with us" (ch. 7:14). Given the thorough duality of the entire scene, there is an ironic duality even in this name. It looks unambiguously positive: "God with us." The child's development to the point of "knowing enough to reject the bad and to choose the good" (vs. 15-16) will measure the removal of the threat from Aram and Ephraim. Yet there await the days of trouble, "such times as have not come since the day Ephraim departed from Judah" (v. 17). The sign, then, is not simply a promise but is also a threat. *'Immānû'ēl* means not only "God with us" but perhaps also "God against us."[19] When we observe that in ch. 8:8 the name is ironically double in meaning, the possibility of its dual connotation in ch. 7 extends the ironic duality of the confrontation between prophet and king and brings the unity of the passage into focus.

A fourth paronomastic technique is the use of words to mean their opposite. In ch. 5:22, Isaiah uses extravagant but sardonically qualified praise words:

> Woe to heroes — at drinking wine;
> Mighty men — at mixing liquors!

A similar use of a term with opposite meaning is in a rather difficult oracle in ch. 7:21-22. The context strongly suggests that the oracle is a threat of extreme hardship: "And in that day, a man will keep alive a young cow and two sheep. And from the

[18] With Volkmar Herntrich, *Der Prophet Jesaja* (ATD, Vandenhoeck & Ruprecht, Göttingen, 1950), p. 126. Sheldon Blank separates threat from promise by analysis in "The Isaiah of Legend and the Seventh Chapter," *Prophetic Faith in Isaiah,* pp. 9–31. On the other hand, I cannot agree with Joh. Lindblom, *A Study on the Immanuel Section in Isaiah* (C. W. K. Gleerup, Lund, 1958), pp. 9–10, who argues an unambiguously positive meaning to the name.

[19] The preposition *'im,* "with," frequently means "with" in the sense of "against," e.g., with verbs like *nilcham,* "to fight," *rîb,* "to strive" (either in combat or in court, hence often to carry out legal proceedings "against" someone).

abundance of milk produced, he shall eat curds. For the whole remnant in the midst of the land will eat curds and honey." [20] The precise connotations of "curds and honey" are unclear. In v. 15, the curds and honey are ordinarily taken as evidence of prosperity, but, if the context is indicative, they can hardly mean prosperity in vs. 21-22, and therefore "the abundance of milk produced" means its ironic opposite. Of the same order is the ironic threat to Syria in ch. 17:3: "And the remnant of Aram shall become like the glory of Israel's sons." As the succeeding verses show, the "glory" (*ḳābôd*) will be humbled and entirely inglorious.

A fifth type of wordplay is the play on sounds, of which Isaiah is very fond. Alliteration is one of his more common poetic devices, occurring from the very beginning of the book: *shim'û shāmayim wᵉha'ᵃzînû 'erets* (ch. 1:2). Note, for example, the irony of the alliterative lines from ch. 22:2:

> *chᵃlālayiḳ lô' chalᵉlē chereb*
> *wᵉlô' mēthē milchāmāh*
> ("Your slain are not sword-slain, nor battle-dead.")

In the context of the wildly celebrating city the statement itself is ironic, and the alliterative phrasing compounds the irony. Another example, involving rhyme rather than alliteration, is in the statement of the people in ch. 30:16: "On horses we will speed" (*'al sûs nānûs*), which the prophet echoes ironically: "Therefore you shall speed [*tᵉnûsûn*] indeed!" The soundplay is continued in the next verse with the word "beacon":

> Until you are left . . .
> Like a beacon [*nēs*] on a hill.

[20] There may be some duplication of phrases in the text, but it makes perfectly good sense as it stands. Herntrich, *op. cit.*, p. 139, omits certain words to make the oracle promise rather than doom.

Sometimes the sound of one word will suggest another that the poet intends to be in mind. An example is ch. 17:6:

> Gleanings will be left in it
> As when an olive tree is beaten:
> Two, three berries
> At the very top,
> Four, five
> On the fruit tree's branches.

The " fruit tree," *pôriyyāh,* brings to mind, by sound and perhaps etymology, the name Ephraim (cf. the similar wordplay, using the word *pôrath,* in the oracle on Joseph in Gen. 49:22). Isaiah's most famous soundplay is, of course, the end of the Song of the Vineyard, ch. 5:1-7, where the poet manages a feat of virtuosity that cannot be reproduced in English:

> *way<sup>e</sup>qaw l<sup>e</sup>mishpāṭ*
> *w<sup>e</sup>hinnēh miśpāch*
> *lits<sup>e</sup>dāqāh w<sup>e</sup>hinnēh ts<sup>er</sup>āqāh*
> (V. 7.) [21]

A fourth major form of ironic expression is *litotes,* or *understatement,* as seen in the description of Assyria's intentions in ch. 10:7:

> But he does not intend it so,
> His heart does not conceive it so;
> For in his mind is destroying,
> And cutting off not a few nations.

[21] G. H. Box, *The Book of Isaiah* (Isaac Pitman, London, 1908), p. 41, tried to reproduce this: " For measure he looked — but lo massacres! / For right — but lo riot." It does not quite work. Jean Steinmann comes closer in French, in *Le prophète Isaïe: sa vie, son oeuvre, et son temps* (LD 5, Les Éditions du Cerf, Paris, 1955), p. 69: *" Il en attendait l'innocent, et c'est du sang, le droit et c'est le cri d'effroi! "* The lines may be literally translated: " And he looked for justice / and behold, bloodshed, / for righteousness, and behold, a cry."

The understatement is, "Not a few" (*lô' mᵉʿaṭ*). Another example is at the end of the prophet's enigmatic parables in ch. 28:23-29. It is difficult to know the precise meaning of these two agricultural analogies, but it is clear that the prophet's rhetorical questions are ironic.

> Give ear, listen to my voice,
> Pay attention, listen to my words.
> Is it all the time
> That the plower plows for sowing,
> That he opens and harrows the soil?
> If he has leveled its surface,
> Does he not scatter dill, throw cummin,
> And put wheat in rows
> And barley in plots [22]
> And spelt in the border?
> And he is properly instructed;
> His God teaches him.
>
> But dill is not threshed with a thresher,
> Nor is a cart wheel rolled over cummin.
> But dill is beaten with a stick,
> Cummin with a rod.
> Bread grain is crushed,
> But not endlessly,
> One carefully threshes it. [23]
> But he drives his cart wheel,
> And the hoofs [24] do not crush it. [25]
> This too has come
> From Yahweh of hosts.
> He makes wonderful counsel,
> He magnifies wisdom.

[22] The translation of *nismān* is a sheer guess, as is every translation proposed for the word. It occurs nowhere else in the Old Testament.

[23] Reading *dôsh* for MT *'ādôsh*.

[24] Reading *pᵉrāśāw* for MT *pᵉrāshāw*.

[25] Reading *yᵉdûqûnû* for MT *yᵉdûqennû*.

The last verse suggests the point of both parables. The different techniques of sowing and harvesting for different crops are well known to every farmer. Isaiah is saying the obvious. By analogy, he suggests that Israel should quite naturally follow Yahweh's wise counsel, vouched for by history as " wonderful " (cf. ch. 9:5 for another combination of " wonderful " and " counsel ") and evident to all. By calling so solemnly for attention, as if he were about to say something striking and new, and then supplying the listeners with what sounds superficially like an extract from the opening lecture in Agriculture 1, the prophet underlines his irony.

A fifth ironic technique is the opposite of the previous. Namely, *exaggeration*. In ch. 5:11-12, the prophet bitterly satirizes those who are devoted to their own limited pleasures but not to Yahweh's work:

> Woe to those who get up at dawn
> To chase after liquor,
> Who tarry into evening
> While wine inflames them.
> And there are lyre and harp,
> Drum and flute,
> And wine at their feasts.
> But the deed of Yahweh they do not regard,
> And the work of his hands they do not see.

The oracle is a satiric caricature, pointing up the ironic disparity between what the people think is important and what is actually occurring.

The sixth technique of irony may be called *conceptual irony*. Its purpose is to demonstrate the distance between assumption and reality, as in ch. 5:11-12, above. This is done in various ways. For example, the prophet's combination of the metaphors of height and depth in ch. 2:6-22 sharply etches man's abasement

before Yahweh's exaltation, ironic because man pretends to be
high.

> But man is to be humbled,
> And men to be brought low —
> Do not lift them up! [26]
>            (V. 9.)

> The haughty eyes of man shall be lowered,
> And the height of man shall be humbled,
> And Yahweh alone exalted
> In that day!
> For Yahweh of hosts has a day
> Against all that is prideful and high,
> Against all that is lifted and haughty.[27]
>            (Vs. 11-12.)

Another example of conceptual irony is the " schoolroom scene "
in ch. 28:9-13. The passage is usually analyzed as a dialogue between one or more onlookers (vs. 9-10) and the prophet
(vs. 11-13).[28] This makes perfectly good sense of the passage,
though it requires the emendation of *'ābú'* in v. 12 to *'ābú*, omitting an aleph with some Hebrew manuscripts. It would also be
possible, however, to see the passage as a more complex dialogue,
as follows:

ONLOOKER:   Whom will he teach knowledge?
            Who will understand his message?

ISAIAH:     Those weaned from milk,
            Those too old for the breast.

---

[26] The line is usually translated, "Forgive them not! " But that misses the
metaphorical force of the verb *nāśā'*, " to lift."

[27] Reading *weɡābô*ᵃ*h*, with LXX, for MT's strange *weshāphēl*, " and low."

[28] So, e.g., Scott, *loc. cit.*, p. 316; Kissane, *op. cit.*, pp. 316–317; Skinner,
*loc. cit.*, pp. 223–224.

ONLOOKER:    But it is
             *Tsadē-tsadē, tsadē-tsadē*
             *Qôph-qôph, qôph-qôph,*[29]
             The lad here, the lad there!
             For with stuttering language
             And an alien tongue
             He speaks to his people.

ISAIAH:      To whom he [God] said,
             "This is rest:
             Give the weary rest.
             And this is repose — "?

ONLOOKER     (breaking in):
             I did not come [30] to listen [to that]!

ISAIAH:      So Yahweh's word to them will become
             *Tsadē-tsadē, tsadē-tsadē*
             *Qôph-qôph, qôph-qôph,*
             The lad here, the lad there!
             In order that they may go and stumble backward,
             And be broken and snared and captured.

The irony of the interchange is unmistakable. The onlooker
mocks the prophet's elementary introduction comparable to teaching lads the alphabet. But Isaiah points out that Yahweh's word
is utterly clear. If the people refuse to comprehend plain Hebrew,
Yahweh must, as it were, teach them the alphabet all over again.
No matter how the passage is analyzed, the irony of the point
is unquestionable.

These six techniques — metaphor, attribution, wordplay, un-

---

[29] Letters of the alphabet; the onlooker mocks the prophet for giving first-
grade instruction. Cf. William W. Hallo, "Isaiah 28:9-13 and the Ugaritic
Abecedaries," *JBL*, Vol. 77 (1958), pp. 324–338; G. R. Driver, *Semitic Writing
from Pictograph to Alphabet*, rev. ed. (British Academy, London, 1954),
pp. 89–90.

[30] Reading *'ābô'* for MT *'ābû'*.

derstatement, exaggeration, and irony of concept — cover all of
Isaiah's ironic statements. The passages cited may suggest the
range of Isaiah's powers as a poet, as well as some of the themes
on which his ironic vision turns. His irony falls upon those who
fail to regard or comprehend the work of Yahweh, a theological
judgment; upon those whose failure to regard the work of Yahweh produces the deadly fruits of international chaos, a political
judgment; and upon those whose failure to regard the work of
Yahweh threatens their own internal collapse, an ethical judgment.

## A NATION AGAINST GOD

Isaiah does not refer to Israel's past, as the other prophets do.[31]
He has little, if anything, to say about the exodus, nothing about
Moses, hardly anything about the formative historical tradition.
He concentrates on the meaning of the present, casts his gaze
toward the future, insists that the decisive moment faces the
nation now. The nation's relation to Yahweh, its faith, stands at
the center of his concerns. He is a theologian. That theology, the
articulation of the divine action and imperative, informs Isaiah's
irony from the start.

Yahweh is at work, and therefore Judah's business is also to
be at work. That is the burden of the parables about agricultural
technique (ch. 28:23-29) discussed above. " This too comes from
Yahweh of hosts. He makes wonderful counsel, he magnifies
wisdom." " A counsel," says Vriezen, " is a preparation for action
and in many cases decides the future." [32] The comparison of the
farmer's wise " counsel " in his sowing and harvesting with the

31 Cf. Th. C. Vriezen, "Essentials of the Theology of Isaiah," in *Israel's
Prophetic Heritage: Essays in Honor of James Muilenburg,* ed. by B. W. Anderson and Walter Harrelson (Harper & Brothers, 1962), pp. 128–129.

32 *Loc. cit.,* p. 142. Cf. chs. 5:19; 14:26; 30:1 (*'ētsāh*); 14:24, 26, 27; 19:12
(*yāʿats*).

nation's implicit failure to recognize Yahweh's "wonderful counsel" (cf. ch. 9:5) implies that the action the future is about to bring will produce strange results.

> For as at Mount Perazim
> Yahweh will rise,
> As at the valley in Gibeon he will bestir himself,
> To do his deed — strange his deed! —
> And to work his work — alien his work!
>
> (Ch. 28:21.)

The allusions to Mt. Perazim and the valley of Gibeon may be among Isaiah's rare citations of the past, perhaps the victories of Yahweh over Israel's enemies narrated in II Sam. 5:20, 25.[33] To refer to Yahweh's victories as analogies to his coming work, and then to interject the chillingly ironic "strange his deed . . . alien his work!" reverses the expected meaning of the analogies. Judah cannot adduce the past to predict the future, cannot confine him who "makes wonderful counsel" to the action he has already done. Rote allegiance, the spewing of phrases, to which the prophet refers in ch. 29:13, will make Yahweh "again do marvels [haphlî'] with this people" (v. 14). But the "marvels" are the ironic opposite of their apparent meaning. The work is afoot, but the expectations are mistaken.

Frequently Isaiah speaks of the ironic reversal of expectation. Israel (the Northern Kingdom) will meet it:

> In that day, this will happen:
> The wealth [ḳābôd] of Jacob will become poverty,
> And his fat flesh will become lean.
>
> (Ch. 17:4.)

---

[33] So Scott, loc. cit., p. 320. "The valley of Gibeon" might refer to Josh. 10:1-27, especially to v. 12.

The prophet continues with two ironic agricultural metaphors:

> And it will be
> Like the reaper gathering the standing grain,
> When his arm reaps the ears —
> And it will be like the harvester of ears
> In the valley of Rephaim.
> Gleanings will be left in it
> As when an olive tree is beaten:
> Two, three berries
> At the very top,
> Four, five
> On the fruit tree's branches.
>
> (Vs. 5-6.)

The olive harvester was required to leave gleanings for the poor (cf. Deut. 24:19-22; Lev. 19:9-10; 23:22). The purpose of the metaphor here, however, is to say that the olive crop is so sparse that little is left for the poor. With the implied wordplay on Ephraim in "fruit tree" (*pôriyyāh*), the metaphor depicts the riches-to-rags decline of Israel. The nation has clearly failed to respond to the divine counsel. The prophet falls back again on an agricultural metaphor in what is the next thing to an allegory:

> Let me sing for the beloved a love song about his vineyard.
> The beloved has a vineyard
> On a very fertile hill.
> And he dug it and took out stones
> And planted in it choice vines.
> And he built a tower in the middle,
> And dug a vat in it.
> And he expected it to produce grapes —
> But it produced stinking weeds.
>
> So now, dwellers of Jerusalem,
> Men of Judah,

Judge, please, between me
And my vineyard.
What more is to do for my vineyard
That I have not done in it?
Why, when I expected it to produce grapes,
Did it produce stinking weeds?
So now I will tell you
What I will do for my vineyard.
I will remove its hedge,
And it will be burned;
Breach its wall,
And it will be trampled.
And I will make it desolate;
It will not be pruned or hoed,
But thorns and thistles will grow.
And I will forbid the clouds
To give it rain.

(Ch. 5:1-6.)

The seventh verse, with its virtuoso play on sound, sets out the outlines of the allegory. The vineyard is Israel, Judah is the delightful garden. The irony of the divine expectation provides the theme of the " song." The question (v. 4), echoing the statement (v. 2): " Why, when I expected it to produce grapes, did it produce stinking weeds? " turns into the devastating irony of Yahweh's expectations, expressed in that wordplay quoted above that comes across only in Hebrew. In spite of all that God could do for Israel, Israel has failed. Yet she is not prepared for the judgment that ensues.

And what will you do at the visitation day
And at the ruin (from afar it comes!)?
To whom will you flee for help?
And where will you abandon your honor?

(Ch. 10:3.)

The questions, with their innocent assumption that those addressed have considered "the visitation day" and its "ruin," convey the irony of the fact that Israel has failed even to give thought to the consequences. "To whom will you flee for help?" (You will, of course, have to flee.) "Where will you abandon your honor?" (You will, of course, have to fling it aside along the road somewhere.) "Strange" — "alien" — indeed is the work.

Israel has failed basically to regard the work of Yahweh. Those who chase all day after alcohol (ch. 5:11-12) "do not regard the deed of Yahweh, and the work of his hands they do not see." The prophet implies, of course, that their eyesight is too impaired to see anything very clearly, like that of the priests and prophets who stagger about at their tasks after long draughts of liquor (ch. 28:7-8). The image of drunkenness conveys that oblivion to what is actually transpiring, pictured in ch. 5:11-12. It is the same with those who, at the threat of Sennacherib's siege, took such care with Jerusalem's defenses.

> So you looked that day
> To the weapons of the arsenal,[34]
> And the breaches of David's city,
> You saw, were many.
> And you collected the waters
> Of the lower pool.
> And you counted the houses of Jerusalem,
> And you knocked down houses
> To strengthen the wall.
> And you made a reservoir between walls
> For water from the old pool.

[34] If that was the function of "the house of the forest," which is Isaiah's phrase. Scott, *loc. cit.*, p. 291, refers to I Kings 10:17, which seems to me not utterly clear that the "House of the Forest of Lebanon" was an armory but suggests that it might have been a treasury.

> But you did not look to its maker,
> Him who planned it long ago you did not see.
>                              (Ch. 22:8b-11.)

The ponderous piling up of detail is not mere pedantry. The prophet laboriously rehearses the difficult task of preparation for defense to prepare the irony of the last two lines. The attention paid to the siege produced sweat and curses, and, as vs. 1-2 show us, it succeeded. But no attention was paid to the purpose of what was actually happening or, more important, to the purposer.

> And the Lord, Yahweh of hosts,
> Called that day
> For weeping and wailing,
> For baldness and wearing sackcloth.
> And behold, joy and happiness,
> Slaughtering cattle and killing sheep,
> Eating meat and drinking wine —
> " Eat and drink,
> For tomorrow we die! "
>                              (Vs. 12-13.)

The prophet is mourning (v. 4), for the occasion calls for repentance. It calls forth precisely the opposite from the people, however: irresponsible celebration, utter heedlessness of what is really happening. " Eat and drink, for tomorrow we die! " That is bellowed in the bars and restaurants of Jerusalem to the accompaniment of raucous laughter. Yesterday it was their only sign of courage. Today they recall yesterday's fears and, knowing nothing but relief, are able to mock them. But the mockery is turned back on them.

> Yahweh of hosts has revealed it in my ears:
> " This iniquity shall not be forgiven you
> Until you die," says the Lord, Yahweh of hosts.
>                              (V. 14.)

The people mock at a death they have not avoided after all.

Ridicule of Yahweh's work, like failure to regard it, calls forth the prophet's irony in ch. 5:18-19:

> Woe to those who drag iniquity along
> With ox harness,
> And sin with cart ropes — [35]
> Who say, " Let it speed!
> Let his work hurry
> So that we can see!
> Let it draw near and come —
> This counsel of the Holy One
> Of Israel — that we may know! "

This sarcastic eagerness to see, this apparent desire to regard the work of Yahweh, is ironically quoted. Those who, like the ox, are yoked to their sin and drag it along like a heavy sledge scoff at the knowledge the prophet would convey. They call for knowledge but have no desire for it. To give them ignorance was the duty ironically assigned the prophet at his call:

> Go and say to this people:
> " Hear indeed, but do not comprehend!
> See indeed, but do not be informed! "
> Fatten the heart of this people,
> Weight down its ears and shut its eyes,
> Lest it see with its eyes
> And hear with its ears
> And its heart understand,
> And it turn and be healed.
>
> (Ch. 6:9-10.)

The prophet is commanded, as it were, to be an antiprophet, to do the opposite of what a prophet does. The passage has greatly em-

---

[35] See notes 13 and 14 above for my emendations in these lines.

barrassed Old Testament exegetes, for it seems to impute to God the deliberate intent to condemn without possibility of redress. Alternatively, scholars have regarded the words as the prophet's later reflection on his career, producing the realization that the terrible result of his prophecy had been the deepening of the people's guilt. If that were the result, Yahweh must have intended it, and when the prophet narrates his call he sets down the condemnation as the command given him. If, however, we recognize the irony in the command, we need worry neither about the morality of God nor about the psychological pilgrimage of the prophet, neither of which is accessible to us. The command is the counterpart of the ironic quotation in ch. 5:19, where the people sarcastically express their eagerness to see and hear. And the command ironically says, "Try to make them worse than they are! Give them more ignorance, extend their incomprehension!" That is not, of course, what the prophet has done, nor is it what he is supposed to do. He is confronted from the very first with this fundamentally ironic perception of the nation's life, that its business is knowledge, its pleasure, ignorance.

It is the same with the "schoolroom scene" (ch. 28:9-13) discussed above. The mockery of teaching, expressed by the onlooker, is turned to the teaching of mockery by the prophet. The motto that opens the entire book expresses the same irony:

> Hear, O heavens,
> And give ear, O earth,
> For Yahweh speaks:
> "Sons I have reared and brought up,
> But they have revolted against me.
> The ox knows its master
> And the ass its owner's crib.
> Israel knows not,
> My people comprehends not."
> (Ch. 1:2-3.)

The contrast between the "knowledge" of the stupid animals and the willful ignorance of Yahweh's people casts the ironic vision upon the whole life of the people. Not only do they fail in knowledge, they pervert it. They think they speak truth when they are speaking falsehood (ch. 29:16). They deny the work of prophets and the presence of God himself (ch. 30:10-11).

"To know" meant to Israel something different from what it ordinarily connotes to us. English, in common with Hebrew, does not have two words to designate different kinds of knowledge, such as the German *kennen* and *wissen* or French *connaître* and *savoir*. But where the English verb "to know" means on the whole to have something in the mind, to possess the result of the intellect's work, the Hebrew verb carries with it more particularly a "knowledge" that is personal and relational. "Adam knew his wife." (Gen. 4:1.) That does not mean that he possessed information about her, but that they were mutually related in the most intimately personal way. When, therefore, Isaiah accuses Israel of failure to know, he does not mean merely that information, data, or theory are missing. More importantly, he means that Israel lacks firm and steadfast loyalty, allegiance, and commitment of life to God.

Allegiance is finally at issue. That is what theology is all about. Hence, Isaiah is bitterly ironic about the people's failures of allegiance.

And when they say to you, "Seek out the mediums and soothsayers, who chirp and mutter " — should not a people seek out its God? Does one consult the dead on behalf of the living for teaching and testimony? [36] (Ch. 8:19-20.)

[36] With Kissane, *op. cit.*, p. 109, I take the words *lᵉtôrāh wᵉlitᵉʿûdāh* with the previous sentence. Ordinarily, as in RSV, they are taken as an independent exclamation: "To the teaching and to the testimony! " That, however, is in direct contradiction to the "binding" and "sealing" of teaching and testimony among the disciples (v. 16), apparently in anticipation of Yahweh's deed (cf. v. 17). In addition, it is probably necessary either to take the verb *yidrôsh* in

Mediums and soothsayers deal with what is dead and powerless, and they do not speak words but "chirp and mutter." What can the dead give Israel for "teaching and testimony" that the living God cannot give? The ironic questions reveal the prophet's astonishment at the perversion of allegiance.

The same perversion is the theme of the complex and difficult poem in ch. 2:6-22. It is a kind of poetic aria, moving across metaphor, allusion, description, to provide a superb poetic effect. The structure of the poem is chiastic. The center strophe (vs. 12-16) is flanked on both sides by almost identical refrains (vs. 11, 17), before and after which are ironic reflections on idolatry (vs. 7-10, 19-21). The opening (v. 6) and the closing (v. 22) reflect the general tenor of divine rejection.

> For thou hast deserted thy people,
> The house of Jacob.
> For they are filled with sorcerers [37]
> And soothsayers like the Philistines,
> And they clap hands [38] with foreigners.[39]
>
> And their land is filled
> With silver and gold,
> And their treasuries are endless.
> And their land is filled with horses,
> And their chariots are endless.
> And their land is filled with little gods —

v. 19 to govern both clauses of the sentence or to add, perhaps with LXX (*ti ekzētousin*), *mî yidr<sup>e</sup>shû* at the beginning of the second clause.

[37] Reading *miqqôs<sup>e</sup>mîm* for MT *miqqedem*.

[38] Reading *bidê* for MT *b<sup>e</sup>yaldê*.

[39] A possible alternative translation would be, "And they have plenty of foreigners' children," retaining MT *b<sup>e</sup>yaldê* and taking *yaspîqû*, with LXX and Syriac, from the verb *śāphaq*, "to suffice," rather than from *sāphaq*, "to slap, clap." Neither verb occurs elsewhere in the Hiph'il stem. The meaning of the alternate translation is that the people fill their land with foreign slaves, who exert a baleful influence, as well as with foreign cults.

To the work of their hands they bow,
To what their fingers have made.
But man is to be humbled
And men to be brought low —
Do not lift them up!
Enter the rock
And hide in the dust
From the terror of Yahweh,
From his majestic splendor! [40]

The haughty eyes of man shall be lowered,
And the height of men shall be humbled,
And Yahweh alone exalted
In that day!

For Yahweh of hosts has a day
Against [41] all that is majestic and high,
Against all that is lifted and haughty.[42]
Against all Lebanon's cedars —
Tall and lifted up —
Against all Bashan's oaks,
Against all high mountains,
Against all lofty hills,
Against all high towers,
Against all fortified walls,
Against all seafaring ships,
Against all lovely vessels.[43]
And man's haughtiness shall be humbled,

[40] LXX inserts "When he rises to terrify the land," as in MT at v. 19.
[41] *'al*, literally, "over."
[42] Cf. note 27 above.
[43] For these two lines, see G. R. Driver, "Difficult Words in the Hebrew Prophets," in *Studies in Old Testament Prophecy: Presented to Theodore H. Robinson on His Sixty-fifth Birthday August 9th, 1946*, ed. by H. H. Rowley (Charles Scribner's Sons, 1950), p. 52, where the difficult *sheḳiyyôth* is read *shiḳtē* and referred to Egyptian *śḳti* and Ugaritic *tḳt*, "boat, ship." I have not accepted in its entirety Driver's reading of the two lines.

And men's height lowered,
And Yahweh alone exalted
In that day!

[44] And they shall enter the caves of rocks
And the holes of dust
From the terror of Yahweh
And from his majestic splendor
When he rises to terrify the land.
In that day, men will throw out
Their silver idols
And their golden idols —
Which they made themselves to bow down to —
To the moles [45] and the bats,
Entering the rocky caverns
And the clefts of the crags
From the terror of Yahweh
And from his majestic splendor
When he rises to terrify the land.

Stop yourselves from man
In whose nostrils is breath.
For what value has he?

Irony pervades the poem. We notice the combinations of opposites — the land " deserted " by Yahweh but " filled " with
idolatry and the fruits of idolatry, man who is to be " humbled "
and " lowered " and by no means " lifted up," the genuine
" majesty " of Yahweh, his " exaltation," his day "against "
(" over ") the opposition, as opposed to the spurious " majesty,"
" height," " haughtiness " of man. The land, " filled " with all
that is specious and false and already " deserted " by Yahweh,

[44] I omit v. 18 as a gloss, on the rather subjective grounds that it seems to
me out of place. Herntrich, *op. cit.*, p. 37, replaces it after v. 9.

[45] With almost all scholars, I combine MT's two words, *lachpôr pērôth,* with
Theodotion's translation into one: *lach*e*pharpārôth.*

is abandoned by its prideful inhabitants, who descend into the
rocks and the dust, the caves and the holes. They take the silver
and endless gold with which their land was filled and throw
them out in terror as garbage for the moles and bats when the
God who is God " rises up " over their pitiful lowliness. Man's
height is lowered, man's fullness emptied because in the light of
Yahweh's height and fullness they are recognized as illusions.
The final verse, which has seriously troubled commentators,
harks ironically back to the opening theme, to those whose " fill-
ing " Israel had actually caused it to be " deserted." The nation
is exhorted to desist from dependence on man. " For what value
has he? " We see that man, in comparison to Yahweh, has no
inherent value at all. False allegiance leads to man's " mole-ifica-
tion." Man's self-dependence rather than allegiance to Yahweh
makes him not more man but less. Hence " Yahweh of hosts has
a day against all that is majestic and high." That is why the
" work " of Yahweh, which is the prophet's constant refrain,
shows up the irony of Israel.

## The Irony of Politics

Spurious self-sufficiency, so thoroughly aired in ch. 2:6-22, is the
fundamental problem of Israel's relation to the nations. Ephraim
expresses this confidence:

> " Bricks have fallen,
> So we will build with dressed stone.
> Sycamores have been cut down,
> So we will substitute cedar for them."
>                     (Ch. 9:10 [Heb., v. 9].)

We noted, before, the irony of the " fallen " bricks, echoing the
judgment " fallen " upon Israel (v. 9). Here the irony is conceptual, the disparity between arrogance, which assumes under

judgment that only a little hard work is required to reconstitute
the nation, and the ultimacy of the divine judgment, the word
that has "fallen" on Israel. Ephraim's arrogance is described
ironically again in the metaphorical poem of ch. 28:1-4:

> Ho, haughty wreath of Ephraim's drunkards,
> Drooping flower of its leafy beauty,
> Which is at the head of a rich valley! [46]
> Behold, the Lord has a strong one and a mighty,
> Like a hailstorm, a destroying wind,
> Like a downpour, mighty, flooding,
> Thrusting down the land with his hand.
>
> Under foot it will be trampled,
> The haughty wreath of Ephraim's drunkards.
> And the drooping flower of its leafy beauty
> Which is at the head of a rich valley
> Will become like an early fig [47] before summer,
> Which he who sees it
> Will swallow while it is still in his hand.

Again we have the combination of opposites. What is "haughty"
(gĕ'ûth — perhaps a soundplay with gĕ', "valley") is at the
same time "drooping," and then "trampled under foot" and
"thrust down with the hand." The hailstorm devastates the
"leafy beauty" and, in a rather badly mixed metaphor which is
suggestive but does not come off too well, the flower turns to an
early-ripe fig, eagerly snatched for eating. The poem shows
Ephraim's inevitable fate when it puts too much stock in its
"haughty wreath," and v. 5 following, certainly secondary (see
below), casts a further ironic light on this poem by speaking of

---

[46] Omitting, as a gloss derived from vs. 7-8, hᵉlûmē yayin, "overcome by
wine."

[47] Reading kᵉbikkûrāh without the aspirated hē suffix of MT.

Yahweh as " a wreath of beauty."

The same rejection of Yahweh's promise in favor of the nation's own meager resources lies behind the richly paronomastic irony of ch. 30:15-17:

> For thus said the Lord Yahweh,
> The Holy One of Israel:
> " In turning and rest you shall be delivered,
> In quietness and trust shall be your strength."
> But you would not,
> And you said, " No!
> On horses we will speed."
> Therefore you shall speed indeed!
> " We will ride on the swiftest."
> Therefore your pursuers shall be swift!
> A thousand shall flee [48]
> From the threat of one,
> From the threat of five you shall flee
> Until you are left
> Like a pole on top of a mountain,
> Like a beacon on a hill.

The irony in rejecting Yahweh's safety is unmistakable (cf. ch. 8:6-8). The wordplays underline the futility of this self-sufficiency, and the final ironic simile of the remnant like a bare pole on a mountaintop, a flickering beacon on a hill, is not unlike the simile of the lodge in a cucumber field in ch. 1:8 (and cf. the equally ironic simile of a remnant in Amos 3:12).

The attempted self-sufficiency in the nation produces an irony similar to what we saw in such passages as chs. 2:6-22; 22:1-14. The irony deepens when the nation depends not on its own resources but on those of another nation. Some of Isaiah's most sardonic comments are reserved for Egypt.

[48] Reading, with Kissane, *op. cit.*, p. 341, *yānûsû* for MT *'echād*.

> Ho, you who descend to Egypt for help,
> Who lean upon horses,
> Who trust in chariots — for they are many —
> And in horsemen — for they are very strong.
> But they do not regard the Holy One of Israel,
> Nor do they seek out Yahweh. . . .
> And Egypt is man, not God,
> And their horses flesh, not spirit.
>
> (Ch. 31:1, 3.)

The number of Egypt's chariots and the strength of its horsemen are no less a limitation than Israel's own resources. Neither will serve to oppose divine power.

More subtle is the very difficult poem, apparently on the Ethiopian dynasty of Egypt, in ch. 18:1-7, which is full of obscure and shifting allusions, with abrupt changes from one metaphor to another and then back again.

> Ho, land of rustling wings [49]
> Which is beyond the rivers of Cush,
> Which sends ambassadors by sea,
> In papyrus boats [50] upon the water.
> Go, swift messengers,
> To a nation tall and smooth,[51]
> To a people feared
> Near and far,
> A nation mighty [?] and conquering,
> Whose land rivers divide.
>
> All you inhabitants of earth,
> You who dwell in the world,
> When a signal is raised on the mountains, look!

---

[49] Or " winged ships," that is, ships with large sails. Cf. G. R. Driver, " Difficult Words," p. 56.

[50] Reading *bik̄elî* for MT *ûbik̄elî*.

[51] Read (?) *mᵉmôrāṭ* or *môrēṭ* for MT *môrāṭ*.

When a trumpet is blown, listen!
For thus Yahweh said to me:
" I will be quiet and gaze in my dwelling,
Like dazzling heat in the light,
Like a cloud of dew in harvest heat."
For before the harvest, when budding is finished,
The blossom has become a ripening grape,
He will cut away the shoots with pruning hooks,
The branches he will hew off.
They shall be left together
To the mountain birds,
To the beasts of earth,
And the birds will summer on it,
And all the beasts of earth
Will winter on it.

At that time,
Gifts will be brought to Yahweh of hosts
From a people [52] tall and smooth,
From a people feared
Near and far,
A nation mighty and conquering,
Whose land rivers divide,
To the place of the name
Of Yahweh of hosts:
Mount Zion.

The relation between vs. 1-2 and v. 7 is obvious, but v. 7 is in the different context of a new attitude. In vs. 1-2, the messengers are presenting an ultimatum. In v. 7, they are the image of obsequiousness, which renders the description of high reputation in vs. 1-2 ironic. The middle section, vs. 3-6, contains a curious but explicable metaphorical shift. Verse 3 is a call to the nation to attend to signs of war. Then in vs. 4-5, Yahweh speaks, under

[52] Read *mē'am*, with LXX and Vulgate, for MT *'am*.

the harvest metaphor, of waiting in quietness. That seems to be, but is not, a contradiction of the preparations for war in v. 3, for Yahweh is quietly waiting for the proper moment. In v. 5, the proper moment comes ironically before the regular time for harvest as an unexpected, drastic catastrophe. Verse 6 returns to to metaphor of war, describing the aftermath of the devastation, depicting the field of battle strewn with corpses on which the birds of prey and the beasts feed (recalling the rather grisly passage on a similar theme in Ezek. 39:17-20). With the reference to " summer " our attention is called back to the " heat " of v. 4; with that to " winter " we think of the now useless harvest. The epilogue of v. 7, repeating the words of v. 2, shows the earlier Egyptian arrogance to be ironic pretension in the face of Yahweh's power. The ironic force of v. 7 depends on the welter of shifting metaphors in vs. 3-6. Perhaps the poetic technique here is not on a par with that, say, of chs. 2:6-22 or 22:1-14. But it makes the irony of Egypt unmistakable.

More direct yet is ch. 28:15, which opens another of Isaiah's "set pieces." Here, I suggested before, we have in effect a parody on a communiqué from Judah's state department:

> Because you say:
> " We made a covenant with Death,
> With Sheol we made an agreement.
> The flooding scourge, when it passes,
> Will not come to us.
> For we have made lies our refuge,
> And in falsity we are sheltered."

Isaiah turns on Egypt some of the same language he used of the Assyrian danger. Judah has bound itself to Egypt in fear of the " flooding scourge " that Isaiah describes so graphically in ch. 8:7-8. But dependence on Egypt is as deadly as the flood it attempts to avoid. And, as in the context of the Assyrian threat (cf. ch. 7:4), the prophet exhorts the people to quiet trust in Yahweh: "He who has faith will not be hasty" (ch. 28:16; cf. the ironic name given to Isaiah's second son, ch. 8:1: *Mahēr-shālāl-chāsh-baz,* "Speedy the spoil, hasty the prey.")

Egypt alone does not incur the prophet's irony, however. In the earlier crisis with Damascus and Israel, when Ahaz decided to relieve Judah's burden by calling in Assyria, Isaiah retaliated with some ironic pronouncements, most notable of which are the two related passages in chs. 7:1-17 and 8:5-8. The confrontation with Ahaz (ch. 7:1-17) uses several of Isaiah's ironic techniques, the ironies of metaphor, of quotation, of wordplay, of concept. In the light of the mildly ironic note at the end of v. 1 ("They were not able to bring the battle about") we contemplate the terror of Ahaz (v. 2), who is more frightened by the near enemy than by the far. When Isaiah is told to go and talk with him, his son is named and declared present through the entire episode: "A remnant shall turn." The first interchange has explicitly to do with Damascus and Ephraim. Ahaz is exhorted to courage, and the prophet insults the enemies. He calls the Syrian Rezin, meaning perhaps "one crushed," instead of his real name, Razon, which would mean in Hebrew something like "favor." He refers to the Ephraimite king, Pekah, by his father's name alone, a stinging insult.[53] The ironic metaphors of the smoldering firebrands and the "heads" of Damascus and Samaria (vs. 4, 8-9) demonstrate Ahaz' unnecessary timidity. "It shall not stand, nor shall it happen." (V. 7.) In the sparkling wordplay of v. 9b, the prophet puts the principle in negative terms: "If you will not stand firm, you will not be confirmed." Irony lies over both the intentions of Damascus and Ephraim and the cowardice of Ahaz, "the house of David" as Isaiah sarcastically calls him (vs. 2, 13). Now Ahaz is invited to be shown the truth of Yahweh's promise: "Ask for a sign from Yahweh your God; it can be as deep as

[53] Cf. Lindblom, *op. cit.,* p. 11.

Sheol or as high as what is above " (v. 11). Ahaz piously refuses: " I would not ask such a thing, nor would I put Yahweh to the test " (v. 12). A. J. Heschel thinks that we have no reason to question the king's sincerity.[54] But the savagely ironic exclamation of v. 13 shows enough reason to question it: " Listen to me, ' house of David '! Is it too little that you weary men, but you must weary my God as well? " Ahaz' refusal to accept the offer of a sign is another indication that his career has all along been an offense, that he is not prepared to " stand firm." If the prophet did not doubt the king's sincerity, the sign would not be forced upon him. The child's development is certainly the sign, oddly double-sided like the name of the other child in the chapter, Sheʾar Yāshûb.[55] On the one hand, " Before the child knows how to reject the bad [unpleasant] and choose the good [pleasant], the soil whose two kings you dread will be deserted " (v. 16). " God with us " — the child is well named for promise. But, on the other hand, " Yahweh will bring upon you and your people and your family such times as have not come since the day Ephraim departed from Judah " (v. 17 [56]). " God with/against us " — the child is well named for threat. " A remnant shall return." " A remnant shall return." (Cf. ch. 10:21-22.) Ahaz, however, fears the wrong threat, which is the point of the sardonic metaphors of the oracles in vs. 18-25, whether or not they were spoken at this same time. The choice between the Damascus-Ephraim coalition and Assyria, unambiguous as it may seem to

[54] Abraham J. Heschel, *The Prophets* (The Jewish Publication Society of America, 1962), p. 64.

[55] The many interpretative skirmishes that have swirled about v. 14, e.g., on the identification of the " young woman " (*hāʾalmāh*) or the importance of the LXX translation of the word by *parthenos,* do not concern me in this context. The sign is not the child's birth but his growth, and I fail to see any messianic import to the passage. The mundanely chronological character of the child's growth seems to me sufficient disproof of any mythological ingredient.

[56] The glossator who added " the king of Assyria," plodding literalist though he was, was correct. Lindblom, *op. cit.,* pp. 26–27, attempts to show that this verse is a promise. I find his reasoning too tortuous to accept.

the beleaguered Ahaz, is a limited choice indeed. To choose
Damascus-Ephraim is out of the question; to call in Assyria
against them is a counsel of desperation.

The despair resulting from desperation comes to the fore in
the oracle of ch. 8:5-8. " This people " rejects the quiet but life-
giving lordship of Yahweh, shakes in terror before the ludicrously
feeble Damascus-Ephraim coalition, and prefers the waters of the
mighty Euphrates. But, with the water metaphor that serves him
so precisely, Isaiah points out the danger of demolition from this
river. The " waters of Shiloah, which flow gently," give no threat
of flood. The " waters of the river " will sweep away the entire
nation, " O Immanuel! " We cannot avoid the double-edged irony
of the name. The choice between Damascus-Ephraim and Assyria is a limiting choice. The prophet insists on a third: Yahweh,
Lord of hosts. In the light of that choice, either of the others must
be ironic.

By vacillating among the choices, Judah fails to perceive the
true political situation. Once the decision is made, however, and
Assyria becomes the true and evident enemy, Isaiah turns the heat
of his irony on Assyria. Chapter 10:5-15 shows both Isaiah's consistency and his inconsistency. He is inconsistent in preaching
Judah's frightful doom at Assyria's hands in 734 B.C. and then
turning about in this oracle to proclaim Assyria's doom in comfort for Judah in 701.[57] But he is consistent in seeing everywhere
the irony of politics, whether Judah's politics, Ephraim's, Egypt's,
or Assyria's. National and international power is sharply limited
for Isaiah because God exerts overarching power in human affairs.
Assyria, appointed the " rod of God's anger, the staff of his fury,"
the agent of judgment on a faithless and corrupt Judah, is also
the object of that same anger, fury, and judgment. We have already noted the irony of the passage. It amounts to a metaphor

[57] A few scholars earlier wanted to date ch. 10:5 ff. in 717 or 711 B.C. The
majority opinion is now 701 B.C.

carried to a logical conclusion. Assyria is the tool of God, but he claims autonomous action and power. That, indeed, is the problem of political action in a world dominated by divine providence. But the fact that Assyria is the agent of God is no proof against his being kept in his place.

> Does the ax vaunt itself
> Over him who hews with it?
> Does the saw magnify itself
> Over him who wields it?
> In the same way, a rod wields him who lifts it;
> In the same way a staff lifts what is not wood.
>
> (V. 15.)

A heavy-footed glossator has laid down the prophet's meaning for us in v. 12, fearing that we might miss it. Irony is a dangerous tool, for it risks misunderstanding, and the literalist will always gloss it in the interests of unmistakable clarity.

Political power is at issue also in an odd little passage in ch. 8:12-15. The irony is somewhat obscured, and the passage is difficult. It is unclear whether it is poetry or prose, and certain expressions are difficult.

Do not call alliance [58] all that this people calls alliance, and do not fear what it fears nor be terrified. But Yahweh of hosts, be in alliance with him,[59] with him your fear, him your terror. And he will become a sanctuary [60] and a stone of offense and a rock for stumbling to both houses of Israel, a trap and snare to Jerusalem's

[58] See Kissane, *op. cit.*, p. 103, for this translation. The word is apparently patent of a double meaning, either that of alliance openly arrived at or conspiracy.

[59] Reading *'ittô tiqsherû* for MT *'ôthô taqdîshû*.

[60] A very strange word in this context. Some scholars emend *miqdāsh* to *môqēsh*, "snare," but *môqēsh* appears later in the verse. I do not think that *miqdāsh* was Isaiah's word, but I have no alternative emendation to offer. A form from the root *q-sh-r*, which appears in the passage, would fit, but I am unable to identify a suitable form.

dwellers. And many shall stumble on them, and they shall fall and be broken, snared, captured.

The problem is the uselessness of the alliances into which Judah has entered. The prophet has been opposed to them all, and the reason finally comes clear: the "alliances" the people are entangled in are actually "conspiracies." The double-edged noun *qesher,* "alliance" or "conspiracy," may suggest that the prophet has been accused of subverting the interests of the state. But he insists that the proper "alliance/conspiracy" is with Yahweh. Allegiance is again the issue. To be allied with the nations is to conspire against Yahweh. And this shifts the allegiance, the fear, and the terror to what does not deserve such attention. Yet, in the second part of the oracle (vs. 14-15), Isaiah promises that the proper alliance will not magically produce safety or happiness any more than do those illicit alliances to which he is opposed. Perhaps the irony of being Yahweh's people is that no external security lies in it. Yet less security lies in Judah's belonging to anyone else, Assyria, for instance, or Egypt. Judah's life moves in a realm where the normal configurations of national and international power do not, in Isaiah's opinion, apply. His "eyes have seen the king, Yahweh of hosts" (ch. 6:5).

## REFLECTIONS ON THE ETHICAL

Isaiah reserves most of his irony for the vast theological and political issues of his day. His concern for the internal ethical situation, though far from absent, is not so pervasive as his concern for the nation's cosmic and international condition. Isaiah is more theologian than moralist, in contrast, for example, to Amos, who is more moralist than theologian.

Consider, however, his ironic symbolization of Judah's rote and false piety:

> Hear the word of Yahweh,
> Rulers of Sodom;
> Give ear to our God's instruction,
> People of Gomorrah!
>
> (Ch. 1:10.)

Isaiah proceeds to detail Judah's devotion to its liturgical piety, a fact that makes this opening reference to Sodom and Gomorrah, the quintessence of moral corruption (Gen. 13:13; 18:20 to 19:28), a piece of biting irony. Another, perhaps unintended, irony is the fact that the reference to Sodom and Gomorrah is a catchword linking this oracle with the preceding one, which closes:

> Had not Yahweh of hosts
> Left us a few survivors,
> We should have been like Sodom
> And become like Gomorrah.
>
> (Isa. 1:9.)

This is to say, "We did not become like Sodom or Gomorrah," but v. 10 reverses that optimism.

Again, in what looks like a courtroom scene, Judah is invited to present its case:

> Come along, and let us argue the case, says Yahweh.
> If your sins are like scarlet,
> Like snow they shall be whitened!?
> If they are red like crimson,
> They shall be like wool!?
>
> (V. 18.)

Most translations treat the third and fifth lines declaratively, as if this were a promise, but this treatment fits badly with the severe conditions laid down in v. 19. The statements are made in

mocking irony, to be inflected almost as if they were questions.[61]
Scarlet is to be turned to white! Marvelous!

The opposite movement, the good turning bad, is also treated
ironically by Isaiah.

> How the faithful city
> Has turned harlot.
> She filled with justice,
> With whom righteousness lodged —
> But now assassins.
> Your silver has turned to dross,
> Your wine is mixed with water.
>
> (Vs. 21-22.)

The irony lies in the procession of metaphors. The city, formerly
the "faithful" (ne'emānāh) wife, has become a harlot. Living
previously in legal marriage ("righteousness"), she now lies in
promiscuity (lodging with "assassins"[62]). The metaphor changes
to the adulteration of fine things, the change of silver to dross,
the mixing of fine wine with water to weaken it. The change of
silver to dross is a little strange, since dross ordinarily means what
is removed from the ore to obtain silver in the purification process

---

[61] I have adopted the punctuation (in reversed order) used by Napier, *Song
of the Vineyard*, p. 225. Cf. also Scott, *loc. cit.*, p. 175. Another interpretation
is given by Blank, in his unpublished paper, "Irony by Way of Attribution,"
p. 5. We are, says Blank, to understand some parenthetical interpolations within
the lines (designated below by italics), which would be conveyed originally by
the speaker's tone of voice:

> Though your sins are like scarlet,
> They shall be white as snow, *you say,*
> Though they are red like crimson,
> They shall become like wool, *you fondly imagine.*

The difference of this from that proposed in the text is that Blank wants to
understand the thought not as the prophet's thoughts but as those of his opponents.

[62] The word is odd in this combination of metaphors. Perhaps it bore a con-
temporary connotation, not now recoverable, that made it appropriate.

(cf. Prov. 25:4), although perhaps the word can also mean the metal with impurities in it before purification (cf. Ezek. 22:17-22). The point is clear: what was fine about the city has unaccountably become bad. The poet does not account for the change; he states it. His suggestiveness, his odd combination of opposites and his failure to provide all the mental links, makes this passage ironic. Not only is it incredible that the bad could turn good (Isa. 1:18), it is equally and ironically incredible that the good has in fact turned bad.

In several passages public officials of the nation come under the whip of Isaiah's irony. In ch. 22:20-25, he singles out a particular individual, Eliakim, who will be made steward over the palace (though this may sound like a butler's position, actually it was a very high government post, perhaps very close to prime minister). Eliakim is described in glowing terms, in contrast to his predecessor, Shebna, who is condemned in vs. 16-19. The metaphor of the " peg hung in a sure [ne'²mān] place " portrays Eliakim's responsibility and others' dependence upon him. Suddenly, however, the metaphor crashes to its conclusion: the " peg " gives way and falls from its " sure place," bringing down all with it (v. 25). Some curious factors in the entire passage have frequently been noticed. The whole seems to be a speech to Shebna, the incumbent who is about to be removed. Why does Isaiah describe to Shebna not only the accession of his successor but also that successor's downfall? If the end is in sight from the beginning, why does he trouble to praise Eliakim so thoroughly? Is it a warning to him? [63] But the oddity of the abrupt reversal of Eliakim's fortunes may be mitigated if we understand the entire description to be directed not to Shebna but to Eliakim himself, as an ironic prediction of Eliakim's excellence. The entire glowing praise, in particular the metaphor of the peg hung in a " sure [faithful, unmoving] place," is ironic. In the end of the day, the

[63] Kissane, op. cit., p. 255, thinks Eliakim is being warned against nepotism.

nation is no better off with Eliakim than it had been with Shebna, bad as he was.

The chaos resulting from corrupt officials is canvassed even more directly in the first verses of ch. 3. Isaiah threatens that the mainstays of society will be removed for its corruption. What will be left is sheer chaos:

> And I make boys their princes,
> And babies shall rule them.
> And the people shall oppress themselves —
> One man another,
> A man his neighbor —
> The boy shall be arrogant to the old man,
> The dishonorable to the honorable.
>
> (Vs. 4-5.)

All normal order in the society is reversed; children rule, and the young and base lord it over the old and upright. The chaos is continued in the following verses (vs. 6-8). All proper criteria for the leadership are upset, and the possession of a cloak is considered sufficient qualification to be king. In the background, of course, lies Isaiah's assumption that the people has its proper ruler in Yahweh himself. The depiction of the nation's chaos and its fumbling through the rubble in search of spurious order takes its irony from that assumption.

In the same category is the rather vicious satire on the women of Jerusalem (chs. 3:16 to 4:1). As in ch. 2:6-22, the metaphor of the specious high that becomes low dominates the passage. The women are " high, haughty " (gābô⁴h), very proud of themselves, with noses in the air and adultery in their eyes, with exaggerated step and clanking ornaments on their feet. Their sole thought is to call attention to themselves. It is a splendid description, one of few such descriptions in the Old Testament. The outcome, however, will be reversal. The ostensibly respectable will become

obviously prostitutes ("The Lord will uncover the heads of
Zion's daughters," v. 17 [64]). The staggering list of female cos-
metics in ch. 3:18-23 (probably a gloss) leads up to the ironic
substitutes in v. 24:

> Instead of a sweet smell, it will be a rotten,
> And instead of a sash, a rope.
> Instead of a coiffure, baldness,
> Instead of a fine robe, a burlap shift.

With the final verse (ch. 4:1), the prostitution theme recurs. The
women will seek desperately for any means of respectable identity, will even support themselves in exchange for being somebody once more.[65] Yet even this is an illusion, a fiction recognized by the women themselves, which provides a double irony
to the description. The entire satire plays upon the society's false
pride and moral corruption.

Against this inner corruption comes the prophet's ironic reference to the only heroism he can find in the society — the heroic
consumption of wine and the mighty mixing of liquor (ch. 5:22).
It is the same corruption to which he refers, perhaps not in ironic
speech but certainly with ironic thought, in the same context:

> Woe to those who say
> Of evil, "It is good!"
> And of good, "It is bad!"
> Who make dark into light
> And light into dark;
> Who make bitter into sweet
> And sweet into bitter.
>
> (Ch. 5:20.)

[64] Reading *pashshēṭ* for MT *śippach*. In the Assyrian Laws the uncovered
head is the sign of prostitution; cf. par. 40 of the "Middle Assyrian Laws,"
*ANET*, p. 183. The MT word must be distorted to produce RSV's meaning,
"smite with a scab." I owe this understanding of the passage to a suggestion
made orally by Prof. Isaac Mendelsohn.

[65] Ch. 3:25-26 is a gloss, perhaps from the beginning of the exile, by a
reader who allegorized the satire into a threat against the city itself.

Those are the ethical reflections of a theologian. The entire
scheme of things is reversed, turned upside down, as he says to
the people in ch. 29:16. The moral structure of the nation is the
blatant reverse of its proper structure; it is an antimorality as the
prophet is, in a sense, an antiprophet. For all its seriousness and
its indignation, the prophetic criticism of Israel and the world
conveys the fundamentally ironic vision of an incredible confusion of bad for good, of faithlessness for faith. The vision is ironic
because the prophets sought Israel's redemption by God. And
that lies close to the center of any prophetic vision of the world
and its ills.

## IRONY AMONG THE GLOSSES

We are not finished with the book when we have isolated and
interpreted what is authentically from the lips or pen of the
original prophet. Particularly is this true with The Book of
Isaiah, which is the receptacle for so many oracular oddments
from varied sources. We may start with a slyly humorous point,
not strictly a gloss but an easily overlooked piece of Masoretic
punctuation. In ch. 7, when Damascus and Ephraim are plan-
ning their invasion of Judah, they propose to put on the throne
of Judah a puppet, pliable to their own purposes, whose name
was evidently Tabeel (*tob'ēl*), meaning " Good is God " (v. 6).
The Masoretes, however, vocalized the name *tob'al,* which can
be rendered, " Good for nothing." [66]

An unintended irony may be present in the gloss in ch. 28:5,
which deepens the irony of the oracle on which it expands
(vs. 1-4). Isaiah's oracle, on which I commented above, turns
upon the metaphor of the " haughty wreath " of Ephraim, which
will be " trampled under foot." The glossator extends the metaphor: " In that day, Yahweh of hosts shall become a wreath of

[66] Cf. also Herntrich, *op. cit.,* p. 118: *Taugenichts.*

beauty and a garland of loveliness to the remnant of his people "
(v. 5). We see the same words as in the original oracle: " wreath "
(*ᵃṭereth*, cf. vs. 1, 4), " beauty " (*tsᵉbî*, cf. vs. 1, 4), " loveliness "
(*tiph' ereth*, translated " leafy " above, vs. 1, 4). The " drunkards
of Ephraim " (v. 1) put much stock in their "haughty wreath,"
which is rudely trampled under foot. Yahweh is the proper
" wreath of beauty " for Ephraim, but he will be recognized only
by " the remnant of his people." The glossator probably did not
notice either the irony of Isaiah's oracle or the ironic effect of
the first part of his gloss, for the second part, v. 6, is a straightforward promise.

In several passages is an ironic contrast of a future with a
present. In ch. 32:1-8, for example, the principal contrast comes
in v. 5:

> No longer will the fool be called noble,
> Nor will the knave be said to be generous.

When this was written, values were reversed (cf. ch. 5:20). But
it is the nature of periods of corruption to refuse to recognize
their corruption. To this poet, only when the future brings a
righting of the wrong will the present upheaval appear in its
true ironic light. A similar contrast of future with present is in
ch. 33:18. When the period of oppression ceases, the fate of the
oppressor will seem ironic:

> Your mind will meditate on the terror:
> " Where is the counter, where the weigher?
> Where is the counter of the towers? "

The precise meaning of the terms, in particular the connotation
of " the counter of the towers " (*sôphēr eth-hammigdālîm*), is uncertain. One may surmise that they denote occupation army officers. The contrast is promised for a time when the " terror " is
over, though for the writer and his readers this time has clearly

not come. The "insolent people" (v. 19) are very much with
them. But in the future, Israel will meditate ironically upon the
fate of those who now perpetrate the terror.

An implied ironic contrast with the present from a poet with
a very dramatic mind is found in the oracle on Tyre in ch. 23.
The unknown prophet sarcastically exhorts, "Wail, you inhabitants of the coastland!"[67] (v. 6b). He then piles up the irony
with his questions:

> Is this your exultant one,
> Whose beginning is from ancient times,
> Whose feet brought her
> To sojourn afar?
>
> (V. 7.)

Tyre is (hypothetically?) destroyed. To call it now an "exultant
one" is profoundly ironic; the reference to its "ancient" (*qedem*)
beginnings casts irony on its sudden ending. The description of
Tyre's far-flung commercial and colonial dealings as a distant
"sojourn," underlining its temporary quality, compounds the
irony of the questions. But the poet is not finished. The shocked
observers of Tyre's fate ask questions that are deeply ironic in
effect:

> Who has purposed this
> Against Tyre, the crown-giver,
> Whose businessmen were princes,
> Whose tradesmen were honored worldwide?
>
> (V. 8.)

The poet proposes the ironic contrast of destruction with the
commercial and political preeminence of Tyre, who gave crowns

---

[67] K–B, *s.v.* *'i*, equates the expression with "Phoenicians." The word *'i* may
mean either "coastland" or "island," and without qualification it is always
difficult to choose between the two meanings.

and won renown. But, by putting the contrast in the mouths of
the observers, he displays irony by attribution. The situation is
profoundly shocking to those who have assumed Tyre to be in-
destructible, wholly capable of maintaining herself in power before any threat. To him who affirms the power of God, it is ironic.

The praises heaped upon Babylon in ch. 13:19 carry the same
ironic contrast:

> And Babylon, beauty of the kingdoms,
> Loveliness of the Chaldeans' pride,
> Shall become like God's overthrow
> Of Sodom and Gomorrah.

The praise words (cf. ch. 28:1-4) mean their opposite in the light
of the comparison with Sodom and Gomorrah (and cf. ch. 1:9
and 10).

An ironic double meaning is to be found earlier in the same
oracle on Babylon. The day of Yahweh is a day of destruction,
where pride and arrogance are to be rooted out (ch. 13:11), the
cosmos shaken from its foundation (v. 13). In v. 12 is the curious
remark:

> And I will make a man rarer than pure gold,
> And mankind than Ophir's gold.

The principal connotation of the lines is that men will be rare
because they will be hard to find, a rarity comparable to that of
particularly good gold. On the other hand, to be " rare " may
also mean to be eagerly sought, which becomes ironic when,
in v. 17, the Medes, Babylon's destroyers, are said to " take no
delight in gold." For this poet, man's rarity will not make him
precious.[68]

---

[68] There may, in addition, be a soundplay between the first and last words
of the verse, 'ôqîr and 'ôphîr.

Within the composite oracle on Tyre (ch. 23) is the ironic application to Tyre of the Song of the Harlot (*shîrat hazzônāh*). Quoted in v. 16, this may have been a popular ballad.

> Take up a lyre,
> Go around the city,
> Forgotten harlot.
> Play well on the strings,
> Sing many songs,
> So that you may be remembered.

That Tyre, of worldwide fame, should be so soon "forgotten" is an ironic comment on her actual importance. The exhortation to the erstwhile great commercial power to bring herself again to people's attention so cheaply is ironic. In particular, the controlling image under which Tyre is described, that of a harlot past her prime of attractiveness, out on the streets trying desperately to drum up trade with an out-of-tune lyre and a cracking, ancient voice (such is the ironic implication of the song), is a piece of irony that, from the compiler's point of view, is little short of vicious.

An ironic metaphor, the referent of which is extremely obscure, is to be found in ch. 33:23a:

> Your ropes are drooping,
> They cannot hold their mast in place,
> They cannot spread the sail.

The little poem certainly occurs here because of its pictorial connection with the ships mentioned in v. 21, though it is not of a piece either with what precedes or with what follows it. We may guess that it is an ironic comment upon an enemy with great plans but little efficiency, under the metaphor of a sailing ship. The irony lies, of course, in the observation of a ship rigged in a landlubberly fashion, with slack shrouds and loose sheets.

We must turn finally to a long, magnificently virtuoso expansion on a metaphor, ironically applied to Babylon, the "taunt song" in ch. 14:4-19a:

> How the oppressor is resting,
> The assault (?) has come to rest.[69]
> Yahweh breaks the staff of wicked men,
> The rod of rulers.
> He who smote peoples in fury
> Is smitten [70] without ceasing;
> He who drove nations in anger
> Is pursued without check.
> The whole earth rests, is quiet.
>
> (Vs. 4b-7a.)

The sarcastic reference to "resting" (*shābath*) surely means death, as later images show (cf. vs. 9-11, 15, 19). Were the tone not so vitriolic, we might call it ironic understatement. There may also be a wordplay between "rest" (*shābath*) and "break" (*shābar*). The lines on smiting and being smitten, on driving and being pursued, present the irony of an action turned back upon the actor. And with the final line, the meaning of the initial "resting" comes clear. Now that Babylon is down, the world may have genuine rest and quiet.

We now have in a short, four-line strophe, a new picture not of quiet but of joyous noise:

> Even the junipers burst into a shout,[71]
> Lebanon's cedars rejoice at you:

[69] The usual emendation of MT *madhēbāh* to *marhēbāh* is followed.

[70] Reading the Hoph'al participle, *mukkeh*, for MT *makkeh*. In the next line, I retain the reading of MT, *murdāph*.

[71] I have changed the line arrangement in the interests of sense. The last words of v. 7, *patsᵉchû rinnāh*, contradict the quiet of the previous line and form an excellent parallelism with *samᵉchû lᵉkā* in v. 8.

" Since you lay down, no longer
Does the woodsman come up against us."
(Vs. 7b-8.)

The entire cosmos is rejoicing as in Isa. 55:12. The exultant shout
of the trees picks up the motif of " resting " with " lying down "
(shākab), which is contrasted with ." coming up " (yaᶜᵃleh), a
contrast of movement down and up that we will see later.

Sheol beneath is agitated at you,
To meet your coming
Rouses up the shades for you.
All the earth's leaders [72]
Get up from their thrones,
All the kings of nations.
They all answer and say to you,
" You too are weak like us,
You have become a byword to us." [73]
(Ch. 14:9-10.)

The earth is quiet (v. 7a), but the dead are in motion. Once
again we meet the motifs of lying down and getting up (" rouses
up," out of sleep, in v. 9) and of the movements down (" Sheol
beneath ") and up (" rouses up," " get up from their thrones ").
But the irony lies in the mock respect paid by the dead kings of
earth in rising to greet Babylon with their gloating taunt. The
irony is intensified in the next strophe, corresponding to the earlier
four-line strophe of vs. 7b-8:

Your pride is brought down to Sheol,
The sound of your harps.

[72] The word is " he-goats " (ᶜattûdîm), a term apparently used as a metaphor
of rulers or leaders in Zech. 10:3 and (?) Jer. 50:8.
[73] Taking nimshaltā to mean what the noun māshāl means, a proverb or
" taunt," as in the caption to the present poem in v. 4a.

> The maggot under you is your mattress,
> Your blanket the worm.[74]

(V. 11.)

We have again the contrasting movements up and down. " Pride "
(*gā'ôn*), the " swelling upward " of thought, has been " brought
down " (*yārad,* Hoph'al) to Sheol. With Babylon's resting place
upon the maggot and his grisly blanket of worms we have re-
turned to the sleeping-resting metaphor which we saw in vs. 4, 7,
8, and 9. This metaphor draws the ironic contrast between the
tyrannous activity of Babylon's previous doings and the enforced
inaction of its present condition.

Now the contrasting movements up and down predominate:

> How you have fallen from the sky,
> Day-Star, son of Dawn!
> You have been struck to earth,
> Who prostrated the nations.
> But you, you said to yourself:
> " I will ascend to the sky;
> Above God's stars
> I will raise my throne.
> I will sit on the mount of assembly
> In the north's far reaches.
> I will ascend the cloud's backs,
> I will make myself like the Highest."
> Yet you are brought down to Sheol,
> To the pit's far reaches.

(Vs. 12-15.)

The initial downward tone of v. 12, with the ironic descent of
the mythological Day-Star, is supplanted by the ironically re-

---

[74] The last two lines are translated paraphrastically. Literally:
> The maggot is spread out [as a couch] under you,
> The worm is your covering.

counted boast of Babylon. All the verbs and nouns now denote rising, ascending, being high: " ascend," " above," " I will raise," with the sitting on the " mount " in the " north's far reaches," a mythological allusion to the habitations and assemblies of the gods in the Canaanite literature. In v. 14 we have again " ascending " upon the cloud (Baal is called " rider of the clouds " in the Ugaritic myths, and cf. Ps. 68:4), and the climax comes with the overweening last step in attaining height: " I will make myself like the Highest ['elyôn]," equal to the God whose high is beyond all highs. The irony of this entire amazing speech is crystallized in the restrained but devastating response of the last two lines, with their sudden descent (" You are brought down ") and their ironic echo of Babylon's boast with the words "the pit's far reaches." [75] The next strophe also suggests ironic contrast:

> He who looks at you will gape,
> Will ponder over you.
> " Is this the man who made the earth tremble,
> Who shook kingdoms,
> Who made the world like a desert
> And broke down his cities?
> He did not open the prison for his prisoners." [76]
>                                         (Isa. 14:16-17.)

The irony of the contrast lies more in its implication than in its language. One almost has the impression that the previous strophe exhausted the poet's creative faculties, for the poem begins to disintegrate here. In the question, " Is this the man who made

[75] I could wish that v. 15 had more than two lines, since the expression 'el she'ôl tûrad, " you are brought down to Sheol," is so much like that in v. 11, hûrad she'ôl ge'ôneḵā, " your pride is brought down to Sheol." Another refrain-like strophe, such as those in vs. 7b-8 and 11, would round out the poem's structure.

[76] The final line is conjecturally emended in desperation, to read bêth hakkele' for MT bêthāh ḵôl. In either case, the line is so obscure as to defy my understanding it.

the earth tremble [*margîz*]?" is an ironic echo of Sheol's being "agitated" (*rāgᵉzāh*) in v. 9, pointing up the contrast between past and present. The agitation of Sheol is no threat to earth, which is now "quiet" (v. 7).

With the final strophe,[77] we return to the "resting" image with which the poem began:

> All the kings of the earth
> Have lain down in honor,
> Each in his own house.
> But you were cast out from your grave
> Like an abominable shoot,[78]
> Clothed with the slain.
>
> (Vs. 18-19a.)

Even in death, Babylon has no proper "rest." Other kings have "lain down" (*shākab*, cf. v. 8) with glory (*kābód*), but Babylon is even cast out of its grave. Here the vicious irony of the poem comes to its completion. Perhaps we should qualify the use of the term "irony," for we must certainly say that this poet was not concerned for Babylon's amendment. He cared only for its destruction, which he contemplated with a savage joy. His method may be ironic; his thought is not.

[77] I call this the final strophe, failing to see any connection in thought, language, or poetic form with what follows. Other scholars continue the poem to v. 20b or through v. 21.

[78] The word *netser* has troubled commentators, who want to emend it. Note, however, its occurrence in Isa. 11:1; Dan. 11:7 of kings, and in Isa. 60:21 as a metaphor of the nation. Combined with the qualifier "abominable," the word seems entirely appropriate here.

# VI

## QOHELETH:
## THE LIMITS OF WISDOM

THERE is a certain pious assumption that anything in the Bible must be true; the question easily becomes not whether a book or passage has truth but what its truth is. But it is by no means self-evident that Qoheleth [1] has a stance in truth. To be sure, a follower, who perhaps wanted to reassure readers or even to reverse the book's effect, claimed that he did: "Qoheleth sought to find pleasant words, and he wrote truthful words uprightly" (ch. 12:10). But many of those who have studied Qoheleth most closely are not at all convinced that that judgment is sound. Morris Jastrow titled his book on Qoheleth *A Gentle Cynic*. D. B. Macdonald thinks that Qoheleth inculcates amorality (not, mark well, immorality) on the basis of the divine amorality. [2] Terms like "fatalism," "pessimism," "nihilism" are often used of Qoheleth. And Lauha holds that the only reason to maintain the book in the Biblical canon is that its negativity clarifies Scripture's positive faith, because this book's darkness shows how impossible life is without Scriptural faith. [3]

[1] I prefer to use the Hebrew name of the book instead of the cumbersome Greek Ecclesiastes.

[2] D. B. Macdonald, *The Hebrew Philosophical Genius: A Vindication* (Princeton University Press, 1936), Ch. V, *passim*.

[3] Aarre Lauha, "Die Krise des religiösen Glaubens bei Kohelet," in *Wisdom in Israel and in the Ancient Near East*, ed. by M. Noth and D. Winton Thomas (Supplements to *VT*, Vol. 3 [E. J. Brill, Leiden, 1955]), pp. 183–191. Cf. the

The major difficulty in understanding Qoheleth is that the book seems not to present a thoroughgoing, well-organized argument. The observation that it contradicts itself raised grave doubts among the early rabbis about retaining the book in the canon. On the one hand,

> The wise man's mind is on the house of mourning,
> But the fool's mind is on the house of rejoicing.
> (Ch. 7:4.)

And on the other hand:

I lauded rejoicing, because there is no good for man beneath the sun except to eat and to drink and to rejoice. (Ch. 8:15.)

Again:

The destiny of men's sons and the destiny of the beasts are the same destiny. As the one dies, so does the other, and all of them have the same spirit. And the advantage man has over the beast is nil. So the whole of it is vanity. They all go to the same place: all have come out of dust, and all return to dust. Who knows the spirit of man? Will it go upward? And the spirit of beasts: will it descend down into the earth? (Ch. 3:19-21.)

But:

> The dust returns to the earth as it did,
> But the spirit returns to God who gave it.
> (Ch. 12:7.)

Examples could be set side by side for several more pages. It is a baffling book that exhorts not to be " overly righteous " nor " overly wicked " (ch. 7:16-17) but closes with the injunction to

---

paper's concluding sentence: " The function of the Book of Ecclesiastes in the Biblical canon, consequently, appears to be to disclose the hopelessness and untenability of the secularist concept of life and thereby to proclaim indirectly the living reality of God and the indispensability of a personal struggle of faith."

keep the commandments of God (ch. 12:13). Can we ascribe to such a book a "stance in truth"?

Scholars have ordinarily solved the dilemma by postulating an original author and one or more editors and glossators. The most elaborate theory, propounded by Siegfried in 1898, was that the book was written by a philosophical Jew influenced by Greek thought, and comments were added by three other persons: a Sadducean Epicurean, who suggested that we enjoy life while it lasts; a "wise man" (*chākām*), who set forth the advantages of wisdom; and a "pietist" (*chāsîd*), who referred to the divine judgment. Further additions, according to Siegfried, were made by a glossator concerned with wisdom, two redactors, and three contributors to the epilogue (ch. 12:8-14).[4] The flaw in such a theory is that one decides beforehand what the thought and style of the "original" author were and ascribes anything inconsistent with them to an editor or glossator. It is always a circular argument, and one seldom fails to come to the conclusions with which he originally started.

One reaction to the theory of multiple authorship is found in the work of Kurt Galling, who argues that the book is made up of a string of independent poems, two to fifteen lines in length, by the same author but absolutely unrelated to one another (the epilogue, ch. 12:8-14, and the beginning, ch. 1:1-11, are later additions).[5] Galling insists on the mutual independence of these poems

---

[4] Siegfried's view, propounded in his commentary, *Prediger und Hoheslied* (HKAT, Vandenhoeck & Ruprecht, Göttingen, 1898), is set forth quite fully by O. S. Rankin, "Ecclesiastes," *IB*, Vol. 5, p. 8. Other writers followed Siegfried more or less closely, although most were dubious of that Sadducean Epicurean, and he has tended to disappear. Small loss!

[5] See Galling's commentary, "Die fünf Megilloth" (HAT, J. C. B. Mohr, Tübingen, 1940 [a new edition is in process]), and his articles, "Kohelet-Studien," *ZAW*, Vol. 50 (1932), pp. 276–299; "Stand und Aufgabe der Kohelet-Forschung," *TR*, Vol. 6 (1934), pp. 355–373. The view that the first verses of ch. 1 are from a later editor seems to be recently accepted by Galling, as indicated by Oswald Loretz, "Zur Darbietungsform der 'Ich-Erzählung' im Buche Qohelet," *CBQ*, Vol. 25 (1963), p. 46, n. 1.

to the point of refusing to consider that the way a word is used
in one poem has any bearing on its use in another. Yet Galling
comprises all these separate pieces in the mind of the single author. We are not to search for conceptual unity or for an overall
structure that will make sense of the mishmash. The unity is
the unity of the man, not of his work.[6] The difficulty, of course,
is that we cannot work with the man but only with the book.
Whatever the man has to say can reach us only through the
work. If the work seems to speak out of both sides of its mouth,
it is slight comfort to appeal to the unity of an author. One
can argue, as Galling does, that this demonstrates human inconsistency. But here the question of truth emerges again from
the wings.

Perhaps we are too certain that we know what a " book " is:
a unified, logically argued and constructed whole.[7] When we
discover that Qoheleth as it stands does not fit the definition, we
are baffled. We are forced to assume, therefore, either that its
disunity, lack of construction, and failures of logic are illusions,
to be dispelled if we work hard enough,[8] or that somebody has
been tampering with the original, which must, *ex hypothesi,* have
corresponded to our definition of a " book." So we search out
the " original," brush aside all that rings falsely with it, and bask

[6] Cf. " Kohelet-Studien," *ZAW*, Vol. 50 (1932), p. 281: "*Ihre Einheit —
nicht Einheitlichkeit — muss in der Einheit des Menschen Kohelet, ihre Wider-
sprüche, Spannungen und Gebrochenheiten müssen in eben diesem Widerspruch,
der Spannung und Gebrochenheit des Menschen Kohelet geschaut werden. Es
gilt, die Kräfte des dynamischen Schaffensprozesses abzutasten, um ohne Nivel-
lierung, Addition und Subtraktion die ganze Fülle der Lebensschau und Leben-
shaltung in diesem Menschen und in seinem Werk zu erkennen.*" Similar views
are stated by Lauha, *loc. cit.,* p. 183.

[7] I am indebted for this argument to the important article of Oswald Loretz
referred to above in n. 5. Cf. especially p. 54.

[8] H. L. Ginsberg sets out a coherent outline for the book in " The Structure
and Contents of the Book of Koheleth," *Wisdom in Israel and in the Ancient
Near East,* pp. 138–145. It is an extremely interesting argument, but when I try
to follow Ginsberg through the text, I simply get lost, and the structure disappears.

in the warm assurance that once again we have justified our definition of a " book."

The fact is that we have before us a " work." To our minds, trained in certain ways and on certain assumptions, the work appears a scattered, miscellaneous, unstructured, and internally inconsistent congeries of remarks. Perhaps — the hypothesis has been proffered — it was a diary in which the writer set down thoughts without telling us when or why, or a kind of commonplace book in which the writer mixed ideas of his own with quotations that he fancied, or miscellaneous meditations of the author somewhat on the model of Pascal's *Pensées*. Perhaps it is any or none of these. Does it really matter? To analyze the book's origin is not necessarily to solve its problem. The issue is to permit it to speak for itself so far as it will, and not to decide prematurely what it must say. The unity of the book, if unity there be, must emerge from the book itself, not from the student's predispositions, little as those predispositions can be totally obliterated. But we must above all avoid the modernizing error of confusing the person of an author with the integrity of the work. In Qoheleth we have to do with the work, not with a hypothetically reconstructible author. If in the pages that follow I use the pronoun " he," I do not mean by it any securely grasped and analyzed personality. The purpose of interpretation is at any rate not to reconstruct and analyze a personality but to grapple with truth — or with falsehood.[9]

I believe, as will shortly appear, that there is a basic unity of thought in the book. If that requires the postulation of a single

[9] For this reason I find it hard to accept Gordis' statement: " An appreciation of his personality is impossible without a comprehension of his style and, conversely, his style cannot be evaluated without an understanding of the man." (*Koheleth — The Man and His World*, 2d ed. [Bloch Publishing Company, 1955], p. 74.) It seems to plead the necessity of a knowledge that can be no more than hypothetical, namely, the knowledge of a writer's " personality." Fortunately, Gordis does not rigorously follow his own principle.

author, I am prepared to postulate a single author. But I fail to perceive a clear formal structure to the book.

## Some Basic Axioms

Qoheleth was no systematician — or, if he tried to be, he failed spectacularly. But certain axioms seem to hold true for the entire book. Primary among them is that every man must find the significance of his life within that life, not beyond it. The references to death point out that man must make the most of life.

> The wise man's eyes are in his head,
> And the fool walks in darkness.
> But I also know
> That one destiny
> Befalls them all. . . .
> The wise man dies just as the fool does.
>                          (Ch. 2:14, 16.)

This life is all we have. Meaning is to be found here or not at all. " Who can bring [man] here to see what will come after him? " (Ch. 3:22; cf. chs. 6:12; 7:14; 8:7; 9:10; 10:14.) It may be unfortunate that we cannot look beyond life, that all we do may go over to someone unworthy of our toil (cf. chs. 2:18-21; 4:8; 5:12-16). It may even drive one to despair and to hatred of life (ch. 2:17, 20). But nothing is to be gained by brooding over life's limits. What is left is rejoicing at what one has to rejoice over: eating, drinking, the toil one is given to do, the wife with whom one lives, youth and vigor (cf. chs. 2:24-26; 3:12-13, 22; 5:17-19; 6:1-6 [negatively]; 9:7-10; 10:19; 11:7-10). It is useless to look either to the past or to the future. The past is forgotten (ch. 1:11), and the future cannot be possessed (ch. 3:22). We have the present, and there life makes sense or does not make sense. But it must also make sense in the light of the boundary that death

sets to human aspirations. " The living know that they will die,
but the dead know nothing." (Ch. 9:5.) " For if many years a
man should live, in all of them he should rejoice. But he should
remember the days of darkness — for they too will be many."
(Ch. 11:8.) "Remember your grave [10] in your youthful days,
before the unhappy days come, and the years reach you when
you will say, ' I have no pleasure in them.' " (Ch. 12:1.)

Secondly, it is axiomatic that distinctions are to be drawn in
this life between what is good and what is bad, between righteousness and wickedness, wisdom and folly. To be sure, " what is
good" (*tób*) sometimes means " what is to be enjoyed " (e.g.,
chs. 2:1; 3:13), and " what is bad " (*ra*ᶜ) often means " what is
unpleasant, unhappy " (e.g., chs. 1:13; 5:12, 15; 6:1). Likewise
Qoheleth enjoins:

> Do not be overly righteous,
> And do not be too terribly wise.
> Why should you cause yourself trouble?
> Do not be overly wicked,
> And do not be a fool.
> Why should you die when your time has not come?
>                               (Ch. 7:16-17.)

Even so, there is a difference between them. Wisdom is preferable
to folly (ch. 9:17). There are places where, expecting to find
justice and righteousness, we should be shocked to find wickedness (ch. 3:16), though we should not be surprised (ch. 5:7). It
is not amusing that the wicked are sometimes praised as if they
were righteous, and that men seem bent on doing what is bad
(ch. 8:10-12). Qoheleth finds it strange that " there are righteous
men who are treated according to the works of the wicked, and
there are wicked men who are treated according to the works
of the righteous " (v. 14). But he does not draw the conclusion

---

[10] Read *bórᵉkā* for MT *bórᵉkā*. The latter, " your creator," is very strange
coming from Qoheleth, and the context strongly suggests the emendation.

that nothing distinguishes righteousness from wickedness. Moral distinctions are to be drawn; that is so axiomatic that Qoheleth does not even ask or implicitly answer the question, "How do you know?"[11]

Thirdly, it is axiomatic that the circumstances of life come from God. Qoheleth does not argue the point; he states it. "There is nothing better for a man than that he should eat and drink and show himself a good time in his toil. I saw that this too comes from God's hand. For who can eat, and who can have pleasure, apart from him?" (Ch. 2:25-26.) That is God's "gift" (ch. 3:13). "For any man to whom God gives riches and property and makes him master of it, to eat of it and to take his lot and to have joy in his toil — that is God's gift." (Ch. 5:18.) "Consider the things God does. For who can straighten out what he has made crooked? In the day of prosperity, be happy. And in the day of unhappiness, consider: God has done both the one and the other, in order that man may not figure out anything after him." (Ch. 7:13-14.) The work of God has a certain inscrutability. Man cannot "figure it out" (cf. ch. 3:11). "The righteous and the wise and their works are in God's hand," but man is not certain whether this means love or hate (ch. 9:1). Qoheleth does not, then, set limits to the kind of life God may give man. Whatever a man has, he can thank (or blame) God for it. One may therefore justly use the term predestinarian of Qoheleth. "Every happening is predestined by God and takes place at the moment which he has appointed for it."[12] The famous passage in ch. 3:1-8 is usually taken as the schematic account of the divine determinism,[13] but I do not think that those

---

[11] Cf. Sheldon H. Blank, "Ecclesiastes," *IDB*, Vol. 2, p. 12. Rankin, *loc. cit.*, p. 33, interprets ch. 1:17 to mean that Qoheleth sought to determine the principles distinguishing wisdom from folly.

[12] Ginsberg, "Structure and Contents," p. 145.

[13] Cf., e.g., Friedrich Nötscher, *Kohelet* (Echter-Bibel, Echter-Verlag, Würzburg, 1954), p. 12. D. B. Macdonald makes a great deal of the idea, arguing that Qoheleth conceives of God as amoral, thus inculcating amorality in man. Cf. Macdonald, *op. cit.*, pp. 86–90. Cf. also Gordis, *Koheleth*, pp. 218–219.

verses mean that every event has been given its time beforehand. Rather, I interpret it to mean that there are times appropriate to all kinds of actions, and no kind of action may be excluded a priori as inappropriate. Hence neither side of any pair can overweigh the other, and all cancel each other out with regard to the determination of final meaning. "What profit [yithrôn] has the worker in what he has toiled over?" (V. 9.) That is the real question of the passage, and we shall return to it later.

Much more compelling to show Qoheleth's predestinarianism is ch. 6:10: "Whatever has been was named long ago, and its destiny was known." [14] Blank rightly points out that Qoheleth, like most predestinarians, adds to his affirmation of the divine control the exhortation to man to decide, as if man had the power of deciding.[15] That exhortation, indeed, sets off Biblical predestinarianism from determinism. For the determinist will assert the folly of human decision, will scorn and mock it; the predestinarian will not. God is in control, and man must decide about his own acts. One may argue, if he likes, that you cannot have both God's control and man's decisions. But in Qoheleth, as in the Bible generally, we do have both.

## VANITY

In view of this account of Qoheleth's axioms, we must now attend to the difficult saying that we may take as the book's motto:

> Vanity of vanities, says Qoheleth,
> Vanity of vanities, all is vanity.
> (Chs. 1:2; 12:8.)

[14] For this translation, cf. Mitchell J. Dahood, S.J., *Canaanite-Phoenician Influence in Qoheleth* (Pontificio Istituto Biblico, Rome, 1952), p. 40.
[15] "Ecclesiastes," *IDB*, Vol. 2, p. 12.

This motto seems to justify the assumption that Qoheleth has no stance in truth, that he looks resignedly on life as useless, as a mere vapor (which may be the etymological basis of the word *hebel,* " vanity "). If etymology were the last word, we could as well translate the motto, " A mere breath." Ginsberg thinks that the word means, in effect, " zero." [16] Macdonald translates it as " transitoriness or transitory." [17] Staples, connecting it with the Israelite view of Canaanite cultic rites, assumes that it refers to " incomprehensibility." [18] Nötscher says, " frail, nothing, without result," [19] Barton, " fruitless, ineffectual, unavailing." [20] Gordis thinks the basic meaning is " unsubstantial." [21]

We must not assume the word's meaning beforehand, but need to see how and where Qoheleth uses it. He uses words with meanings peculiar to himself. The fact that Third Isaiah can use *hebel* to mean a " vapor " (Isa. 57:13) does not mean that Qoheleth must do so.

Let us note what Qoheleth describes by the word *hebel.* " All the deeds that are done beneath the sun " are *hebel* (ch. 1:14). More specifically, " all my deeds which my hands have done and my toil at which I toiled " are *hebel* (ch. 2:11; cf. v. 17). But those deeds and that toil are *hebel* because " I must set it by for the man who will succeed me. And who knows whether he will be a wise man or a fool? Yet he will lord it over all my toil for which I toiled and used my wisdom beneath the sun. This too is *hebel* " (ch. 2:18-19; cf. v. 21). It is also *hebel* that " to the man

[16] *Loc. cit.,* p. 138.

[17] *Op. cit.,* Ch. V, *passim.* Cf. also A. D. Powers, *Ecclesiastes, or The Preacher* (Longmans, Green & Co., Ltd., London, 1952), pp. 144–145.

[18] W. E. Staples, "The 'Vanity' of Ecclesiastes," *JNES,* Vol. 2 (1943), pp. 95–104. Staples takes the term $r^{e'}\hat{u}th$ $r\hat{u}^{a}ch,$ " striving after wind," not as synonymous with *hebel* but as complementary to it, " the striving of (or by) spirit," which drives man on despite the " incomprehensibility " of all things.

[19] *Op. cit.,* p. 7.

[20] G. A. Barton, *A Critical and Exegetical Commentary on the Book of Ecclesiastes* (ICC, Charles Scribner's Sons, 1908), p. 72.

[21] *Koheleth,* p. 195.

who is good in [God's] sight he gives wisdom and knowledge and joy. But to the sinner he gives the business of gathering and collecting, only to give it to the one who is good in God's sight " (v. 26). Hence, the whole of toil and its restlessness are *hebel* (v. 23). The man who toils unremittingly without an heir, never asking himself for whom he is working, is *hebel* (ch. 4:7-8), as is the fact that toil and skill derive from a man's jealousy of his fellow (v. 4).

Pleasure too is *hebel* because it accomplishes nothing (ch. 2:1). But it is also *hebel* that a man who has all that heart could desire never has pleasure from it, but someone else does (ch. 6:2). Yet he fails to enjoy it for another reason:

> The lover of money
> Is not satisfied with money,
> Nor is he who is in love with wealth
> Satisfied with profits.
> That too is *hebel*.
>
> (Ch. 5:9.)

There is even *hebel* connected with wisdom:

And I saw that there is an advantage to wisdom over folly just as there is an advantage to light over darkness. The wise man's eyes are in his head, but the fool walks in darkness. But I also know that one destiny befalls them all. And I said to myself, " What befalls the fool will also befall me. So why have I been so extremely wise? " And I told myself that this too is *hebel*. (Ch. 2:13-15.)

When death enters the picture, the apparent advantage of wisdom over folly turns out to be an illusion. " For what is the wise man's advantage over the fool? And what the poor man's who knows how to walk in life? Better the eye's sight than the soul's [or

desire's] wandering. That too is *hebel* and a regard for wind."
(Ch. 6:8-9.) Yet wisdom is better than folly; the "poor and wise
youth" is preferred to the "old and foolish king." "And that
too is *hebel* and a regard for wind." (Ch. 4:13-16.) [22] At the same
time, "man's advantage over the beast is nil," for they have "the
same spirit" and come to "the same destiny." That too is *hebel*.
"All go to the same place. All have come out of dust, and all return to dust." (Ch. 3:19-20; cf. Gen. 3:19.) We seem to have the
same sentiment, referring only to man's destiny, in ch. 9:2, if we
read *hebel* for MT's *hakkôl*, "all of it": "*Hebel* it is, that one
destiny comes to all, to righteous and wicked alike," etc.

Clearly *hebel* is connected with the question whether man or
some group of men have any profit or advantage (*yithrôn* or
*yôthēr*). The difficult passage in ch. 6:10-11 suggests this:

Whatever has been was named long ago, and its destiny was
known.[23] Man is not competent to plead a case with him who is
mightier than he. For the more words, the more *hebel*, and what
advantage [*yôthēr*] is that to man?

In trying to overcome the scheme of things, man multiplies *hebel*
and increases words: "For in many dreams there are also *hebels*,
and words increase. But you fear God." (Ch. 5:7 [Heb., ch. 5:6].)
To increase words is to find *hebel*, as the fool does (cf. ch. 5:2).
Dreams, then, like the "soul's wandering" (ch. 6:9), come out
to *hebel*. "For God is in heaven and you on earth. Therefore
make your words few." (Ch. 5:2 [Heb., ch. 5:1].)

Qoheleth points also to the *hebel* involved in moral perception:

There is a *hebel* that occurs on earth, namely, that there are
righteous men who are treated according to the works of the

[22] I accept the interpretation of this passage suggested by William A. Irwin,
"Ecclesiastes 4:13-16," *JNES*, Vol. 3 (1944), pp. 255–257.

[23] Cf. Dahood, *op. cit.*, p. 40, reading *'ashrēhû* for MT *'ªsher hû'*. *'Ādām* is
therefore to be taken with the next sentence.

wicked, and there are wicked men who are treated according to the works of the righteous. I said that that too is *hebel*. (Ch. 8:14.)

One might not expect, and surely would not hope, that that would happen. But it does happen, and it is twice called *hebel*. Similar to it is the difficult passage preceding it:

And then I considered wicked men buried; they had come in and gone out of the holy place, and were even praised in the city where they had acted so. That too is *hebel*. Because the sentence on evil deeds is not executed quickly, men's sons fill their minds with the doing of such deeds, because a sinner can do evil a hundred times and still prolong his life. (Ch. 8:10-12.)

The passage is textually difficult, though some such sense as that can be made of it. The *hebel* seems to point to the incongruity of act and public reaction. Going deeper in the same direction, but more like ch. 8:14, is ch. 7:15:

I have considered all this in my days of *hebel*: there is a righteous man who perishes because of his righteousness, and there is a wicked man who prolongs his life because of his wickedness.

This is followed by the advice not to indulge in too much wisdom or in too much wickedness (ch. 7:16-17).

In ch. 7:6c, it is difficult to know the referent of *hebel*. It follows a list of pairs in which one is " better than " the other. Perhaps *hebel* refers to the entire list, or perhaps it refers only to the first part of v. 6, or perhaps to the last saying, vs. 5-6. It is possible, on the other hand, that *hebel* refers not to what precedes it but to what follows in v. 7, or in vs. 7-8. In that case, we should have to take *kî* in v. 7 to mean " that," as a relative adjective, rather than " because ": [24]

[24] So A. Lukyn Williams, *Ecclesiastes* (CB, Cambridge University Press, Cambridge, 1922), p. 76. Gordis, *Koheleth,* pp. 259–261, takes *kî* to refer to what follows, but understands " this " (*zeh*) to refer back to " the wise man's reproof," v. 5. That seems to me impossible.

And this too is *hebel*,
That oppression makes a wise man mad,
And a bribe destroys the heart.

Qoheleth refers to *hebel* twice in his advice in ch. 11:

For if many years
A man should live,
In all of them he should rejoice.
But he should remember the days of darkness,
For they will be many —
All that comes is *hebel*.
Rejoice, young fellow, in your youth,
And be cheerful of heart in your young manhood.
And go as your heart directs you
And with the sight of your eyes.[25]
But put vexation away from your heart,
And put away sadness from your flesh,
Though youth and its black hair alike are *hebel*.

(Ch. 11:8-10.)

The youth is to " rejoice " in spite of the *hebel* of what is coming and of youth itself. We meet the same theme elsewhere in the book, for example, in ch. 9:9: " Enjoy life with your wife (if *r$^e$'ēh* means " enjoy " and not " consider ") whom you love all the days of your life of *hebel*," because that is " your portion." On the other hand,

Who knows what is good for man in life, the sum of the days of his life of *hebel*, which he accomplishes like a shadow, so that who can tell what will happen next beneath the sun? (Ch. 6:12.)

Life can be referred to in general as " a life of *hebel*" (cf. ch. 7:15), and that may be meant by the obscure saying that a prema-

[25] With some uncertainty, I conclude that the sentence following (" But know that for all these things God will bring you to judgment ") is a marginal gloss.

ture fetus " comes into *hebel* [or " in *hebel* "] and goes into darkness " (ch. 6:4).

The problem, then, is, what does *hebel* mean? Apart from general remarks like " all that comes is *hebel*," the references to life as *hebel*, and the book's motto, " all is *hebel*," the word is used to point out incongruities. It is incongruous that a man's work may go for the advantage of someone he does not know who has not done the work. It is incongruous that wise and fool, good and bad, pious and impious, come to the same destiny. It is incongruous that the righteous and the wicked are treated as if they were the opposite, that the wicked should be praised for doing badly. It is incongruous that a man toils merely to keep up with the Joneses. It is incongruous that, although rejoicing is the best thing for man to do, it accomplishes nothing. It is incongruous that man should foolishly multiply his dreams and his babblings before God. The whole of life, the motto says, is a tissue of incongruity.

That is, Qoheleth uses the term *hebel* to mean something very close to " irony " and " ironic." Wherever he uses it, the subject is treated ironically. Labor and the acquisition of goods are ironic because no man can know the future, and therefore he cannot know for whose benefit he is toiling. The piling up of wealth is ironic because nobody is ever satisfied with his pile but wants a bigger one. The sinner's toil is ironic because it goes to enrich the pious man. Wisdom is ironic because it lacks the power to alter a man's final fate, even though for the time it may preserve him alive.

That these are " vanities " does not mean that Qoheleth rejects the whole. He is engaged in pointing out the incongruities because only when the incongruities are perceived, only when the ironies of life are felt, can life have any integrity. The significance of life, whatever it may be, must be found in life. But the discovery will be possible only if we look at life without clouds of darkness over our eyes. "Better is the sight of the eyes than the soul's wandering." (Ch. 6:9.)

## BUSINESS AND PLEASURE

Dahood makes the intriguing observation, which he does not work out, that the book's vocabulary is shot through with commercial terminology.[26] Most of the key terms are in the list: "advantage or profit" (*yithrôn, yôthēr,* and *môthār*), "toil" (*'āmāl*), "occupation, business" (*'inyān*), "money" (*keseph*), "portion" (*chēleq*), "success" (*kishrôn*), "riches" (*'ôsher*), "owner" (*ba'al*), "lack, deficit" (*chesrôn*), etc. "The overall picture delineated by Ecclesiastes suggests a distinctly commercial environment."[27]

We have seen that many of the ironic "vanities" to which Qoheleth draws attention are commercial in character. The toil (*'āmāl*) at which men labor produces all kinds of incongruities (chs. 2:11, 17-26; 4:7-8). It is ironic that the capitalist is never satisfied with his capital (ch. 5:9). Vanities are also characteristic of wisdom, for although wisdom would seem to show an advantage (*yithrôn*) over folly, the wise and the fool come to the same end (ch. 2:13-16).

I suggest that Qoheleth is musing upon a society dominated by commerce, an acquisitive society that sees the meaning of man's life in his assertive achievement. But Qoheleth is very dubious about this philosophy. "What profit has man from all his toil at which he toils beneath the sun?" (Ch. 1:3.) "And then I turned to all the deeds my hands had done and to the toil I had given to do them. And behold, all that was vanity and a regard for wind, and there is no profit beneath the sun." (Ch. 2:11.) "What profit has the worker in what he toiled over?" (Ch. 3:9.) "And I looked at all the toil and all the skill of work,

[26] *Canaanite-Phoenician Influence,* pp. 52–53.      [27] *Ibid.*

but this is a man's jealousy of his fellow. And that too is vanity and a regard for wind." (Ch. 4:4.) "The lover of money is not satisfied with money; nor is he who is in love with wealth satisfied with profit. That too is vanity." (Ch. 5:10.) It is not that Qoheleth speaks only of business and commerce. But he takes especial aim at those constellations of commonly held values in a primarily commercial society. And he is, if not thoroughly disillusioned, at least concerned to dispel many illusions about life.

Qoheleth's irony is directed first of all at that extension of commercial values to cosmic validity which seems to characterize the acquisitive society. When he speaks in the first person, he uses this rhetorical fiction not to mean that he himself has gone through it all but to point to what is obvious to anyone who reflects upon it. He describes, for example, the "compleat capitalist":

I did great works: I built me houses, I planted me vineyards. I made me gardens and parks, and I planted all kinds of fruit trees in them. I made me pools of water with which to irrigate the forest that sprouted trees. I bought slaves and maids, and some were born in my house. I also had great holdings of cattle and flocks, more than all who preceded me in Jerusalem. I collected me silver and gold and a kingly treasury and provinces. I got me singers, men and women, and those delights of men's sons, one lover after another.[28] And I was great; I surpassed all who preceded me in Jerusalem. Yes, my wisdom stood by me. And anything my eyes requested I did not withhold from them. I did not hold back my heart from any pleasure, but my heart was pleased by all my toil. And that was my reward from all my toil. But then I turned to all the deeds my hands had done and to the toil I had given to do them. And behold, all that was vanity and a regard for wind, and there is no profit beneath the sun. (Ch. 2:4-11.)

[28] The last phrase is hypothetically translated.

The reason there is no profit is clear: "Because I must set it by for the man who will succeed me. And who knows whether he will be a wise man or a fool? Yet he will lord it over all my toil for which I toiled and used my wisdom beneath the sun. This too is vanity" (vs. 18-19). A man gives himself to the strain and grief of business, piling up the profits that go finally to someone else (vs. 21-23). Death evens out the balance sheet, and there is no profit, no ultimate gain. "Just as he came out of his mother's womb, he shall return, naked as he came, with nothing to show for his toil which he can take in his hand." (Ch. 5:14.) Even a premature fetus is to be preferred, for a fetus is at least delivered from the frustration of failing to profit (ch. 6:2-6).

Time too cancels out profit. "For everything there is a time, a proper time for every enterprise under heaven." (Ch. 3:1.) There follows the famous list of pairs, often interpreted to mean a determinism of inexorable law. "Everything occurs when it must occur. . . . Man is not a free agent. He is not master even of his life within." [29] I argued before that this is not the point of the passage, that the key to it is the question following: "What profit [yithrôn] has the worker in what he has toiled over?" (v. 9). Man's actions add up to nothing, each balanced by one from the other side. Hence, ironically, as man acts responsibly with the deed appropriate to every present moment, he ensures that he does not come out ahead. "I turned then and considered beneath the sun, that the race is not to the swift nor the battle to the heroes nor bread to the wise nor wealth to the competent nor favor to the knowledgeable. But time and chance befall them all." (Ch. 9:11.)

It is useless, then, to look for profit in life. There is none. That is not the way the world spins. The meaning of life is not to be found in a ledger, because everyone finally goes to the same place (chs. 3:20; 9:2-6, 11-12). Death writes "Canceled" over the

---

[29] Rankin, loc. cit., p. 44.

entire transaction. The search for profit is finally man's effort to
establish himself, to assert his own meaning, to wrest something
by and for himself out of life. But it comes to nought. " All of
a man's toil is for his mouth, but he does not even fill his belly."
(Ch. 6:7.) [30] And, not troubling with picayunish consistency:
" Sweet is the sleep of the hireling, whether he eats little or much.
But the rich has too full a belly; it lets him get no sleep."
(Ch. 5:11.)

Death, then, means that "the advantage man has over the
beast is nil" (ch. 3:19). What a man has sought to secure for
himself is wiped out, " for there is neither deed nor device, neither
knowledge nor wisdom, in Sheol, to which you are going "
(ch. 9:10). There may, of course, be a relative aid in gregarious-
ness. " Two are better than one, for they get a good return for
their toil." (Ch. 4:9.) But it is only relative: " A three-strand cord
will not quickly be broken " (v. 12).

When Qoheleth argues the absence of *yithrôn* (" profit ") from
the world, he is not presuming cynically that the world is meaningless, but is standing on the axiom we noted before, that the
circumstances of life come from God. If *yithrôn* were available
to man, he could fashion his own meaning, could assert himself,
could come to the end satisfied that he had " made it." But precisely that Qoheleth denies. He works over the incongruities of
the profit motivation in order to demonstrate the irony of men's
projecting their commercialism onto the meaning of life.

What, then, is the point of being wise? Though Qoheleth
claims great wisdom, still using his first-person rhetorical fiction,
he comes finally to an ironic conclusion. " What befalls the fool
will also befall me. So why have I been so extremely wise? And
I told myself that this too is vanity." (Ch. 2:15.) " For what is
the wise man's advantage [*yôthēr*] over the fool? And what the

[30] The sardonic irony of this verse leads me to disagree with Rankin, *loc. cit.*,
p. 62, who thinks that it is a gloss.

poor man's who knows how to conduct himself in life?" (Ch. 6:8.) [31] The answer is ambiguous: "Better is the eye's sight [or perhaps "enjoyment"] than the soul's wandering. That too is vanity and a regard for wind" (v. 9). Whatever the precise meaning of the cryptic remark about eye and soul, the net result seems to be the ironic one that the wise man finally has no noticeable *yôthēr* over the fool. And wisdom is difficult, if not impossible, of attainment. "I said, 'I will be wise.' But that was far from me. Distant is that which has been, and deep, deep indeed. Who can figure it out?" (Ch. 7:23-24.) [32]

When I set my mind on knowledge and wisdom, and on consideration of the business that occurs on earth, that neither night nor day do one's eyes see sleep, then I considered all the work of God, that man is not able to figure out the happenings that occur beneath the sun, on account of the fact that man toils to seek, but he cannot figure it out. And even if a wise man says that he knows, he is unable to figure it out. (Ch. 8:16-17.)

Life simply does not turn out as man would fashion it.

To be sure, there is relative value in wisdom. "Better a poor and wise youth than an old and foolish king who still does not know enough to take advice." (Ch. 4:13.) "The wise man's eyes are in his head, and the fool walks in darkness." (Ch. 2:14.) "Wisdom strengthens the wise man more than ten rulers who are in the city." (Ch. 7:19.) When the king commands something potentially unpleasant, "the wise man's heart knows the right time and the proper procedure" (ch. 8:5), that is, the right way to go about the matter with the least possible unhappi-

[31] The second clause could be translated: "And what the poor man's? He knows how to conduct himself in life [or before the living]."

[32] Qoheleth uses the verb *mātsā'*, "to find," to mean intellectual penetration, mental discovery of truth or insight. Cf. its uses in chs. 3:11; 7:14, 27-29; 8:17; 9:15; 11:1. The occurrence in ch. 12:10 is different, but that is in the secondary epilogue.

ness.[33] The story of the poor wise man who delivered the little town from siege by his wisdom is a " great " example of wisdom. As might be expected, no one appreciated the man, " but I said, ' Wisdom is better than heroism, though the poor man's wisdom be despised and no one listen to his words ' " (ch. 9:13-16). " The words of the wise, listened to in quiet, are to be preferred to the bellowing of a ruler among fools." (V. 17.) " Wisdom is advantageous toward success," Qoheleth says (ch. 10:10), referring ironically to the fact that if one will bother to sharpen his ax, chopping wood will not exhaust his weary muscles.

But the relative value of wisdom does not assure success, as the story of the poor wise man and the siege shows (ch. 9:13-15). " There is no memory of the wise man or of the fool for very long, for in the coming days all of it will be forgotten." (Ch. 2:16.) Being " too terribly wise " may cause " trouble " (ch. 7:16). The wise, with the righteous, are in God's hand, but " whether love or hate, no man knows all that is ahead of them " (ch. 9:1). And wisdom is by no means invincible. " Wisdom is better than weapons of war, but one sinner can overcome much good. Dead flies make the perfumer's oil stink; a little folly is costlier than wisdom and honor." (Chs. 9:18 to 10:1.) And the acquisition of wisdom has its ironic twist. " For in much wisdom is much grief; when one increases knowledge, he increases sorrow." (Ch. 1:18.)

The irony of wisdom is that it may turn into a means of man's attempted self-assertion. Qoheleth's continual pricking of wisdom's bubble, his ironic tone in laying bare its limitations, can only mean that he is speaking to those who expect wisdom to provide the certainties of life and the means of power. But ignorance is much more pervasive in life, Qoheleth argues, than knowledge. And knowledge, taken seriously, produces still more ignorance.

[33] For the translation of *mishpāṭ* as " proper procedure," see William A. Irwin, " Ecclesiastes 8:2-9," *JNES*, Vol. 4 (1945), pp. 130–131.

I turned my mind to knowledge, to penetrate and seek out wisdom and logic,[34] and to know the wickedness of foolishness and the folly that leads to madness.[35] And I came up with this [gravely limited conclusion]: more bitter than death is the woman whose heart is nets and snares, her hands fetters. He who pleases God escapes from her, but the sinner is caught by her. "Consider this that I figured out," says Qoheleth, "putting one and one together to figure out the logic which my soul has sought again and again, but I could not figure it out. One man out of a thousand I figured out, but not a single woman among them all could I figure out. Consider this alone, which I did figure out: that God has treated man uprightly, but they have sought out many dodges." [36] (Ch. 7:25-29.)

In that last verse, frequently analyzed as a gloss,[37] is a central key to Qoheleth's point. For here the basic axioms come together. Every man must find the meaning of his life within that life, not beyond it. Distinctions are to be drawn in life between what is good and bad, what is wise and foolish, what is righteous and wicked. And, keystone of all, the circumstances of life come from God. Those who are not prepared to admit the last point Qoheleth deftly skewers on the point of his irony. For if men refuse the third axiom, if they "seek out many dodges," they are doomed with regard to the first two. In affecting to ignore and escape God's "upright" treatment of them, they bypass the

[34] I translate *cheshbôn* so with some trepidation. It means, perhaps, "device, scheme," and in the context of intellectuality here, "logic," if not taken in a technical sense, seems as good a rendering as any.

[35] Rankin, *loc. cit.*, p. 68, translates this: "to know that wickedness is foolishness and folly is madness."

[36] In *chishsheᵇbônôth*, "dodges, devices," is a wordplay on *cheshbôn*, "scheme, logic," which emphasizes the irony of this remark. The "dodges" are a ludicrous substitute for "logic." I translate the verb *'āśāh* "to treat, deal with," which it often means in the Old Testament, because Qoheleth never uses it of God's creative power. The apparent exception in ch. 3:11 actually means "to do, make happen" (cf. Ginsberg, "Structure and Contents," p. 140).

[37] Cf. Rankin, *loc. cit.*, p. 68.

possibility of life's meaning and the perception of the necessary distinctions.

To be sure, Qoheleth confesses ignorance about the quality of the divine sovereignty. No one knows whether it means hate or love (ch. 9:1), though it involves both prosperity and unhappiness (ch. 7:14). The "times and occasions" through which men pass consistently evince this duality (ch. 3:1-8). But this is not merely whimsy or blind destiny. " [God] has done it all as lovely in its time." (V. 11a.) God is not blind; man is. " But he has put ignorance into [men's] hearts, so that man cannot figure out the deed which God has done from beginning to end." (V. 11b.) [38] Neither man's wisdom nor his toil can overcome the fundamental fact of life, that all depends on God. Qoheleth is well aware of the anguish this can cause (cf. chs. 2:17-18; 4:2-3). Man far prefers to be master of his own destiny, but for Qoheleth death, the ineluctable, makes that ironically impossible.

But his solution is neither resignation nor the descent into fatalism. Relative goods are to be found in wisdom, in keeping the eyes open. But the good that he enjoins on men again and again, in a constant refrain, is to live life as it comes *in joy*. "There is nothing better for man than that he eat and drink and show his soul good in his toil. This too, I saw, for it comes from God's hand. For who can eat, and who can have pleasure, apart from him?" (Ch. 2:24-25.) "I know that nothing is good for [man] except to rejoice [*liśmóªch*] and to do what is good in his life. And moreover, all of those who eat and drink and see what is good in all their toil — that too is God's gift." (Ch. 3:12-13.) "Behold, what I myself have seen to be good, that is, lovely, is to eat and drink and see the good in all one's toil at which he toils beneath the sun his whole life long, however

---

[38] Repointing *'elem* for *'ólām*, meaning "hiddenness, obscurity, ignorance, forgetfulness." Cf. Rankin, *loc. cit.*, pp. 46–48, for full consideration of the alternatives.

much God gives him, for that is his lot. For any man to whom God gives riches and property and makes him master of it, to eat of it and to take his lot and to have joy in his toil — that is God's gift." (Ch. 5:17-18; cf. the negative example in ch. 6:1-6.) The remark following may, to be sure, sound a mildly ironic note: "For he does not much recall the days of his life, because God occupies him with his heart's joy." (Ch. 5:19.) That would suggest that God keeps a man sufficiently content not to remember the bad times. The verb "to recall" (*zākar*) might, however, be interpreted to mean "to brood over, to dwell on." Man's "heart's joy," then, is of enough more importance than anything else that he wastes no effort brooding over what he can do nothing about.

This constant harping on joy preserves Qoheleth's injunctions from mere resignation, a mere *carpe diem*. Rather, he urges the potentially positive in a present life that has its boundaries.

And I lauded rejoicing, because there is no good for man beneath the sun except to eat and to drink and to rejoice, for that will attend him in his toil all the days of his life that God has given beneath the sun. (Ch. 8:15.)

We could take that to mean that man has a very limited good ("there is no good except . . ."), or we could take it as an ironic understatement, in which "to rejoice" carries a far more positive meaning than the hedonistic "to enjoy yourself."

Go, eat your bread with joy and drink your wine with a merry heart. For God has already approved your doing that.[39] Let your

---

[39] The sentence is usually translated, "For God has already approved what you do," and is interpreted as sheer determinism. I cannot agree to that interpretation, partly because of the references already cited to God's giving eating and rejoicing, which intimate that those are things which God approves, partly because Qoheleth never seems to me to say that God approves of whatever one does. I cannot, therefore, accept D. B. Macdonald's delineation of the divine and human "amorality" in Qoheleth.

clothing be white for every occasion, and do not stint with the oil on your head. Consider [40] the life with the wife whom you love all the days of your vain life which he [God] has given you beneath the sun, for that is your portion in life and in your toil at which you toil beneath the sun. Whatever your hand finds to do, do it with all your strength, for there is neither deed nor device, neither knowledge nor wisdom in Sheol, to which you are going. (Ch. 9:7-10.)

The clear boundaries of life express not the grim limits within which man functions but the importance of making the most of significance in this life where alone meaning is to be found. God has given his gifts, indeed, not that man may feel frustrated with them but that he may have joy in them. Gordis is emphatically right: " For Koheleth, joy is God's categorical imperative for man, not in any anemic or spiritualized sense, but rather as a full-blooded and tangible experience, expressing itself in the play of the body and the activity of the mind, the contemplation of nature and the pleasures of love." [41]

A man must, of course, bear in mind that life is not endless. " The wise man's mind is on the house of mourning, but the fool's mind is on the house of rejoicing." (Ch. 7:4; cf. v. 2.) That would seem to suggest that the wise man refrains from rejoicing. But Qoheleth is speaking here about the differentiation between wise man and fool, a differentiation that, in the long view of the book, is of a limited value. We have seen above that the joy men are to have is set in the context of the death that puts a stop to it all. Fools do not understand the boundary in their joy. Hence it is " better to go to a house of mourning than to go to a house where they are feasting. For the former has to do with

---

[40] The verb *rā'āh*, ordinarily " to see," is taken by many scholars both here and in several other passages to mean " enjoy." If that is a valid interpretation, it adds weight to my argument, but I am not certain enough of it to put any emphasis on it.

[41] *Koheleth*, p. 119.

every man's boundary, and the living may take it to heart " (v. 2).
The irony, then, is that the joy proper to man, the joy God gives
to lend significance to life, must have its ingredient of sorrow.

> And sweet is the light
> And pleasant to the eyes
> To see the sun.
> For if many years
> A man should live,
> In all of them he should rejoice.
> But he should remember the days of darkness,
> For they too will be many —
> All that comes is vanity.
> Rejoice, young fellow, in your youth,
> And be cheerful-hearted in your young manhood.
> And do as your heart directs you
> And with the sight of your eyes.
> And put vexation away from your heart
> And put sadness away from your flesh,
> Though youth and its black hair alike are vanity.[42]
> Remember your grave in your youthful days,
> Before the unhappy days come,
> And the years reach you when you will say,
> " I have no pleasure in them."
>
> (Chs. 11:7 to 12:1.)

There follows the magnificent, moving, and melancholy sketch
of the day of death (vs. 3-7), a passage sufficiently obscure to
exercise Old Testament exegetes for many decades to come. But
the thrust of the whole is clear. The meaning available to man
will be found in life, and it must come before the onslaught of

---

[42] The word is usually translated " dawn " and interpreted as " the dawn of
life." Etymology might, paradoxically, suggest something to do with blackness,
and Hertzberg first suggested the color of hair as a symbolic description of youth
(cf. Rankin, *loc. cit.*, p. 83).

death's final victory. Here, perhaps more clearly than in any other passage, Qoheleth suggests wherein life's meaning lies: in rejoicing in the years God gives. Those years are full of vanities, incongruities, ironies. But the incongruities to which Qoheleth so sharply points are not incompatible with the joy that is his constant exhortation.

Within that joy, everything else has its place. The joy " attends you " in toil. It makes relative wisdom useful. It renders the puzzles of life bearable. Since God has given joy, the efforts of man to make his own way are quite useless, vain, incongruous. There is no " profit." Man cannot expect that, nor can he wrest it out of life. Indeed, he can exact nothing of life. What is important, what is alone available, God gives. For that, joy is sufficient. The secrets of the universe may remain hidden. The effort to penetrate the future may be abandoned. No one but God knows either the secrets of the universe or the contents of the future.

It is man's " portion " to accept what God gives him with a joyful heart. God, after all, is not to be trifled with.

Guard your steps when you go to God's house. And approach him to listen, rather than setting fools to sacrificing. For none of them know they are doing evil.[43] Do not be hasty with your mouth nor in a hurry in your heart to bring out a matter before God. For God is in heaven, and you are on earth. Therefore, make your words few. "(Chs. 4:17 to 5:1.)

Man's position before God carries that necessary, restraining irony. Only the fool, the man who thinks he can make his own way in life, will hold lengthy discourses with God. He who knows what life is all about is prepared to accept his subordinate status.

---

[43] The sentence is very obscure. As it stands, this is the only way I can find to translate it, for " they do not know how to do evil " seems strained. Is he rejecting the whole cultic machinery? That would be by no means impossible.

The book is not a systematic or complete presentation of a theology, a philosophy, an ethic, a way of life. The large gaps that remain, Qoheleth's sardonic wit might have filled delightfully, but we must leave them blank. He was clearly addressing a society possessed by many of the commercial values that our own has in such abundance, and his reactions perhaps combine some of the best traits of an H. L. Mencken and a Harry Golden. One could wish that he had said more about the religion of his day.

Whatever the shortcomings of his thoughts, Qoheleth stands firmly on a comprehension of truth. Certainly it is not the whole truth; neither is it a rejection of truth. We can too easily be misled by his ironic rejection of his own day's commonplaces into thinking that he saw life very darkly indeed. But he had his eyes in his head. And he saw how useless it is to try to " straighten out what [God] has made crooked " (ch. 7:13).

# VII

## JOB:

## THE IRONY OF RECONCILIATION

The chief enemy of faith in the Old Testament is magic. By magic is meant not the entertaining sleight-of-hand tricks " magicians " do, but the occult power that previous ages took with the utmost seriousness. This is the magic of the horoscope, of the witchcraft hysteria of Salem, the magic black and white of which the late Charles Williams wrote so splendidly in his novels.[1] Magic, the virtual structure of life in the ancient Near East, assumes that a vast blind source of power awaits utilization to fulfill man's desires. When the correct formula is uttered or acted, the power source, which has no motive mechanism in itself, is stirred into the desired action. At the bottom of magic, then, is the very powerful assumption that man has a way to ensure his own success in life.

The magical assumption has always pervaded human life. It lies behind the fertility rites of the ancient world, in which the fulfillment of the correct formulas in word and act was thought to ensure fertility in the ensuing year for soil, beast, and man alike. It lies under all superstitions that assume the right deed at the right moment, or the wrong deed at the right moment,

[1] Cf. such novels as *Descent Into Hell, The Place of the Lion, All Hallows' Eve,* and *War in Heaven.* Williams also wrote a superb study of black magic, *Witchcraft* (Faber and Faber, London, 1941; republished by Meridian Books, The World Publishing Co., 1959).

will inexorably be followed by results good or bad. Permit a black cat to cross your path, and the grinding process of bad luck is set in train. The magical assumption lies, furthermore, behind the conception that man's ultimate relationship with God in salvation or damnation is determined by what man does, thinks, and says. This is the " Judaizing " that Paul opposed under the name " justification by works of the law," the Pelagian doctrine against which Saint Augustine fought, the doctrine of indulgences against which Martin Luther and John Calvin revolted. For the magical approach to man's relationship with God asserts, explicitly or implicitly, that in the last analysis man has the upper hand over God. Man can by his excellence require God to save and accept him or by his unworthiness require God to damn and reject him. The pursuit of moral or theological excellence can be as magical as any voodoo rite of sticking pins into the image of an enemy, and it can be accompanied by an assumption every bit as rigid as the witch doctor's that the cause will inevitably produce the effect. Exalted morality, pursued with the expectation of reward (" honesty is the best policy "), is magic, just as is the Baalist's orgy. The desired effects are different; the methods are not.

Magic, however crude or exalted the language of its rationalization, is the method of life that most threatened Old Testament faith. The issue between them is clear: magic is focused on man's self-fulfillment, faith on the will of God. Not only the external force of Baalism, which so pervaded the preexilic period and exercised its prophets, but also and equally very powerful tendencies within Old Testament thinking were always threatening faith's degeneration into magic. Against such tendencies, perhaps actually dominant in his age, the author of The Book of Job protests. The issue of The Book of Job is *faith,* the true and proper relationship between man and God. We could say that the book shows Job's movement from a position of magical dogmatism to his ultimate stance in faith.

Uncomplicated as this account may sound, The Book of Job is by no means simple. Its author has been called the most learned man known to us from the Old Testament. The learning is so fluent, so lightly borne, that we might continue unaware of it. Yet it lends the subtlety, the complexity, the richness of image and color to the book that makes it so perpetually unfathomable and yet so productive of new depths of understanding. But I cannot agree with those who argue that the purpose of the book is to deepen the mystery of life and of God. In one sense this is so, since the poet insists on maintaining the deity of God and the humanity of man. But in the sense that the poet intends to overwhelm Job at the end with the divine inscrutability, to render God utterly unintelligible to man, the argument is unacceptable. Inscrutable God is, at the end as throughout the book. But finally he is inscrutable in a new way, for Job is now reconciled to him, thoroughly trustful of him as he never was before. Job explicitly repudiates the idea that this is blind faith in the face of impenetrable mystery:

> With ear's hearing I had heard of you.
> But now my eyes see you.
>
> (Ch. 42:5.)

A certain self-irony is in the statement, which marks the final turning of Job's mind from the magical assumption to the assumption of faith. Job has, of course, fallen away from the full magical assumption long before this, but only now has he a satisfactory alternative to it. He has realized before that the magical assumption made no sense of the world, but no other supposition served him better. Now, however, Job has decisively entered the ranks of faith.

This we must show in detail as we study the book's structure

in terms of its irony. To understand The Book of Job, we need
to study the persons of the drama.[2] For the book is a long discussion, unpunctuated by action of any kind, save only in the
prose tale of the first two and the last chapters. We must first
look at the friends, including Elihu,[3] as exemplars of a certain
irony regarding Job. We shall then consider Job's speeches within
the dialogue with the friends (chs. 3 to 31), for the several directions of his irony. Then we must investigate the irony of God,
as it appears in the interchange between God and Job in the
book's denouement (chs. 38:1 to 42:6). Throughout we must
have in mind the irony of the poet, the artificer of the whole
affair.

To be sure, the poet is not the author of the tale in the first
two chapters and the latter part of the last (ch. 42:7-17), nor did
he write the speeches of Elihu (chs. 32 to 37). The hymnlike
praise of wisdom in ch. 28 breaks into the discussion strangely,
though Terrien argues that although this poem does not belong
to the book itself, it was written by the same poet responsible
for the major portion of the book.[4] Certainly the poet was not
responsible for the confusion introduced into the third cycle of
speeches by the complete elimination of Zophar's final speech,
the truncation of Bildad's third speech, and probably the shifting
of material from both of those speeches to the mouth of Job (cf.
chs. 24:13-24; 27:7-10, 13-23, perhaps to be assigned to Zophar;
ch. 26:5-14, probably to be assigned to Bildad). We cannot be

---

[2] I use the word "drama" loosely, not in the more technical sense in which,
e.g., Horace M. Kallen uses it in *The Book of Job as a Greek Tragedy* (Moffat,
Yard & Co., 1918), or into which Archibald MacLeish has turned it in *J.B.*
(Houghton Mifflin Company, 1957). I may add that, in my opinion, *J.B.*, no
matter how fine a play it may be, has completely missed the point of The Book of
Job.

[3] The speeches of Elihu, chs. 32 to 37, are held by practically all scholars to
be interpolated.

[4] Samuel Terrien, "The Book of Job," *IB*, Vol. 3 (Abingdon Press, 1954),
pp. 888, 1099–1100. Cf. also Terrien's *Job: Poet of Existence* (The Bobbs-Merrill
Company, Inc., 1957), pp. 172–173.

certain why these transpositions and distortions have taken place. We may conjecture, but without possibility of demonstration, that the poet brought Job to heights of blasphemy even beyond those he had reached before, and that pious readers and copyists disarranged the material to remove the offense.

## The Friends: The Irony of the Healthy

Our poet has a satirical purpose in the implicit portraits of Job's three friends. By all they say, they represent the unquestioning orthodoxy that the poet profoundly calls into question. United in their assessment of Job's situation, the friends parrot each other's words from time to time, as if the three were one and interchangeable (cf., e.g., the intertwining images of darkness, fire, and flood, spoken by Eliphaz in chs. 5:14; 15:30, 34; 22:16b; by Bildad in ch. 18:6, 15b, 18; by Zophar in chs. 20:26; 24:18; 27:20). At the same time, the poet suggests psychological and slight theological differences among them. Eliphaz appeals to a vision (ch. 4:12-16; cf. ch. 15:17b), Bildad to traditional wisdom (ch. 8:8-10), Zophar to an esoteric wisdom denied to Job but apparently at Zophar's disposal (ch. 11:5-6). Eliphaz is a courtly, urbane debater, more verbose than the other two. One could imagine him with a saintly face and white hair. Bildad is the most concise and the least independent of thought. Privately I have always pictured him as a retired colonel. Zophar, on the other hand, is extremely blunt and argumentative. He has neither the patience of Eliphaz (whose patience emphatically runs out in ch. 22) nor the practical mind of Bildad, but he comprehends better than either the divine transcendence. These portraits are useful chiefly to suggest that the poet's vivid dramatic sense has lent individual characterizations to his dramatis personae. But as the discussion continues, the suggestions of differences among the friends drop more and more from sight. The three represent finally a single position, and they can therefore be considered together.

The position is that of the day's orthodoxy. Recognizing in true Hebraic fashion that God cares for every man's life, and that the business of the faithful is not simply to believe but also to put understanding into action, the friends insist on a direct correlation between life and faith, which is to be sought in terms of cause and effect. The syllogism is simple: righteousness pleases God; God rewards that which pleases him; therefore, the righteous man fares well in this life. The negative of this syllogism is assumed as well. The logic of discovery of the correlation in any particular case, therefore, is equally simple. Since God rewards righteousness with prosperity and conversely punishes wickedness with catastrophe, one may know who is righteous and who wicked by noting who is healthy and who is suffering. We shall return to this syllogism when we consider Job. For the moment we may simply note — as Job notes (ch. 12:5) — that the friends are healthy. They take themselves seriously, as we would expect. Any threat to the logic of their dogma is a direct threat to themselves. But as long as their logic is not assailed, their position is impregnable.

The irony perceptible in the words of the friends is aimed in only one direction: to the wicked, and therefore implicitly and explicitly to Job. The wicked man, says Eliphaz, comes to no good end

> Because he has stretched his hand out against God,
> And against Shaddai [5] he plays hero [*yithgabbar*].
>                                             (Ch. 15:25.)

A *geber* is a strong man, a *gibbôr* a heroic one. The cognate verbal form denotes the sham of the wicked man's " heroism "

[5] The name Shaddai (RSV " the Almighty "), used often in the book, is of uncertain explanation. I am not sufficiently satisfied with any meaning ascribed to it to attempt an English equivalent.

against God. But all such pretences must come to nought, according to the dogma, because whatever the wicked man does must turn out badly. Bildad makes the point:

> His strong steps are cramped,
> And his own plans cast him down.
> For he is cast into a net by his own feet,
> And he walks over a snare cover.[6]
>
> (Ch. 18:7-8.)

The wicked man, all unknowing, is led by his own plans into the inevitable distress. Whatever he may do to secure himself is hopeless, for even if everything appears to be going well, says Zophar (presuming that our rearrangement of the last cycle of speeches is correct), it will all fall to pieces and go for the benefit of the righteous (ch. 27:14-19). Whatever the apparent happiness of the wicked, he has only the dust to await:

> His bones may be filled with youthfulness,
> But it will lie down with him in the dust.[7]
>
> (Ch. 20:11.)

As an allusion to Job, the imagery of a premature death is tactlessly ironic. The poet has his own irony here as well, for only

---

[6] Cf. Artur Weiser, *Das Buch Hiob*, 4te Auflage (Vandenhoeck & Ruprecht, Göttingen, 1963), p. 135, n. 2. The image is that of a pit dug across the path, with a camouflaged covering through which the victim plunges.

[7] The line is difficult because the verb is a singular feminine form. The natural antecedent is " youthfulness," which, however, is masculine plural. Commentators are not helpful. Stevenson, *Notes on the Poem of Job* (Aberdeen University Press, Ltd., Aberdeen, 1951), p. 92, emends confusingly. Kissane, *The Book of Job* (Sheed & Ward, Ltd., 1946), pp. 128–129, transposes the verse to a position after v. 5, where the antecedent becomes the feminine singular " rejoicing " of v. 5. Terrien, *IB*, Vol. 3, p. 1061, seems to suggest that the feminine verb is an ironic metaphorical change, where the " youthfulness " is now referred to as a lover who will lie down with the man but " not on a couch of delight." That would be an acceptable explanation were the metaphorical shift not so sudden.

Zophar's enthusiasm for his own ideas would make him describe Job in his present wretched state as "filled with youthfulness."

Yet the irony of wickedness, as seen by the friends, is not simply the incongruity between what the wicked hopes and what he will assuredly receive. It lies also in the fact, adumbrated in ch. 18:7-8, that the wicked harms himself, that calamity on the wicked is not whimsical and unwilled but actually devised by the wicked.

> For iniquity does not come out of dust,
> Nor does calamity sprout from the soil.
> But man begets [8] calamity,
> As sparks fly high.
>
> (Ch. 5:6-7.)

The ironic metaphor of v. 6, saying that evil and its effects do not arise without cause, shifts through the wordplay between "soil" (*"adāmāh*) and "man" (*'ādām*) to the assertion of man's own responsibility for his calamity. To be sure, there is the sense that man inevitably begets trouble, as sparks inevitably fly upward. And yet the thrust of the ironic simile falls not on the inevitability but on the wicked man's responsibility for his fate. Hence, Eliphaz can turn on Job further along in the debate and accuse him of being his own worst enemy:

> Your own mouth condemns you, not I;
> Your own lips give testimony against you.
> (Ch. 15:6.)

This remark shows the weakness of the position of Eliphaz. From now on he gives up the discussion and turns to accusation and invective, thereby giving the lie to his own disclaimer of condemnation. At the same time, however, the remark reveals

[8] Read *yólid* for MT *yullād*.

the ironic view of the inevitable outcome of wickedness. It is almost as if God did not have to punish evil; it would punish itself. Indeed, if this principle were carried to its logical conclusion, it would leave no place in the universe for a living God, such as him to whom Old Testament faith bears witness.

But most of the irony of the friends emphasizes not only man's sinfulness but also his inherent limitation. Sinfulness, they suggest, comes out of man's disastrous attempt to overcome limitation, and Job himself, in their eyes, is the perfect exemplar. This is almost the first point Eliphaz makes, as he recounts the vision that seems to give him a special line to the divine knowledge. Man cannot be righteous before God, for in the presence of God, the unlimited, everything limited is in error, even the angels (ch. 4:18); therefore much more man, " whose foundation is in the dust " (v. 19b).

> Is not their preeminence pulled from them? [9]
> They die, but not by wisdom.
>
> (V. 21.)

The irony lies in the understatement of the second line. Certainly, Eliphaz argues, one cannot ascribe the causation of death to wisdom. Man dies partly because he is a man, and partly because he errs. For man's knowledge has its insuperable limits:

> Can you find the recesses of God?
> Can you find the limits of Shaddai?
> It is higher than heaven — what can you do?
> Deeper than Sheol — what can you know?
>
> (Ch. 11:7-8.)

Zophar's ironic questions reflect his assumptions both of man's limited comprehension and of God's illimitability. " What can

[9] The translation follows Terrien, *IB*, Vol. 3, pp. 941–942.

you know?" There is that about God — and Zophar rightly emphasizes it — totally beyond man's understanding. It was a heretic who claimed, "I know God as well as he knows himself." [10] But Zophar applies his strictures particularly to Job, when he quotes the ironic proverb:

> An empty-headed man will become intelligent
> When an ass's colt is born a man.
>
> (V. 12.)

The previous two verses may be an answer to some of Job's remarks in ch. 9, and if so, Zophar is accusing Job of so thoroughly misconstruing God's nature and purpose as to be hopelessly mired down in stupidity.

Eliphaz, for his part, does not accuse Job of stupidity. He points ironically to Job's necessary limits of knowledge in words that sound curiously like those Yahweh will use to Job (chs. 38 to 39):

> Were you born the first of men?
> Were you brought forth before the hills?
> Do you listen to the council of God?
> Do you snatch its wisdom for yourself?
> What do you know that we do not know?
> What do you understand that we do not have?
> We have both graybeard and aged with us,
> Much older than your father.
> Are the consolations of God too slight for you,
> The word that is gentle with you?
>
> (Ch. 15:7-11.)

Eliphaz seems to make use here of the old primal man (*Urmensch*) myth, not unlike the one in Gen., ch. 3.[11] He inquires,

[10] The statement is ascribed to the Arian Eunomius of Cyzicus.

[11] Cf. Weiser, *Das Buch Hiob*, pp. 113–114; Gustav Hölscher, "Das Buch Hiob," 2te Auflage (*HAT*, J. C. B. Mohr, Tübingen, 1952), p. 41.

ironically, whether Job, like Wisdom (cf. Prov. 8:25), existed
before the hills. Suggesting a variant on the myth of Prometheus,
he wonders if Job has stolen wisdom out of the very council of
God.[12] The irony of the questions is clarified by the following
remark of Eliphaz, that the whole weight of hoary human wisdom and the insight of the aged is on his side. Then, with a perfectly straight face (though the poet must have written with an
ironic smile), he wonders whether Job finds God's gentle " consolations " too meager. Job pretends to more than human capacities,
and Eliphaz ironically suggests their impossibility. Bildad echoes
the idea that Job is reaching beyond his limits:

> Will the earth be abandoned on your account?
> Or the rock removed from its place?
>
> (Ch. 18:4.)

Alluding to Job's statement in ch. 14:18 that the " rock is removed from its place," Bildad has reversed the meaning, for Job
made his remark in the context of despair, whereas Bildad assumes that Job was grandly demanding the overturn of the
whole cosmic order for his own benefit. Job's problem, says
Bildad, is not God's anger with him, but his anger with God.[13]
Certainly it is Job's titanism that so exercises the friends. No
man has any right to talk of God as Job does. The friends feel
themselves called to God's defense. They say much that is true
and eloquent about God's majesty and sovereignty and about
man's limitations. But they must also overstate the case in the
interests of their own position. Eliphaz does this from the time
he claims a special revelation for the statement that man is es-

---

12 The point must remain uncertain. Terrien, *IB*, Vol. 3, p. 1018, understands the verb in v. 8b to mean " monopolize," which would exclude the specifically Promethean note, for it would simply mean that Job keeps his wisdom
to himself.
13 Weiser, *Das Buch Hiob*, p. 136.

sentially impure before God (ch. 4:17). He is finally forced into
a fundamentally ironic but theologically very dangerous statement:

> Can a man be of use to God?
> But a wise man is of use only to himself.
> Has Shaddai any pleasure if you are righteous?
> Or any profit if you perfect your ways?
> Is it for your piety that he indicts you,
> That he comes with you to court?
>
> (Ch. 22:2-4.)

Anyone would think, from the way Job has been talking, that
man should expect God to care! If Job wants to bring God down,
Eliphaz has to lift him up. But the danger in too exalted a doctrine of divine transcendence is that God may be removed so
far above man that he cannot care. Has Eliphaz not lifted God
too high? If he is right, then Satan correctly argues that man's
true self can be revealed only if God removes himself from the
scene (chs. 1 and 2). But Eliphaz' speech clearly shows that the
effect of so exalting God beyond man is not to make possible a
just appraisal of man but rather to render man beneath notice,
to view him as unworthy of appraisal. After this statement
Eliphaz has nothing to say except to leap maliciously on Job
with utterly unfounded accusations (ch. 22:5-9). Job's suffering
is unquestionably punishment; the dogma says so. " Is it for your
piety [literally, " your fear "; cf. ch. 15:4] that he indicts you? "
With this biting question, Eliphaz drops his irony, and we hear
it no more.

The irony of the friends, then, is directed ostensibly at wicked
and pretentious men but actually at Job himself. They allege the
data of long experience to support their conclusions, but always
they attack Job himself from the standpoint of the dogmatic syllogism laid out above. Job is wicked; he must be. There is noth-

ing for him except submission, which God awaits with impassive patience. No one else can surrender for Job or help him. Eliphaz asks, ironically:

> Call now; is there anyone to answer?
> To whom among the holy ones will you turn?
>
> (Ch. 5:1.)

The " holy ones " are among God's court (cf. ch. 15:15), perhaps participating in that very " council " to which Job could not possibly listen (v. 8). He has no resource outside himself to alleviate his troubles, just as he has put himself where he now is. But to that Job cannot agree.

Before looking at Job's irony, however, we need to turn briefly to the fourth friend, Elihu, the Johnny-come-lately who pops up from nowhere in ch. 32, disappears after ch. 37, and is not heard from again. There are many reasons for concluding that the speeches of Elihu belong to the mind of a poet other than the one responsible for the rest of the book. Elihu deserves a look, however, youngster that he claims to be (ch. 32:6). Indeed, he is ironic, if not sarcastic, about the failure of the elderly to deal properly with Job:

> I said, " Let days do the talking,
> Let many years make wisdom known."
>
> (Ch. 32:7.)

But those possessed of days and years have not succeeded.

> The elderly are not necessarily wise,
> Nor do the old understand rightly.
> Therefore I say, " Listen to me.
> I too shall tell you what I know."
> See, I waited on your words,

> I paid attention to your wise remarks,
> While you were digging around for words.
>                    (Vs. 9-11.)

The brash young man has become irritated with elderly incompetence, and he sees no point in further deference to it.

> They are confounded; they have no answer.
> Words have utterly left them.
> And do I wait while they do not speak,
> While they stand around and have no answer?
>                    (Vs. 15-16.)

It takes a long time for Elihu to get around to saying what he keeps assuring us he is about to say. The young often feel impelled to long prefaces.

When he finally comes to the point, Elihu is worth hearing. Unlike the other friends, he seems to understand the divine grace, and he does not correlate the divine transcendence with man's necessary impurity, as Eliphaz did. But the few ironic utterances directed toward Job are not, finally, different from those of the other three friends. For he suggests, as did Bildad (ch. 18:4), that Job wants God to adjust the world to himself:

> Will he set matters right at your pleasure,
> Simply because you reject? [14]
>                    (Ch. 34:33.)

God's justice does not become justice upon man's accepting it as such. If God is God, argues Elihu, then he is just by definition. Does man gainsay what is divine?

---

[14] The line seems too short. Kissane, *The Book of Job*, p. 235, and Hölscher, *loc. cit.*, p. 83, suggest the insertion of something like " his decision " at the end of the line.

> Do you consider this as just?
> When you say, " I have rights from God? "
>
> (Ch. 35:2.)

Elihu agrees with Eliphaz (cf. ch. 22:2-3) that God has no need
of human assistance. He refrains, however, from ascribing im-
passibility to God, as Eliphaz had implied. Job's titanism looks
ridiculous when set down beside God's infinity, not because God
cannot care but because man cannot contribute to God.

> If you sin, what have you done to him?
> If you multiply your misdeeds, how have you worked on him?
> If you are righteous, what have you given him?
> Or what has he gotten from your hand?
> Your wickedness has to do with a man like yourself,
> And your righteousness with a son of man.
>
> (Ch. 35:6-8.)

Elihu seems to feel that Job expects God to be affected by his
sin or his goodness. Job, of course, has already disclaimed that
(ch. 7:20), and yet he has argued throughout the poem that God
ought to heed his call and respond to his desires. Job has even
implied, with a touch of irony, that God will be sorry (cf.
ch. 7:21). But Elihu suggests the irony of Job's pretensions to such
grand goodness or such huge evil that the almighty God would
be affected. He thinks that God's failure to lash out at Job for
his impious talk has encouraged Job to go even farther.

> Certainly God does not listen to emptiness,
> Nor does Shaddai attend to it.
> Much less when you say that you do not see him,
> That the case is before him, and you await him.
> But now, since he does not punish with his wrath
> And does not attend to great transgression,

Job opens his mouth with vapor,
Multiplies words without knowledge.

(Ch. 35:13-16.)

The passage is difficult. Some scholars read " silence " (*dôm*) for
" case " (*dîn*) in v. 14b.[15] Others read a different form for the
verb in the same line, usually a third person instead of MT's
second person.[16] It seems possible also that we might read a direct
quotation from Job in v. 14, perhaps as follows:

Much less when you say, " You do not regard it [the case]!
The case is before you, and you are delaying it." [17]

In this reading, Job is accusing God of suppressing the case, an
accusation that Elihu calls the height of " emptiness." But God
is beyond men's petty accusations. If Job wants a hearing, he
must do better than he has done.

Finally, in a passage that forms a natural transition to the
advent of Yahweh in ch. 38, Elihu invites Job to consider the
cosmic activity of God, in irony very much like that which
we will hear from Yahweh.

Listen to this, Job,
Stand still and meditate upon God's marvels.
Do you know when God commands them?
And how he makes his clouds shine light?
Do you know how the clouds hang,
The marvels of him whose knowledge is perfect?
You whose clothes are hot
When the land lies silent under the south wind,
Can you spread out the sky with him,
Hard as a molten mirror?

[15] So Kissane, *The Book of Job*, p. 241; Hölscher, *loc. cit.*, p. 84.
[16] Kissane, *The Book of Job*, p. 241.
[17] Reading *dîn lᵉphānekā wᵉtôchēl lô* for MT *dîn lᵉphānāw ûtᵉchôlēl lô*.

Teach us, then, what to say to him.
We cannot confront him because of darkness.
Shall it be told him that I would speak?
Does a man wish to be swallowed up?
                                        (Ch. 37:14-20.)

Job has loudly shouted that he wants to speak to God. Elihu,
with a far gentler irony than the other friends used, asks whether,
considering that God is God, Job actually desires to be " swallowed up." If Job can claim the knowledge and power of God,
if he can overcome his own lassitude when God's summer heat
beats upon him, then perhaps he will be prepared to risk both
the burning light and the frightening darkness to speak to God.
But Elihu doubts that Job is able or desires to do that.

It must finally be said that the poet's irony is at work throughout the speeches of the friends. They say much that is remarkably
true. But the poet certainly differs in viewpoint from them. He
writes in order to undermine their basic assumption, and he sees
their earnest exhortations with an irony of his own that renders
doubly ironic the irony in their own mouths. Not until the book's
solution, however, does the poet's irony upon the friends become
unmistakably clear.


## JOB: THE IRONY OF THE SUFFERER

We saw that the friends assume that prosperity is the effect of
righteousness, calamity of sinfulness. The friends can only condemn Job, for his suffering demonstrates that he is somehow
impious. We must recognize that Job holds the same retributive
presumption. Indeed, this is the source of his problem. Only when
one assumes that suffering is a punishment does the suffering
of the innocent appear unjust. Of course, the friends have no
problem because the suffering of Job indicates to them that he

is not innocent. This is the pass to which they are brought by
the univocal application of dogma to life.

Job lashes out at God on the basis of the same assumption. He
is being punished; he says so again and again (cf. chs. 6:24;
7:20-21; 9:15, 17-19, 28; 10:2, 14-15; etc.). He could make this
claim only if he assumed the inexorable divine action and reaction: for sin, misery; for righteousness, happiness. But something has gone wrong with the machinery. The cause has produced the wrong effect: Job has not sinned, but still he suffers.
In the dialogue with the friends, Job never entirely departs from
the magical assumption.[18] He argues that something is wrong
with the administration. He has not uttered the magical formula
that should have produced his present suffering. God, not Job,
has broken the law. And Job earnestly and repeatedly expresses
his desire to confront God, to set him right. If the world cannot
spin in accordance with justice, then Job wants to get off. He
stubbornly assumes that God will listen to reason, though the
friends (and later Elihu) assure him that God has not the slight-
est interest in reason. But Job is too great a man to take an unreasonable God without protest. And that very greatness leads
Job to the point where the ground may be shifted.

We shall see the shift of ground under the impact of the divine
irony in the next section. We need now to look at the directions
of Job's irony as he wrestles with the friends, with himself, and
with God. It is clear that Job is not groping toward understanding. He does not ask God to justify his actions, and hence the
dialogue is in no sense at all a quest for theodicy. All the par-

[18] Cf. O. S. Rankin, *Israel's Wisdom Literature* (T. & T. Clark, Edinburgh,
1936), pp. 88–93. In pointing out that the retributive dogma informs the dialogue between Job and the friends, Rankin seems to make the point that the
Joban poet never departs from the dogma, apparently feeling that the speeches
of Yahweh as well as those of Elihu are secondary to the poem. I differ with him
with regard to the speeches of Yahweh, and therefore I would want to distinguish
the position of Job and the friends, who maintain the retributive assumption, from
that of the poet, who does not.

ticipants, and Job most vigorously of all, assume that they know
how God acts. Job does not want God's self-justification; he wants
God to justify him. Job asks not for theodicy but for anthropodicy.

Job addresses now the friends, now God, but he is always, as
it were, talking past the friends in the effort to persuade God in
his favor. When, therefore, he addresses the friends directly, he
is generally impatient and ironic, if not sarcastic, with them. He
has two complaints with the friends: (1) that they are no help
to him at all, and (2) that on the whole they talk nonsense.

Job's reproach to the friends, that they are useless as helpers
and comforters, is a constant refrain.

> No doubt you are the people,
> And wisdom will die with you.
> > (Ch. 12:2.)

The remark, often cited as irony, should probably be called sarcasm. Job makes several such comments to and about the friends.

> How offensive honest words are,
> And how your indictment indicts! [19]
> > (Ch. 6:25.)

Job has invited the friends to show him where he has gone
wrong. If they have not indicted error but have misunderstood
honesty, the friends, not Job, have gone wrong. At the end of the
dialogue, Job returns to the same theme, but more powerfully:

> How you have helped him without strength!
> Rescued the arm that has no might!
> How you have counseled him without wisdom!

---

[19] For the connotation of *mārats*, cf. I Kings 2:8; Micah 2:10. The second
line is literally, "And how an indictment from you indicts!" The particle *māh*,
"how?" or "what?" seems to me, against most commentators, to have the
same force in both lines.

> Sound advice declared to the ignorant! [20]
> With whom have you bandied words?
> And whose spirit has come out from you?
>                           (Ch. 26:2-4.) [21]

The sarcastic indictment of the friends is followed by the difficult
questions of v. 4, which I interpret as being on the brink of accusing Bildad of receiving his wisdom from spirits of doubtful
integrity.[22] Bildad and the other two friends with him are " comforters of trouble " (ch. 16:2), whose " comfort " is a contradiction in terms.

There is more, however, to their failure to help Job than these
rather general accusations show. After the firm rebuke in ch. 6:25,
which the friends do not seem to understand, it looks as if they
made a move to go. Job pleads with them to come back, with
a remark of curiously double meaning:

> Come back, please, let no wrong be done.
> Come back now, my innocence is at stake.
>                           (Ch. 6:29.)

Does he mean that he did not intend to insult his friends? Or
does he mean that they should not leave him alone to his fate
with God, since God will surely wreak evil upon him? Surely
he means both, for his " innocence is at stake," not only before
them but also, and more significantly, before God. And somehow
his innocence before God depends on them. They must neither

[20] Reading *labbur* for MT *lārôb*.

[21] Both Kissane, *The Book of Job*, pp. 163–164, and Hölscher, *loc. cit.*, pp.
62–63, assign these verses to Bildad. As was noted above, this is the section of
the dialogue in which some rearrangement is necessary. It is pointed out by
many that the present passage is set in the second person singular, which is characteristic of the friends' address to Job but not of Job's to them. Nevertheless, the
content is so much more like Job's thought than like that of his friends that it
seems best to maintain it in his mouth.

[22] So Weiser, *Das Buch Hiob*, p. 190.

wrong nor take offense at him. His complaint, in the last analysis, is not with them (cf. ch. 21:4), and yet their influence may be evil. He has already expressed his disappointment in them (cf. ch. 6:14-20), a disappointment that comes to its climax in a penetratingly ironic indictment:

> You see [my] terror and you are afraid.
> (V. 21; cf. ch. 12:5.)

The calamity through which Job is passing reduces the healthy to fright, which causes them to turn against him. " There but for the grace of God go I." Such a judgment always implies the fear that the grace might be removed. The accusations of the friends, Job says, are motivated by fear for their own security. So they " pursue " him, " like God," and are " not satisfied with my flesh " (ch. 19:22). That they act like God is, in Job's eyes, no compliment.

Not only do the friends not help Job by their counsel, but they actively harm him. He wishes they would be silent:

> Oh, if only you would keep still!
> And it would be wisdom for you.
> (Ch. 13:5.)

He depends upon the friends, but their words mean nothing. He even turns the tables on them, assuring them with devastating irony that he could do the same thing they are doing:

> I too could talk as you do,
> If you were in my place.
> I could pile up words against you,
> And shake my head over you.
> I could strengthen you with my mouth.
> And my lips' condolence would assuage.
> (Ch. 16:4-5.)

Job's ostensibly positive note is ironically negative. He is describing to the friends how their consolations feel to him who is on the receiving end. But they cannot understand, and, even when they are not a positive hindrance to Job, they do not help him.

His second complaint is that they speak nonsense. He gives considerable energy to refuting their claims, implicit or explicit. Eliphaz had claimed that no man can be considered good and righteous before God, a theological judgment with which few would quarrel (ch. 4:17-21). Job comes back again to this theme in ch. 9:2-4:

> Certainly I know it is so:
> " How can a man be righteous with God? "
> If one desires to oppose him at law,
> He could not answer him once in a thousand times.
> Even the wise of heart and the strong of power,
> Who has been stubborn against him and succeeded?

Job's argument is subtly different from that of Eliphaz. Where Eliphaz had seen no contradiction between the doctrine of an immovable, impassible God and the notion of a reward of the righteous, Job penetrates the idea to its logical conclusion. If man is not righteous before God (there he virtually quotes Eliphaz), then it is pointless to " seek God " as Eliphaz had urged (ch. 5:8), because he is defeated before he starts. Eliphaz' argument is nonsense.

> Your recollections are proverbs of ashes,
> Your shields are made of clay.
> (Ch. 13:12.)

Job even quotes a proverb that seems to approve what Bildad, claiming the authority of ancient tradition, had said in ch. 8:8-10:

> With the aged is wisdom,
> And with length of days comes understanding.
> (Ch. 12:12.) [23]

Job speaks here not in agreement with Bildad but in irony, negating the argument in the very following verse:

> [No!] With him are wisdom and might,
> Counsel and understanding are his.
> (V. 13.)

There is even a certain irony about God in that statement, for it is clear that from Job's present standpoint the praise words " wisdom and might," " counsel and understanding," do not denote unambiguous praise of God.

Job ironically describes the reactions of righteous men to a calamity like his. One might expect the good and the upright to demonstrate some human sympathy, when

> My eye has dimmed from vexation,
> And all my members are like a shadow.
> (Ch. 17:7.)

But they do not:

> Upright men are astounded by this,
> And the guiltless rouses himself against the alienated.
> The righteous holds tight to his way,
> And the pure of hands becomes ever stronger.
> (Vs. 8-9.)

The commentators with one accord are baffled by these verses. Hölscher omits vs. 8-10 entirely.[24] Kissane ascribes v. 8 to Bildad,

---

[23] Weiser, *Das Buch Hiob*, p. 86, and Hölscher, *loc. cit.*, p. 34, set the statement as a question.

[24] *Loc. cit.*, p. 42.

putting it after ch. 18:20, and places v. 9 earlier in Job's speech, after ch. 16:21.[25] Driver and Gray agree with Duhm, placing vs. 8-10 after ch. 18:3.[26] Terrien and Kraeling interpret the verbs as futures, understanding the passage to mean that, "Though for a time the righteous man may be puzzled and dismayed, he keeps steadfastly to his path, realizing that all things must serve to increase his spiritual strength."[27] Weiser, connecting the language of vs. 8-9 to that of cultic psalms, holds similarly that v. 9 points up the firmness of a faithful man in spite of his difficulty, noting the parallel between v. 9b and Isa. 40:31.[28] What is missed on all sides is that Job is speaking ironically. The effect of a righteous man's calamity is to harden other "righteous" men against him. Job does not mean himself by the *tsaddîq* in v. 9, nor can he refer to himself in the plural by *y<sup>e</sup>shārîm* ("upright men") in v. 8. Job has told the friends the same thing before, that they are made fearful by his terror (ch. 6:21), that those who are at ease are readily contemptuous of those who are in trouble (ch. 12:5). Other men's troubles strengthen men in their righteousness, but, Job implies, for the wrong reasons. For if a man pursues excellence from fear of calamity, he is of no human good to the one who is in trouble. And in the next verse Job ironically invites the friends to come on with their arguments again:

> But I will not find a wise man among you.
> (Ch. 17:10b.)

Job has come to the point of denying the minor premise of the syllogism constructed above. The major premise, that righ-

---

[25] *The Book of Job.*

[26] S. R. Driver and G. B. Gray, *A Critical and Exegetical Commentary on the Book of Job* (ICC, T. & T. Clark, Edinburgh, 1921), pp. 153–154.

[27] The quotation is from Emil G. Kraeling, *The Book of the Ways of God* (S.P.C.K., London, 1938), p. 84. Cf. also Terrien, *IB*, Vol. 3, pp. 1031–1032.

[28] *Das Buch Hiob*, pp. 132–133.

teousness pleases God, he firmly retains. He can claim, with eminent justice, that he has obeyed God's ways, has been superlative in moral excellence. But the conclusion to the syllogism, that the righteous man fares well in this life, has not come true for Job. Therefore something must be wrong with the minor premise, that God rewards what pleases him. And Job, continuing to assume that his suffering is punishment, must conclude that though God demands righteousness, he rewards wickedness. He spends most of ch. 21 expounding this remarkable thesis, in answer to the friends' arguments to the contrary throughout the discussion. The center of his argument is his proposal that those who have the easiest time of it are farthest from God.

> They say to God, " Get away from us!
> We have no pleasure in knowing your ways.
> Who is Shaddai that we should serve him?
> How do we benefit from praying to him? "
> (Ch. 21:14-15.)

Righteousness produces no benefit whatever, as Job himself demonstrates. He has done all that should procure for him a life of pleasure and honor. If the argument of the friends is right, then he should be sitting in the city gate, moderating disputes, possessor of authority and object of admiration. But he is sitting not there but here, and the argument of the friends is nonsense. If man wants divine favor, he must have a God he can control.

> The tents of violent men are at peace,
> And security belongs to those who give God trouble,
> Who carry God along in their hands.
> (Ch. 12:6.)

Job propounds a curiously dual thesis, whose parts are so disparate from one another that one wonders how he would propose to hold them simultaneously. On the one hand, he has no

intention of abandoning his righteousness, which he believes is
the divine will. But on the other hand, since he is being punished,
he must hold that the God who wills righteousness in the abstract rewards unrighteousness in the concrete. Job finds a reverse correlation, a negative cause-and-effect relationship, between
piety and prosperity. And that gives rise to some, at least, of
Job's irony about himself, at which we must look briefly before
investigating his ironic attacks upon God.

On the whole, Job takes himself very seriously. That is one of
the sources of his problem. Yet his taking himself seriously is not
incompatible with his self-irony. At the very beginning of the
discussion, even in the midst of his curse upon his own birthday,
the potential irony of Job's death comes through:

> Why did I not die from the womb,
> Come forth from the belly and perish?
> Why did the knees receive me?
> And why the breasts, so that I could suckle?
> For now I would be lying down in quiet,
> I would sleep; then I would have some rest
> With kings and counselors of the earth,
> Who built ruins for themselves;
> Or with princes — gold is theirs,
> They fill their houses with silver.
>
> (Ch. 3:11-15.)

The implied incongruity of a longed-for death and the detested
present life is stated in unusual terms. Life is simply more turmoil
than it is worth. In death, at least, one would be in the presence
of the great. But the great are described ironically, reflecting
irony back upon Job. In death, Job would be with kings and
counselors, the earth's builders — though what they built comes
to ruins; with princes, the rich — though their riches would not
accompany them to Sheol. One is reminded of the cynical Baby-

lonian "Dialogue Between Master and Servant," in which, when
the master proposes to be a benefactor to his country, the slave
cynically talks him out of it:

> Ascend to the ruins of the cities of old,
> Behold the skulls of earlier and latter [men]:
> Who is now an evildoer? Who is now a benefactor? [29]

Yet Job senses an ironically positive note in death, for there
slavery and toil are no more, human status is meaningless, and
release from bondage comes (ch. 3:18-19). Yet the release is not
available to Job, and he closes his first soliloquy with a kind of
resigned, ironical understatement:

> I have no ease, I have no quiet,
> I have no rest, and trouble has come.
> (V. 26.)

Understatement is not Job's normal mode of speech. His ex-
citement mounts, as he explains his position to the friends:

> For Shaddai's arrows are in me,
> Whose poison my spirit drinks.
> God's terrors are drawn up against me.
> Does the wild ass bray over his grass?
> Does the ox low over his mash?
> Does one eat what is flat without salt?
> Is there taste in egg white?
> My soul refuses to touch them;
> They are like the repulsiveness of my bread.
> (Ch. 6:4-7.)

The rhetorical questions are an implicit and ironic answer to
Eliphaz' criticism of his impatience (ch. 4:5). Job wonders how
any man could be patient under such strain.

[29] *ANET*, p. 438.

> What is my strength, that I should wait?
> What is my end, that I should extend my patience?
> Is my strength the stones' strength?
> Is my flesh bronze?
>
> (Ch. 6:11-12.)

He returns to the same point in ch. 21:4:

> As for me, is my complaint against man?
> So why should my spirit not be discontent?

His impatience would be one thing if he were dealing only with men; when he must assert himself against God it is quite another. We see again the persistence of the retributive assumption, understated as "discontent." If Job did not assume that his suffering was from God and that it was undeserved, he would have no complaint at all.

Job's self-irony generally reflects his awareness of weakness. He castigates the friends for failing to help "him without strength" (ch. 26:2). He compares himself to a tree:

> Because for a tree there is hope.
> If it be cut down, it will sprout again,
> And its shoots will not stop.
>
> (Ch. 14:7.)

But for man?

> But a strong man [*geber*] dies and lies prostrate.
> Man ['*ādām*] expires, and where is he?
>
> (V. 10.)

He points out how he can do nothing to alleviate his suffering.

> If I talk, my pain is not assuaged.
> But if I keep quiet, how much of it leaves me?
>
> (Ch. 16:6.)

Hope is utterly gone, and Job depicts its loss with a set of ironic images:

> If I await Sheol for my house,
> In darkness spread out my bed,
> To the grave say, "You are my father,"
> "My mother, my sister," to the maggot,
> Where, then, is my hope?
> And my good, who shall see it? [30]
> Shall they descend with me to Sheol? [31]
> Shall we go down together to the dust? [32]
>
> (Ch. 17:13-16.)

The text is difficult and perhaps in disrepair. If it is granted that the form of the last line requires the foregoing line to be interrogative, then the picture of Job and his hope going down to death together (Terrien compounds the irony of the image by suggesting that it implies the figure of bride and bridegroom [33]) is the ironic picture of a "hope" and a "good," which are their own opposites. This irony is vastly heightened by the horrid images of the hero's embracing the grave and the maggot as his nearest and dearest relatives. To call this "hope" is to cast the entire expectation into darkest irony.

Finally, in his speech of summation, Job indulges in mild self-irony, particularly in the first part, as he depicts his previous happy prosperity, "as in the months of old, as in the days when God watched me" (ch. 29:2). But that benevolent "watching" was of a totally different sort from the "watching" Job has experienced from God lately. In those days Job, in marked contrast to his present hopelessness (cf. ch. 17:13-16), expected as his end nothing but good:

[30] Reading, with LXX, $w^e \underline{t}\hat{o}b\bar{a}th\hat{i}$ for MT's repetition $w^e tiqw\bar{a}th\hat{i}$.
[31] Reading $ha'imm\bar{a}d\hat{i}$ with LXX for MT $badd\bar{e}$.
[32] Reading $n\bar{e}ch\bar{a}th$ for MT $n\bar{a}chath$.
[33] Cf. IB, Vol. 3, p. 1034.

> And I said, " I will perish in my nest,
> And I will multiply my days like sand.
> My root opened out to the water,
> And dew all night on my boughs,
> My glory new with me [every day],
> And my bow renewed in my hand." [34]
>                               (Ch. 29:18-20.)

The entire speech, viewed from the vantage point of our knowledge that Job's situation is totally different now, and from the knowledge of what he will say next (ch. 30), is ironic by comparison to his present situation. But this statement is especially so, as is the final remark of the chapter, with its implied ironic slap at the friends. Job had been at the head of those who were in trouble, had helped and encouraged them, " like one who comforts mourners " (ch. 29:25c).

Job turns his irony, then, upon himself as well as upon the friends. Yet there are times when, even indulging in self-irony, he uses it to cast ironic gibes at God. Job is the most daring of men. Few in the Old Testament are bold enough to use irony on the Almighty. Abraham did (Gen. 18:25), and so did Jeremiah (cf. Jer. 12:1; 15:18; 20:7). It is, however, remarkable that man — even Hebrew man — should take ironic aim at God. And in Job's ironic address to God we see the progress of his position.

He begins mildly enough, as far as God is concerned. The initial curse on Job's day of birth, the irony of which is mostly self-irony, does have one slight ironic allusion to the creation. " That day," says Job, " Let it be darkness " (*yᵉhî chôshek*), echoing the first creative word of the creation: " Let there be light " (*yᵉhî 'ôr,* Gen. 1:3). But as Job moves on, his tone deepens. He turns, toward the end of his second speech (chs. 6 to 7), to

[34] For a different reading of the passage, cf. G. R. Driver, " Problems in the Hebrew Text of Job," in *Wisdom in Israel and in the Ancient Near East,* ed. by M. Noth and D. Winton Thomas (Supplements to *VT,* Vol. 3 [E. J. Brill, Leiden, 1955]), pp. 85–86.

speak to God himself, hinting that God may have forgotten
something:

> Remember that my life is a wind;
> My eyes shall not again look upon good.
> The eye of him who looks at me will not see me;
> Your eyes will be on me, and I will not be.
>
> (Ch. 7:7-8.)

He will say it again. Here, in effect, he is telling God that it
may soon be too late for making amends. But his conclusion is
not simply to await the divine pleasure. Job is far too titanic for
that. He promises unceasing complaint (v. 11), and he mingles
self-irony with irony upon God in a vivid image:

> Am I the sea, or a sea monster,
> That you set a guard over me?
>
> (V. 12.)

Does Job deserve all this attention? The Sea (*yām*) in the Canaanite literature is the cosmic opponent of the forces of fertility,
and we saw with Jonah how in the Old Testament the sea is considered inimical. The sea monster (*tannîn*) reminds us of Leviathan (cf. Isa. 27:1; Job, ch. 41) or of Rahab (cf. Isa. 51:9), possibly two different names for the same mythological enemy of
God. Here Job deliberately and ironically exaggerates. If he were
*yām* or *tannîn* he could understand the unwelcome divine atten-
tions. But he is only man, and this fact gives vent to a devastating
parody of what may have been as familiar a psalm to the poet as
it is to us:

> What is man that thou rememberest him,
> Or the son of man, that thou visitest him?
> Thou hast set him little below God,
> And with glory and honor thou dost crown him.
>
> (Ps. 8:4-5.)

Job's outcry sounds very different:

> What is man that you magnify him so,
> That you set your heart upon him,
> That you visit him at morning time
> And test him every moment?
>
> (Ch. 7:17-18.)

The divine attention to tiny man would rejoice the heart of the orthodox, but it rouses Job to derision. For God's attention, he seems to say, is for the sole purpose of magnifying man so that he may have an excuse to put him on trial. The words that Job uses in common with the psalm are subtly different in meaning. Both contrast " man " ('*e nôsh*) to God, but the psalmist is amazed at God's respect of man where Job is derisively astonished that God pays any attention at all. Both use the verb "to visit" (*pāqad*), but the psalmist means a redemptive visit, Job, a punitive one. The psalmist envisions a ceremony of reward, Job, a court at law.

And he argues that the trial is a waste of God's energy:

> I sin; what have I done to you,
> O watcher of mankind.
> Why have you made me your target?
> Why have I become a burden to you?
> And why do you not pardon my transgression
> And remove my iniquity?
> For now I shall lie down in the dust.
> You will look for me; but I will not be.
>
> (Vs. 20-21.)

" The love of God," says Terrien, " is affirmed and denied at the same time." [35] Would it not be more in keeping with the divine

[35] *Job: Poet of Existence*, p. 65.

majesty to give a pardon? The sin, if sin there be, must anyway
be so slight. Job returns to the hint he dropped before (v. 8b),
that time may be short. God will yet change his mind (" You
will look for me "), and then he will be sorry (" I will not be ").
The struggle through which Job must yet pass is only now
adumbrated for the first time. Now Job wants to avoid a trial,
but shortly he will be shouting for the justice of a trial. Yet he
can only assume that the outcome of the trial is foreordained, and
he will lose. Meanwhile, he wishes to be left alone (v. 19).

In his next speech, however, Job complains that God does
leave him alone. After describing God's allegedly marvelous
cosmic doings (ch. 9:5-10), he remarks ironically,

> Behold, he passes me by and I do not see him;
> He moves on, but I do not perceive him.
>
> (V. 11.)

The praises of the liturgy echoed in vs. 5-10 come to nothing if
God is not perceptible in the acts the liturgy praises. And they
come to less than nothing if the " marvels " (*niphlā'ôth*, v. 10)
are finally to be summed up in a kidnapping:

> Behold, he snatches up. Who can stop him?
> Who can say to him, " What are you doing? "
>
> (V. 12.)

The question is finally simply one of brute force. We see again
how Job shifts the ground in his reply to Eliphaz' assertion of
man's unrighteousness before God. The issue of man's relation
to God only appears to be that of justice (vs. 2-4). It is actually
that puny man is set against mighty God. God is even mighty
enough to pervert justice and prove an innocent man guilty
(v. 20). Job has now come to the point where, desiring a trial,
he is forced to accuse the judge of injustice.

> It is all the same; therefore, I say
> Both upright and wicked he destroys.
> If the scourge suddenly kills,
> He mocks at the despair of the innocent.
> The earth is given into the hands of a wicked one.
> He covers up the faces of its judges.
> If it is not he, who is it then?
>
> (Vs. 22-24.)

The logic is impeccable and devastating. If God is indeed in control, as Job and his friends alike assume, and if there is caprice in the treatment of the good and the wicked, then Job can only conclude that God is not just. He guards himself from the accusation of blasphemy by appealing to an orthodox understanding of providence. God could not permit his world to fall into other hands than his own. " The wicked one," in whose hands it clearly is, must be God. The meaning and tone of the statement are unquestionably ironic.

Once again Job turns to address God (ch. 10). And now he puts his accusation in even more ironic terms to God himself:

> I say to God, " Do not treat me as wicked.
> Make me know why you contend against me.
> Is it a good thing to you that you oppress,
> That you despise the toil of your own hands,
> And shine your light on the designs of the wicked?
> Are your eyes mere flesh?
> Do you see as man sees?
> Are your days as the days of a man,
> Or your years as a strong man's days?
> For you search out my iniquity,
> And you seek for my sin,
> Though you know that I am not guilty,
> And there is no one to deliver from your hands."
>
> (Vs. 2-7.)

Job had agreed before to the transcendence of God. " He is not a man, as I am," he said in ch. 9:32. Now he begins to wonder. " Are your days as the days of a man? " he asks. God seems to be no better than man. Accusing God of injustice, Job can accuse him of failing even to measure up to a good human moral code. And again Job's logic is difficult to assail. If the experience on which he bases his accusation is actual experience, then God is the author of injustice, and if God is the author of injustice, he is not preferable as a judge to man. That is where Job's firm hold on the magical assumption has led him. Now he sees that the "marvels" of God's workings are the "wonderful things you do against me" (ch. 10:16b).

But Job is still surprised at this. He cannot yet understand why God should continue such an animus against him.

> Why do you hide your face,
> And consider me your enemy ['ôyēb]?
> (Ch. 13:24.)

Is the last word a play on the name Job ('iyyôb)? [36] Job follows it with an ironic image that combines self-irony with irony upon the divine action:

> Do you frighten a driven leaf,
> And pursue dry straw?
> (V. 25.)

Job's feebleness does not justify God's pursuit of him. His sins, which he assumes must be the cause of this unwarranted regard by God, are not sufficient to account for it. He continues in the same vein:

> Man, born of woman,
> Few of days, and sated with trouble,

[36] Terrien, *IB*, Vol. 3, p. 1008.

> Comes forth like a flower — and withers,
> Flees like a shadow, and does not stay.
> Is it upon such as this that you open your eyes,
> And bring me to trial with you?
>
> (Ch. 14:1-3.)

Here, Job answers the metaphor of the " sprouting " of man's trouble used by Eliphaz (ch. 5:6-7) and also the image of the papyrus flower and the shadow used by Bildad (ch. 8:9, 11-12). But he turns them to say that man is too ephemeral for God to pursue him unjustly. The incongruity of the entire transaction is brought to a sharp focus by Job's sudden shift from the general third person (" man," ch. 14:1) to the first person (v. 3b). He is not, after all, talking merely about man, but rather about himself. Man's troubles are his troubles; that would be one way to put it. But another way would be to say that Job's appeal to man in general is only a cover for his constant appeal to his own experience. Man is summed up in himself. If God has an answer to Job, he may have an answer to the human problem in general. Perhaps in that sense, Job would give a " Yes " to Eliphaz' ironic question, " Were you born the first of men? " (ch. 15:7). Job is at least honest enough to slip in the occasional first person singular.

Noticeably to this point, in each of his speeches Job turns toward the end and addresses God directly. If we understand chs. 3 and 6 to 7 as a single discourse,[37] we find Job addressing God in ch. 7:7-21. In the next speech, Job turns to address God in ch. 10:2-22, and in the following one, in ch. 13:20, continuing through ch. 14. In each case, the first part of the speech is addressed in the plural to the friends, the latter part in the singular to God. In the following speech, however, Job speaks directly to God only briefly (ch. 17:3-4), and then returns to the third person. In neither ch. 19 nor ch. 21 does he address God. Indeed, only once

---

[37] Cf. Terrien, *Job: Poet of Existence*, pp. 50–51.

again before the end of the dialogue does Job address God, and that with great brevity almost exactly in the center of his final summation in ch. 30:20-23.

What does that mean? We cannot suppose that the poet was not aware of what he was doing. This poet is far too shrewd for that. The fact that Job stops speaking to God and speaks only about him is deliberate.[38] Job has made up his mind. The case is closed, although Job is not finished with it. Job has no hope of a just conclusion to the matter. There is no point in speaking further to God, for God will not render the requisite justice. Job can hope against hope that the constant pleas of justice may reach through to the divine ears. But Job is finished speaking to God directly. Therein, we may suggest, lies the poet's genius in depicting a character. Job's irony now is the irony of maintaining into thin air what he is sure the unjust deity will not heed. It is the irony of a man who perceives the futility of speaking to God but cannot avoid speaking about him. But it is also the irony of a man who has no shadowy doubts of the truth in which he himself stands.

In ch. 23, Job reverts to the wish for a trial (vs. 3-7), sure that if he could only get some legal action he would be acquitted. But it is ironically hopeless:

> Behold, I go east, but he is not there,
> West, but I do not perceive him;
> North, where his deeds are, but I do not see him;
> He hides in the south, and I do not behold him.
>                                                   (Vs. 8-9.) [39]

The last line is the key. God is hiding from Job. Not only is he not seeking for Job, as Job assured him that he would (cf. ch.

[38] It is surprising that, although Westermann notices this cessation of direct speech to God, he makes nothing of it. Cf. *Der Aufbau des Buches Hiob* (J. C. B. Mohr, Tübingen, 1956), pp. 46–55.

[39] For this translation, cf. Kraeling, *op. cit.*, p. 95.

7:8, 21), but he makes certain that Job cannot successfully seek
for him. Job underlines the irony:

> Because he knows the way I take.
> (Ch. 23:10a.)

"The way" is a metaphor for the direction and quality of Job's
life. God knows well that Job is guiltless, and he is hiding from
Job because he cannot afford to permit Job to find him for the
trial, lest the trial should turn out in Job's favor:

> When he has tried me, I shall come out like gold.
> (V. 10b.)

No, that God cannot permit, for it would expose his godhood
as the sham it is. Hence he "makes my heart faint" (v. 16a).
Hence "his days" are not seen by those who "know him" (ch.
24:1b),[40] and evil runs amok among men with no divine inter-
ference (vs. 2-12). Were Job to achieve a trial with God, all of
these injustices would count as evidence in Job's favor. But God
will guard himself.

> From the city the dying groan,
> And the wounded cry out for help —
> But God pays no attention to prayer.
> (V. 12.)

Why does he pay no attention? Does he not hear? Or is it that
he simply must not become involved in justice? It is hard to
avoid the sense that Job is saying the latter.[41] Job betrays his
colossal ego, for he seems to think that God remains stolidly impassive toward all human injustice only in order to avoid the
trial with Job. Job accuses God of doing injustice with other
needy men in order to avoid doing justice with Job.

---

40 That much we can be fairly sure of in chs. 23:17 and 24:1.
41 So Weiser, *Das Buch Hiob*, p. 184.

But finally Job must sum up his case. And it is curious to note that, although he is ironic about himself in his summation speech (chs. 29 to 31), he is rarely if ever ironic about God. Only once does a hint of irony slip out, in ch. 31:3-4:

> Is there not calamity for the evildoer
> And misfortune for the workers of iniquity?
> Does he [God] not see my way
> And count all my steps?

If that is not ironic, then Job has simply retreated to the magical assumption, and his rhetorical questions express self-evident truth. But the poet's characterization is consistent, and Job has now abandoned the magical assumption — at least the assumption that magic works, if not the assumption that it ought to work. We must therefore read these questions ironically. Job is resigned to doom. He has said all he has to say, and he now leaves the matter to heaven. Nevertheless, Job takes the precaution of a last protestation of innocence:

> Here is my *tāw;* let Shaddai answer me.
> (V. 35b.) [42]

The last thing he expects, if we may take seriously his refusal to address God in the latter part of the dialogue, is that God will in fact answer. The fact that God does answer may be the prime instance of the divine irony.


## The Irony of God

The opening speech of God is not calculated to persuade us that Job was wrong, except in one respect: in supposing that God

---

[42] The *tāw* may signify not only the signature, the "mark," but specifically, the plea of innocence. This was suggested to me in conversation by Prof. D. N. Freedman, who suggests a possible connection with the lots, Urim and Thummim. Thummim, beginning with *tāw,* probably signified innocence when the lots were used for judgment by ordeal.

would not speak. The God who has been silent so long now floods his words out as though a dam had broken, and we are treated to an astounding display of poetic virtuosity and of learning. But it is a display of divine irony as well, sometimes bordering on, if not descending to, sarcasm.

> Where were you when I laid the earth's foundation?
> Tell, if you know so much.
> Who sets its measurements? Surely you know!
> Or who stretched the line out on it?
>                                   (Ch. 38:4-5; cf. v. 21.)

The function of the whole of chs. 38 and 39 is to put in high relief the ignorance and impotence of man in general and Job in particular as contrasted with the knowledge and the potency of God. Job is challenged to answer the riddles of the cosmos and to analyze the inner movements of nature, to empower the dawn and to enable the creatures of earth to move. The entire speech is almost viciously ironic.

Yet God has come to speak. That too is ironic, for, though Job has repeatedly demanded this encounter, he has given up hoping for it. Job has called upon God to answer, and now, against all expectations, God is answering. But the answer is ambivalent, for this God instead of answering questions asks them. He gives an answer that is no answer, "a sublime irrelevance."[43] Is the speech of this God ironic? Or is it merely the sarcasm of a God who is, as Job maintained, brute force (cf. ch. 9:3-10), who toys with the feeble man whom he deigns to call, with biting irony, *geber,* " strong man " (ch. 38:3)? So far the tone suggests sarcasm rather than irony.

At the end of the first speech, Yahweh asks an ironic question that harks back to an early theme of Job, which has not appeared since ch. 19, the theme of the heavenly advocate:

[43] R. N. Carstensen, *Job: Defense of Honor* (Abingdon Press, 1963), p. 91.

Shall the disputer with Shaddai yield,[44]
The umpire of God answer it?

(Ch. 40:2.)

In ch. 9:33, Job had denied that there is an " umpire between us " (*môkîᵃch*),[45] but in ch. 16:19 he asserted the presence in heaven of a " witness " on his behalf. And in ch. 19:25 he reaches the peak of his emotion in the assurance of a living *gôʾēl,* an " avenger," against God. These figures do not recur in Job's speech, but Elihu may allude to the idea (cf. ch. 33:23-24). It is not sensible to interpret any of the three to mean God.[46] They represent a grasping at straws on Job's part, the desperate wish that, if God will not grant justice, some advocate might conceivably force it. One may speculate — and leave it at that — that Job originally went farther in the now mutilated third cycle of speeches, so far, indeed, that pious copyists excised the reference. That might explain why the third cycle is in such disrepair. At any rate, in Yahweh's question of ch. 40:2, we meet the " umpire " again, now by implication ironically denigrated. Job has not responded to the challenge of chs. 38 and 39. Would he care to entrust the answer to his hypothetical *môkîᵃch?* Since the *môkîᵃch* is hypothetical, the question can only be ironic.

Job's answer suggests his own residual irony.

Behold, I have been trifling. How should I turn you back?
I lay my hand on my mouth.

[44] Cf. Terrien, *IB,* Vol. 3, p. 1182, for this repointing.

[45] The LXX and Syriac versions, however, have read the negative *lôʾ* as *lûʾ,* with the meaning, " Would that there were a *môkîᵃch* between us! " It still says that there is not such a personage, but the tone is different from MT's flat negative.

[46] I have been convinced of this by Terrien, both from his two books and from study under and conversation with him. Cf. most recently W. A. Irwin, " Job's Redeemer," *JBL,* Vol. 81 (1962), pp. 217–229, who follows the idea out in a way subtly different from Terrien's.

> Once I have spoken, and I will not answer,
> Twice, but I will add nothing.
>
> (Ch. 40:4-5.)

This is usually interpreted as resignation, Job's realization that he is overwhelmed. From there, the continuation of Yahweh's speech is either Job's absolute humiliation, thus proving correct his contention throughout the dialogue that God is arbitrary power, or else the beginning of Job's awakening. Certainly, God has overwhelmed Job. But that is nothing new; Job has claimed this from the beginning. If Job's speech expresses hopeless despair, the motive of Yahweh's repeated question and charge (ch. 40:7 ff.) is not clear. A stronger, profoundly ironic interpretation is more satisfying. "I have been trifling." RSV understands that to mean "I am of small account," I am worthless (KJV "vile"), tiny. But it can also carry the connotation of being lighthearted, too concerned with the picayune. Is Job saying that he now sees that his arguments merely played around the edges of the issue, and if he had known then what he knows now, he would have attacked with heavier weapons? "How should I turn you back?" Again, this is usually translated "How can I answer thee?" But the verb in the Hiph'il stem often means to change something (cf. Num. 23:20), to revoke something (cf. Amos, ch. 1), therefore to change the mind of someone. I suggest that this is Job's meaning:

> Behold, I have trifled with you. How could I change
> your mind?

Overwhelming power he knows already. He has learned nothing new. Brute force raised his irony with God before. Now, if necessary, he is prepared to be ultimately overwhelmed, but he will not speak again. The mark of the poet's superlative genius is that he can portray his rebellious hero, confronted with the over-

powering majesty of the creator, as ironic to God's face and holding fast to his position.

Yahweh requires a better response.[47] He repeats his command
to answer (v. 7), and then raises the key question of the entire
book, the question that finally demonstrates to Job where he has
gone wrong and motivates his reconciling repentance:

> Will you even annul my justice?
> Will you condemn me that you may be justified?
>
> (V. 8.)

There at last, in plain words, is the irony of Job's position against
God. On the magical assumption, he has demanded of God that
he relent in his punishment of the innocent. Receiving no satisfaction, he has accused God of immorality and injustice in punish-
ing the innocent as well as the guilty. But the base of the argument all along has been Job's own righteousness, the fact that
he deserves justification. In the interests of his own fate, Job
would be prepared to dethrone God. He knows God, he argues,
as well as God knows himself. *But never has Job had the slight-
est doubt that his suffering is punishment.* On that point the reconciliation now can ensue. For Job has been pursuing the wrong
line of inquiry. He has assumed all along that he is the victim
of injustice and in the certainty of his own righteousness has
condemned God. Now for the first time, it is suggested that injustice lies on Job's side, not on God's. *Was* the suffering punishment? We have only Job's — and the friends' — word for it. God
never alludes to suffering. But Job was so certain of his cause
that he could thunder titanically into the ear of God, elevating
himself implicitly beyond God. That is the burden of God's challenge (vs. 9-14) to Job to take over and rule the world, put the

[47] Hölscher, *loc. cit.*, p. 5, fails to see the dramatic point in the interchange
between Yahweh and Job and unnecessarily telescopes the two speeches of Yahweh into one, and Job's two speeches also into one.

mighty in their place and prove himself victorious over God.

But Job is in no position even to put Leviathan in his place, to catch him with a hook like a fish (ch. 41:1-2), to force him to plead for mercy (vs. 3-4), to play with him and give him to little girls as a pet (v. 5). And if Job cannot cope with Leviathan, he had better not enter the lists against God (vs. 10-11). Is God's power complex turning up again? Is God finally brute force? No, we have seen that the issue of suffering and punishment has been shifted. Job can no longer assume that they go together, because that assumption has led him to do God injustice. For his being satisfied to know all about God at secondhand (ch. 42:5) and for elevating himself to deity's rank, he now repents (v. 6).

One might almost think that the friends are justified. They had urged Job to repent and make his peace with God. But he has done so for a very different reason. Were Job to submit as the friends urged, it would be a blind agreement to a sin he still did not know. But he repents for a sin he now knows perfectly well, and it has nothing to do with external suffering. No longer is the divine power the horrible threat of punishment. God's irony turns out to be the irony of love. For, though the first impression was that of unbridled force, the result is reconciliation. The apparent sarcasm has become irony, and Job, against all of his own best intentions, has been reconciled to a God who does not hold out carrots on sticks for little donkeys to follow. God's distance from man is maintained, for man cannot control God by being good. But his nearness is also maintained, for Yahweh came to speak to Job, not with the intention of smashing him shuddering into the ground but in order to draw him back to himself.

It is the quietus on magic. The God to whom Job is reconciled is not bound to man's ideas of him, is not required to come at the snap of the good man's moral fingers. The irony of reconciliation is that man is reconciled to God on God's terms, not on man's. That was farthest from Job's mind. He demanded acquittal of an unknown and nonexistent sin. He received acquittal of a known and admitted one. His justification, the anthropodicy for which he sought, has canceled out the grounds on which he sought it. The poet of Job has made his theological point ironically. Job's repentance and reconciliation demand an ironic reading of the poem. Had Job won his case, the poem would be a cynical satire on a God who is not God. Had Job been crushed under God, it would satirize a God who will not let man be man. But God finds man guilty and acquits him. That is the fundamental irony of The Book of Job and of Biblical faith.

# EPILOGUE

## FAITH AND THE IRONIC VISION

IT should be clear by now that the problem of irony in the Old Testament is not exclusively a literary problem. It has much to do with theology, and therefore with faith. To ignore that would be to misrepresent the Old Testament, for the literature of the Old Testament — and therefore its literary study — stand in the service of faith's communication. Although irony, narrowly defined, is a device of style, the guidelines to its identification followed here include the " stance in truth," to which reference has frequently been made. Irony is a way of expressing ideas, but, more than that, irony is also an idea that is expressed, a perception with a content of and assumptions about truth. We have seen its occurrence through six books of the Old Testament; we could have seen it in several others. It is time now to pose the more general theological question: What has irony to do with faith?

Certainly the faith to which the Old Testament bears witness is not a body of doctrines or a set of ideas but a kind and context of life. The context of the life of faith is the covenant, the bond in history between God and Israel. Israel's faith relates her to a God who comes to be known in his acts, who by his acts both brings Israel into being and maintains Israel in being. In the covenantal context, Israel lives in response and obedience to

God's history and comes to be what she is intended by God to be, or kicks over the traces in the futile effort to escape from her weighty responsibility. But the covenant, let it be clear, is understood by Israel as a relationship with God rather than an idea about him, as the structure of life rather than an external description of life. The covenant, or the covenant faith, may be said to be the " indicative " of Israel's life, the given.

Beside this indicative stands an imperative, a kind of life or a style of living. The imperative for Israel derives from the indicative but is necessary to it. Without the imperative, the covenant can be a context in the abstract but not a context of actual life. Without the indicative, the imperative has no ground except arbitrary law. The covenant includes life under the divine claim of specific obedience. It is no accident that Israel set down her corpus of law in the literary context of the giving of the covenant at Mt. Sinai (Ex., chs. 19 ff.), for the elaboration of the demand for obedience into both civil and ritual action stems from the contextual claim of the covenant with Yahweh. The realm of ethics, then, is an intrinsic element of faith, not because it makes faith possible or leads up to faith but because faith is both a context and a kind of life.

Nothing in the foregoing two paragraphs is original. No one remotely familiar with work on the Old Testament during the last twenty-five years will find it in the least surprising. The next thing that must be said, however, is that the faith so described both makes possible and motivates the irony we have seen in the Old Testament. The satiric irony of The Book of Jonah stems from the author's awareness that the covenant God is the God of all the earth, but the covenant people want to keep him in their own possession. The tragic irony of the story of Saul is an interpretation of a man who, failing to trust God's indicative, fell back from the imperative. The multifarious ironies of the book of Genesis go in a number of directions, all basically conveying a relationship between God and man that is constantly surprising man with its stern demand and its consistent love and loyalty. The biting irony of Isaiah of Jerusalem stems from the perception that the indicative cannot stand without attention to the imperative, that a misunderstanding of the imperative introduces a fatal perversion into the living of the indicative. The sardonic irony of Qoheleth discerns a fundamental misconception of the indicative by those who seek their own " profit " out of life, whereas what man has out of life is God's own indicative. And the poet of Job, protesting a more profound search for " profit " by the use of the magical power of morality, proposes again that the indicative is a living, personal faithfulness between man and God.

The irony in the Old Testament, then, receives its meaning in the context of Old Testament faith. Writers of the Old Testament frequently point ironically to the incongruities in relationships among men, in men's self-perceptions, in men's relationships to the world of nature. They often see the other nations ironically (Isaiah of Jerusalem is a notable example), apparently assuming that the nations ought to — and do — know better. But the Israelite ironists expend their strongest energies theologically, concerning themselves with the articulation of faith and its implications. The ironic vision is integral to the style of Old Testament faith. For the ironic vision is a perception of human life as it is lived and a vision of life as it ought to be lived.

The faith can make free use of irony precisely because the covenant indicative has liberated Old Testament man from the requirement of shaping his own destiny. In magic, man must make his own way, and must therefore take himself and his powers with cosmic seriousness. Old Testament man has no need for such self-importance, and the defensive solemnity affected by Job's friends, for example, comes across as a kind of morose comedy. If the life of faith is embedded in the covenantal indicative and actuated in the ethical imperative, then man is free of all demands save those of God. I do not mean that everyone in Israel saw it so. We find in the characters and some writers of the Old Testament the same kind of self-righteous, self-seeking, narrow-minded arrogance that we find anywhere else. We must not romanticize the actual men who were entrusted with living Old Testament faith. But true irony is possible only in true faith, and the Old Testament's irony rests in a liberty from bondage, save bondage to God, that renders bearable the perceptions of incongruity.

Indeed, I would suggest that the presence of irony is a possible touchstone to the presence of liberating faith. I do not mean that liberating faith must invariably produce irony in all its adherents, for there are always those to whom the ironic style is neither attractive nor natural. But no faith genuinely liberating will produce irony's antithesis, the fanaticism or the arrogance always produced by a shaky, unstable faith. Liberating faith is the condition of the true irony that fears neither to perceive nor to state the ironic incongruities of which human life is so full. And liberating faith will also aim at the amendment of those incongruities, the extension of its liberty among men, which is the fundamental aim of irony. If, then, a faith *cannot* produce irony, it is hard to conceive that it can be a liberating faith. It is noticeable, for example, that the Communist faith has no room for the ironic vision. Sarcastic communism can be and often is, but sarcasm is the only type of humor available to fanaticism.

To be sure, as we have seen in our own century with fascism, nazism, and communism — all faiths that are founded in man's self-salvation — fanaticism often succeeds. But Isaiah, Qoheleth, and Job have all taught us that success is no guarantee of truth. It cannot, therefore, be the guiding principle for the strategy of faith. That our age faces issues so awesome as to beggar solution might trap us into premature bondage to rigidities and irrelevant programs, whether political or social. But faith, being freedom, is our best resource against bondage. And as long as we retain the possibility of irony upon our own efforts at the solution of our generation's problems, we retain the possibility of remaining free to solve them.

I certainly do not suggest that faith is to be cultivated for the nation's sake. That sort of specious religiosity, which adopts the greater good for the aims of the lesser, has often been the target of truly aimed theological irony. Nor do I mean to argue that Biblical faith alone liberates man from bondage. But certainly Biblical faith is liberating faith. And if faith is a kind and context of life that provides liberty from less than divine bonds, then faith possesses a necessary clue to understanding human life, and its proclamation in the present dilemma of mankind carries considerable urgency.

But the Old Testament must remind us that the urgency lies with faith, not with the faithful. If the proclamation is merely the extension of institutions that have often demonstrated their pathetic irrelevance, then faith must laugh it down. The issue of faith is the freedom of human life. The point of the gospel, for those of us who hold to the gospel, is not to swell the ranks of contributors to the church but to convey the liberty of the divine grace (and the two may sometimes, though not necessarily always, be antithetical). The faithful must turn the light of irony upon themselves too, and of that the Old Testament is our best witness — a better witness, let it be said, than the New Testament. To argue that faith holds a necessary clue to the character and conduct of human life is not to urge campaigns for money or membership on the church. Such efforts are usually the mark not of faith but of unbelief. It is to affirm that faith provides a freedom spacious enough to permit both a self-irony that is not self-destructive and an irony on the world that is not arrogant. For in faith man knows that he can take only God with ultimate seriousness. All else is susceptible to the ironic vision: the believer, the community of believers, the theology of believers, the societies in which believers live, the institutions in which they work.

Biblical faith, then, provides the basis for an ironic view of the world. That man finds genuine humanity in his relationship to God means that faith can look with liberating irony upon men's frantic search for alternative sources of humanity, for other fulfillment. That the problem of human alienation from God is solved for faith by the reconciling divine action sheds the light of irony upon the solemn programs by which men would manipulate either alienation or reconciliation for their own partial ends. Since the subject of faith is God, faith is bound in servitude only to him and can be bold enough to refuse theoretical or practical divinity to the importunate powers of the world. And since faith is wrought by God upon man, the man of faith can refuse the arrogant powers of the world the right to treat him or any man as less than man. We are neither gods nor worms, and hence we neither grovel before the great nor strut before the lowly. Indeed, in the context of redemption, we laugh about both exaltation and humiliation.

We can talk, then, of a human comedy, or, to use Dante's phrase in a way different from his use of it, of a divine comedy. Faith can laugh both because God's world is splendid and because it is ridiculous. But its splendor does not reduce us only to tears, though tears and laughter lie close enough together. It moves us also to the laughter of joy. Nor does the world's ridiculousness lead to despair, though it is frustrating enough. We ourselves, precisely in the faith that is true life, participate in both the splendid and the ridiculous. Hence, faith can laugh the laughter of mocking irony at the pretensions of those who consider themselves only splendid and the laughter of joyful irony with those who consider themselves only ridiculous. The world does not comprehend its ridiculousness, and hence faith can be ironic about unbelief. But faith's irony about unbelief points to the world's true splendor, that the world is the sphere of redemption. The irony of faith is finally its radical sense of redemption, its freedom in God. For faith, God alone is sacred, and all else is dispensable. Yet God is free to redeem even the dispensable.

# INDEX